The Business Ethics Field Guide

The Essential Companion to Leading
Your Career and Your Organization to Greatness

by Brad Agle, Aaron Miller, and Bill O'Rourke

Tosh,

You're incredible! Keep

up the great work.

-Aaron

Ethics Field Guide LLC
3655 Foothill Drive
Provo, UT 84604
www.EthicsFieldGuide.com

Ordering Information:
Special discounts are available on quantity purchases by corporations, associations, and others.

>   *Merit Leadership*
>   *www.EthicsFieldGuide.com*
>   *(888) 717-1226, International +1 801.717.1226*

Printed in the United States of America

Cover and book design by Carly and Peter Miller

Publisher's Cataloging-in-Publication data
Agle, Brad; Miller, Aaron; O'Rourke, Bill.
The Business Ethics Field Guide: The Essential Companion to Leading Your Career and Your Organization to Greatness.

ISBN 978-0-9910910-3-4

First Edition
August 1, 2016

To my beautiful wife, Kristi—my love, my support, and my partner in all things; our wonderful grandchildren; and our marvelous children and their spouses, Erik (Darlene), Lindsay (Derrick), Christian, and Amanda (Phillip), who believed that Dad would never actually finish a book. —Brad

To my lovely wife, Katie, and our four boys, Luke, Sam, Thomas, and Seth. You make me laugh, bring me joy, and inspire me to be better every day. —Aaron

To my wonderful, supportive wife, Elena; our children, Ryan, Heather and Dmitry; their spouses, Teresa, Andrew and Olga; and our grandchildren, A.J., Quinten and James. You bring meaning and sunshine to my life. —Bill

Praise for The Business Ethics Field Guide

The Business Ethics Field Guide is a unique and practical resource for learning about and applying business ethics based on cutting-edge research. The authors are noted and well-regarded academically in the ethics space, and Bill O'Rourke is a Master Storyteller who brings a timeless, sage and real world focus to each of the ethics dilemmas addressed. If you think you are ready to explore today's territory of business ethics, you're going to need a bigger map! The Field Guide belongs on the bookshelf of anyone studying business ethics or the layperson who wants a useful and timely guide to this rapidly evolving discipline. This is a book that would be a valuable resource and tool for the Ethics and Compliance Program in every organization

Earnest Broughton
Senior Advisor, Ethics & Compliance Initiative and Former Executive Director, Ethics Program Coordinator, USAA

The Business Ethics Field Guide was sorely needed at Enron, my former employer. When faced with an ethical dilemma in the work place, the most common response is what I call "the deer in the headlights" phenomena – we freeze in place with no instinctive action to take. Unfortunately, taking no action translates as acceptance and we are swept along to a place we do not want to go. The practical lessons in this "guide book" will equip you for the ethical challenges you will likely face as you advance in your career. I love this book!

Sherron Watkins
Enron whistleblower, Time Person of the Year 2002; and author of *Power Failure*

Based on the authors' outstanding description and analysis of numerous real-world examples, The Business Ethics Field Guide looks set to become the quintessential manual for understanding and navigating the real world ethics challenges faced by businesses like ours every single day.

Mark Russell, President & COO, Worthington Industries

Growing up my parents taught me the importance of doing what's right and serving others. In my business career, I've attempted to follow their counsel, but find that good intentions are not always enough. The Business Ethics Field Guide provides terrific practical guidance for those who want to do the right thing and change the world for the better. I recommend it highly and plan to use it in teaching my own children."

Josh Romney
President, The Romney Group; son of Mitt and Ann Romney

Agle, Miller, and O'Rourke have produced the navigation guide to ethical decision making that surely has already been written – but it has not. Shelves are crowded with well-intended, informative books on societal impact with retrospective pathologies on corporate social responsibility failures, Sunday school bromides on moral codes of conduct, prescriptions ensuring employee voice, fairness, or product safety; financial regulatory rules on transparency; and calls for philanthropic generosity distributing fruit of success to those in need. While all that is important, the reality is good people can often fail to see the paradoxes and choices around them in real time. Business complexities, empowered work teams, and fast moving conditions make it hard to identify buried personal accountability and alternative responses. The Business Ethics Field Guide moves past sermons and scolding to blend genuine experience and social science–providing the searchlight for righteous, timely solutions.

Jeffrey A. Sonnenfeld
Senior Associate Dean for Leadership Studies, Lester Crown Professor of Leadership Practice, Yale School of Management; Founder, President, & CEO of the Chief Executive Leadership Institute; and author of *The Hero's Farewell* and *Firing Back*

The Business Ethics Field Guide is, hands down, the best book on ethics I have encountered. It highlights the thirteen most common ethical dilemmas found in the world of work, and it contains a large number of real-life (not fictitious) ethical dilemmas along with the solutions actually put into practice. More importantly, it provides insightful questions to guide analysis of each of the thirteen dilemmas as well as the potential pitfalls associated with each dilemma. Every person I know could benefit from this book inasmuch as we all face these ethical dilemmas in everyday life. A renowned ethics scholar and a senior executive provide the practical guidance we all need.

Kim Cameron
William Russell Professor of Management & Organizations, Ross School of Business, University of Michigan; former Dean of the Weatherhead School of Management at Case Western Reserve University; and author of *Positive Leadership*

Most leaders think they've already mastered ethics; great leaders know that ethical leadership is a skill set that needs to be developed. This book is a useful resource for developing that skill set. It's an engaging practical guide to organizational ethics—for professionals and for students.

Adam Grant
Class of 1965 Wharton Professor of Management at the University of Pennsylvania and New York Times bestselling author of *Originals* and *Give and Take*

'You can lead a horse to water, but you can't make him drink.' Similarly, 'you can lead a person to the university, but you can't make him think.' Too many business ethics books nowadays speak at readers instead of engaging them. Enter The Business Ethics Field Guide, a compendium of remarkable, real-life dilemmas that force readers to think and decide. World-class authors from both academe and the C-suite make this book a must-read.

Tom Donaldson
Mark O. Winkelman Professor in Ethics and Law at the Wharton School at the University of Pennsylvania; Co-Founder and Past President of the Society for Business Ethics; and author of *Ties that Bind: A Social Contracts Approach to Business Ethics*

An excellent guide to developing an understanding and culture of value-based leadership within a business. The real-life examples and ethics-based analysis are thought provoking and follow principles that lead from troubling dilemmas to practical solutions and the 'right' outcomes.

Pat Hassey
Chairman, President, and CEO of Allegheny Technologies, retired.

No one wants to be caught off guard, especially when split-second decisions could lead to a potential career mishap, or worse. This book takes the smart, persuasive, and influential approach that not only gives the reader immediate solutions to real-world dilemmas, but could lead to significant organizational shifts in policies to avoid being in those difficult situations in the first place.

Sharlene Wells-Hawkes
Chief Marketing Officer, StoryRock; award-winning ESPN Sportscaster; Miss America 1985

The Field Guide is a must read for executives and anybody who understands that enduring business success and reputation is based on values and sound ethics. It offers a treasure chest of hands on guidance, essential to navigate every day's business life. The authors not only succeed in showing how to deal with dilemmas. They also show how solving dilemmas builds personal and organizational strength

Georg Kell
Founder, United Nations Global Compact; Vice Chair, Arabesque Partners

Honor and Integrity are absolutely critical to leadership. People expect their leaders to have integrity. It is not just a nicety but an absolute necessity. If you are not willing to put in the work to develop your integrity you should not be in the leadership business. The Business Ethics Field Guide is a wonderful tool for helping you cultivate honor and integrity. I highly recommend it to any aspiring leader.

General Robert C. Oaks
Four-Star General, US Air Force, retired

Finally, a handy reference for the ethical realities of business. Ethical dilemmas are part of the natural terrain in business, yet it is often hard to figure out a path from ethical theory to those practical realities. This Field Guide does that, starting from common ethical challenges that arise in business and then providing guidance based on examples and ethical theory. An important reference for academics and managers alike.

Joshua Margolis
James Dinan and Elizabeth Miller Professor of Business Administration,
Harvard Business School

"Doing the right thing" becomes significantly more complex when two apparent moral imperatives collide. Often obeying 'the one' results in transgressing 'the other', thereby exposing a true ethical dilemma not easily solved. Enter The Business Ethics Field Guide! Packed with universal examples and stories from authentic field studies, this workbook can aid and assist us in tackling such moral predicaments and help us find effective solutions that work. A superb guide to personal and organizational ethics!

Stephen M. R. Covey
The *New York Times* bestselling author of *The Speed of Trust*,
and coauthor of *Smart Trust*

20 years ago, Brad Agle introduced me to the study of Ethics and it made a huge impact on my life. This book is a powerful tool for business leaders, anywhere in the world. Yes, reading it will pose difficult questions and even cause immense discomfort. But that's why you must keep it close!

A V Somani
Chairman, Everest Industries Ltd., India

Sitting in my sixth floor office in the heart of the Silicon Valley watching the determined faces of the future United Nations walk on to our bustling campus and into the business building's hi-tech classrooms leaves a junior professor feeling incredibly humbled, inspired, and focused. It's awesome to have a book that is up to the significant task of being an innovative companion to those professors who are seeking to make a difference in the discovery and development of character for their amazing business students. The Business Ethics Field Guide is that textual companion. Our students here at the Lucas College of Business and I have relied on this clear and compelling material for three straight semesters in our well-rated and intensely experiential 'Professional and Business Ethics' course with a highly positive and overall meaningful effect. It is and will continue to be our standard text. Well done Brad, Aaron, and Bill.

M-C Ingerson
Assistant Professor of Management, San Jose State University;
and Master Teacher Award Recipient 2015

As a recovering deal junkie with Entrepreneurial DNA forever laced in my gene pool, it was a joy to read The Business Ethics Field Guide. With nearly 50 years of business experience in my rear view mirror I have run abreast of many of the ethical dilemmas rehearsed in the book. It was fun rehashing how I had handled many of those situations and the times I made great choices and the other times I could have done better...but learned from each one. It would have been wonderful to have had the Guide Book to read 'before' I learned first hand the difficulties I often faced when trying to keep my reputation from being tainted while at the same time trying to keep financially afloat. Life is full of 'opportunities' and any advanced warnings of the potential pitfalls would have been wonderful.

James Ritchie
Founder, Ritchie Enterprises

Wonderful book! Guides the reader over serious business issues through a very practical process with real life experiences. It pushes you to think, self-analyze, plan for prevention and even solve dilemmas. A nice combination of principle learning and its application in a world where more and more grey areas cause business leaders to enter into pitfalls of no return.

Danilo Talanskas
former President of the Brazilian Subsidiaries of Otis Elevator Company and Rockwell Automation, and Managing Director of GE Healthcare

This book is FANTASTIC!! I love it. I want to use it in my MBA class. It offers a unique approach to discussing ethical dilemmas with students. The questions following each case highlight the nuances in ethical decision-making and Bill's commentary adds a dimension of realism to the cases that students will appreciate. I highly recommend The Business Ethics Field Guide.

Tara Ceranic Salinas
Associate Professor of Business Ethics, University of San Diego

The Business Ethics Field Guide offers something unique: a practical approach to tackling ethical conflicts that is organized around the different types of dilemmas themselves. Particularly useful are the questions you are encouraged to ask in each of these situations, as well as the authors' discussion of the common decision traps associated with each type of situation. This is an excellent resource for students and executives alike.

Jared Harris
Samuel L. Slover Associate Professor of Business Administration, Darden School of Business, University of Virginia

The Business Ethics Field Guide is a wonderful volume on ethics. I have read the entire book, and it is a jewel. The next time I teach an ethics class, I'm going to use it in my classroom. It illustrates that organizational ethics are not simple. Most decisions are very close and require insights in being able to even understand one's own inner voice. This excellent new book solidifies Brad Agle, Aaron Miller, and Bill O'Rourke's position as leading authorities in America on business ethics.

Senator Larry Pressler
Retired three-term United States Senator and Chairman of the U.S. Senate Commerce Committee; described by the *Washington Post* as one senator who "would not be bought."

Keeping ethics top of mind requires you to remember where you came from and what your morals and values are. That's why I love this book. It is engaging, fresh and informative, and motivates me to do better.

Art Wing
President, Wing Enterprises (Little Giant Ladders)

The Business Ethics Field Guide provides keen and insightful tips and practical advice that all compliance and ethics professionals will want to have in one easy-to-read reference book full of real ethical issues and dilemmas frequently encountered by all types of businesses around the globe. I keep a copy of this book right next to our Code of Business Conduct to help me more thoroughly resolve all types of compliance and ethics matters.

G. Sonny Cave
Executive Vice President, General Counsel, Chief Compliance and Ethics Officer, Chief Risk Officer and Corporate Secretary, ON Semiconductor Corporation (named a 2016 World's Most Ethical Company® by the Ethisphere Institute)

There are a number of ethics books that purport to tell you what the "right thing" to do is, when facing an ethical dilemma in a business setting. But the Business Ethics Field Guide is the best resource I have found that has helped me decide what the right thing to do is, for the right reasons, at the right time.

R. Brad Oates
Chairman, Stone Advisors, LP

Take it from an observer and a participant in the "wild west" known as the high tech industry in Silicon Valley, this "Business Ethics Field Guide" should be a must-read for managers and employees alike, especially as startups endeavor to mature into viable businesses with productive business cultures.

George Harrington
retired CFO at Virtual Instruments and a veteran corporate executive at Symantec, BMC Software, and IBM

Ethical problems are like beasts in a jungle that can attack at any time. The Business Ethics Field Guide offers practical advice on how to steer clear of these beasts and how to confront them when they cannot be avoided.

Professor Joanne B. Ciulla
Coston Family Chair in Leadership and Ethics, University of Richmond; President of the International Society of Business, Economics, and Ethics; and author of *Ethics: The Heart of Leadership*

The Business Ethics Field Guide presents a perfect balance of academic knowledge about ethical dilemmas in the workplace and practical know-how for solving these dilemmas. Managers hoping to distinguish themselves as true leaders in their organizations would do well to consider this as a primary resource.

Scott J. Reynolds
Professor of Business Ethics, Weyerhaeuser Faculty Fellow, University of Washington

When I read the chapters and cases presented in The Business Ethics Field Guide, I come away with confidence in ethical decision-making. This work is unique, is very readable, and when it is used, provides the reader a 'steel-in-the-spine' point of reference that can make it possible for our best ethical intentions as good people to be realized – even in the toughest of situations. A great read, very timely, and a for sure keeper in my library and in my teaching. (Also now on my gift list for all those I care about.)

Ronald K. Mitchell
J.A. Bagley Regents Chair in Management, Rawls College of Business, Texas Tech University; Fellow, The Wheatley Institution; and Distinguished Visiting Winspear Scholar, University of Victoria

Agle, Miller and O'Rourke's Field Guide does not prescribe "one right way" to navigate the topography of business ethics. Conditions and terrain vary and there are often no trails in the wilderness. But with case studies to map where others have been, the compass of moral theory and social science to help provide directions, and helpful insights from a veteran trekker, this book will help readers lead their organizations reflectively along this fraught journey. The challenges presented here are common to all levels of organizations and are recognizable to businesspeople from the first day on the job to retirement and beyond.

Robert Phillips
David Meade White, Jr. Chair in Business, University of Richmond; former President of the Society for Business Ethics; and author of *Stakeholder Theory and Organizational Ethics*

Brad Agle serves as the George W. Romney Endowed Professor at BYU, and Brad and Aaron both teach in the Romney Institute of Public Management. My grandfather, George W. Romney, was a man of extraordinary integrity who believed that ethical behavior in the public and private sectors is the lifeblood to America's greatness. The Business Ethics Field Guide provides a framework to enable such ethical behavior, masterfully combining ethics principles with practical applications. It is a book he would have savored, celebrated, and gifted to his grandchildren.

Gregory B. Robinson
Founder of RLG Capital, a private investment firm,
and grandson of George W. Romney

This terrific text is rooted in reality, using short, easy to understand case examples most people will face during their careers. While the two professors provide authoritative analysis and a thoughtful structure, Bill's experience assures the reader that these challenges can be recognized, prepared for, and effectively managed. This outstanding, comprehensive field guide will make a fine addition to our business school's courses on individual and organizational professional responsibility. Our courses help students build 'professional responsibility muscle,' and the ethical tools explained in this book will ensure those muscles stay in great shape!

Gretchen A. Winter
Executive Director, Center for Professional Responsibility in Business and Society,
University of Illinois College of Business; Program Director for the Conference
Board's Global Council on Business Conduct, Chair-elect of the Executive Board of
the Association of Practical and Professional Ethics, and former Chair of the Board of
Directors of the Ethics and Compliance Officer Association

Contents

Section 2
Essential Knowledge and Preparation

Section 3

Appendix

Foreword
By Paul O'Neill

You should read this book. You should study this book. You should ponder the lessons and stories in this book.

This book is framed to speak to you as you confront issues and problems with ethical implications—issues and problems that you, as a leader, must navigate well. Keep in mind that ethical behavior, for leaders, is more than avoiding clear wrongs.

In my experience, everything a leader does is examined by the people in the organization. Your people will compare what you do with what you say. What you do defines you and becomes the default standard for your organization.

If you are the leader of an organization and you play golf on workdays and call it work, everyone will know. They may not expect to play golf and call it work, but they will deduce that this is an organization where leadership is not held to the same level of fiduciary responsibility as lower level employees.

If as a leader you condone the practice of not paying suppliers on time in order to improve your working capital ratios, you are defining the non-integrity of your organization. Your organization doesn't honor contract terms, doesn't keep its word—and you, the boss, own that condition.

As you read this book, remember: your every action—and non-action—defines the character of your organization. Ethics is about everything you do.

Paul O'Neill

72nd U.S. Treasury Secretary
Former Chairman and CEO, Alcoa

How to Use This Guidebook
By Bill O'Rourke

The call came at 5 p.m. on a Wednesday. It was one of our environmental engineers.

"Bill," she said, "we found a carcinogen in the water near the Texas plant."

This was bad news—with especially bad timing. Our company had recently acquired the small facility in Texas, and we were under contract to sell the plant to another company soon. Reporting the carcinogen would interrupt the sale and make us victims of unfavorable media. And, truth be told, there was no way to tell whether the trichloroethylene (TCE) even came from the plant operations there. It was just as likely to have come from a nearby service station or dry cleaner.

Our environmental lawyer recommended we stick to the legal requirements: quietly file our groundwater results with the appropriate state agency, but wait until the end of the sixty-day reporting window. Anything more than this could be interpreted as an admission of liability.

Meanwhile, 125 families were drinking water from the tainted aquifer.

As the company leader charged with overseeing environmental issues, handling this crisis was squarely on my shoulders. How was I to respond?

This decision had obvious financial as well as moral implications. My desire to promote our company and do the best for our share-holders seemed at odds with my desire to do the best for the people in one of our communities. And the extent of my duty toward those people, what I needed to do and how quickly, was not entirely clear.

Why You Need a Guide

Difficult decisions were a regular occurrence for me at Alcoa—a metals manufacturing company with (at the time) over 100,000 employees in over 300 facilities around the globe. Alcoa has a reputation for responsible stewardship and exceptional ethics. Still, every company encounters ethical challenges. From unreported safety infractions to demands for bribes, I had dozens of opportunities to respond in ethical, or not-so-ethical, ways. Over time, I learned to handle ethical dilemmas not only with integrity but also with confidence.

Some of my colleagues did not have the same happy ending. I saw capable people felled by ethical missteps—often split-second decisions that ruined their reputations and damaged our company brand. These were my friends, fundamentally good people who wanted to do the *right* thing but buckled under the weight of difficult trade-offs. We learned together that ethical decision-making skills are every bit as critical to organizations as strong management and leadership skills.

The purpose of this field guide is to help you make solid decisions when you have to choose among competing values and the path forward is hard to see. Like a seasoned wilderness expert, this book will assist you in finding your way and in mastering the skills that will allow you and your organization to thrive.

Fortunately for me, by the time I faced the Texas environmental incident, I had learned from some incredible guides, including, among others, my father, Bill O'Rourke Sr., and the values-driven Chairman and CEO of Alcoa, Paul O'Neill.

Dad was a high school teacher and coach who also directed the recreation department of our small town. He loved all sports, especially golf, although raising six kids on a teacher's salary meant he golfed infrequently and with ancient clubs.

As part of his job, Dad regularly purchased equipment from the local sporting goods store. One Saturday morning, the owner of that store pulled into our driveway, where I was washing the family car. He placed a new set of golf clubs in the garage.

"Tell your dad that's for him," he said, then drove away.

When my dad appeared, I was delighted to show him the new clubs in their handsome bag.

But he quickly put them in the trunk of our car and said, "Come with me."

We drove to the sporting goods store. Dad walked in with the clubs, set them on the counter, and told the owner, "I didn't pay for these."

Dad never talked about the incident during our drive to or from the store; he didn't need to. His actions spoke volumes about the man he was.

When I graduated from high school, Dad gave me a small, handmade plaque. On it he wrote:

> *I don't have much to give you, but I give you my good name.*

> *I give it to you untarnished and ask you to keep it that way.*

So when the engineer called that Wednesday afternoon, I was already trying to follow the path set by my dad, as well as my own goals for being an ethical leader: I didn't just want to stay out of trouble. I wanted to do the best I could with the resources I had.

It helped that my goals aligned well with the approach of our CEO, Paul O'Neill. When it came to ethical decisions, his direction was always, "Do the right thing; we'll sort out liability later." Our vision statement at the time read, "We aspire to be the best company in the world."

Within hours, I gathered my team. We agreed that any decent company would disclose this information right away. That choice, though it might be costly, was easy to make. But what should we do for the affected families? Several team members felt we didn't need to do anything to clean up this community problem. Chances are, the TCE was not even our fault. Our ethical duty was simply to disclose.

Then someone asked what the best company in the world would do. The feeling in the room immediately changed. Together, we decided on a plan.

Starting at 8 a.m. the following day, our company engineers went to all the homes in the city to disclose what we had found. Another contingent brought the news to the Texas government officials. We delivered drinking water to the residents and offered to replenish it over the next few weeks while we installed filters to keep the carcinogen out of their wells, at a cost of $1 million. We would do what we could to help the residents, whether the TCE came from our plant or not.

Despite our best efforts, there was litigation—costly litigation. A lawyer from California came to town and recruited each family for a class action lawsuit. Every family signed up. But I never had to take the witness stand or sit for a deposition, because it was clear to all parties that I had not withheld information. Ultimately, the court concluded that liability for the TCE could not be ascertained.

In reviewing the ethical decisions of my career, I realize that almost every situation could have been handled better. Many of my choices were right, but I believe many could have been *more* right. I also believe that many situations could have been totally avoided, had I benefitted from the experience of a guide.

Based on my own observations, I do not believe that we are born with ethical maturity. I believe we must develop our moral compass in the way we develop most other skills: through experience, formal learning, trial and error, and observing the good examples of others.

So I was glad when my friends Brad Agle and Aaron Miller invited me to contribute my experiences to this book. I hope that my triumphs and failures will guide a new generation of leaders as they develop ethical decision-making skills.

About My Fellow Authors

Brad and Aaron are exceptionally qualified guides. Brad has a PhD in management and is a thought leader in ethics research. Together with two colleagues, he more or less "wrote the book" when it comes to balancing the competing needs of various organizational stakeholders, an ethical problem that most leaders encounter daily. Aaron is a lawyer who specializes in helping grow businesses with social impact. Both are dedicated professors who teach and study business ethics, and both have won multiple teaching awards.

More important, Brad and Aaron exemplify integrity. They sincerely care for others and treat all people with dignity and respect. Working with Brad and Aaron has helped me to refine my own moral compass.

What to Expect

In this book, Brad and Aaron will guide you through thirteen types of ethical dilemmas. You might think of them as wilderness challenges. These are real stories from real people at various career stages, trying to do the right thing. Sometimes the actors have to choose between harming one stakeholder or another; between being true to themselves or to the goals of their company. The right thing to do is not readily apparent. In fact, there may be no single "right" thing to do at all.

Remember that ethical decisions are always personal, influenced by the decision makers' values and their company culture. I hope you'll disagree with some of the decisions in the stories—even the "good" decisions. I hope you'll come up with better solutions than we did. Or, best of all, you might think of prudent actions that could have helped us completely avoid the dilemma.

Following the dilemmas is Section 2, which contains critical information I wish I'd had early in my career. These chapters cover just about everything you need to know to become an ethical guide—the perils you will face, the decision-making tools that can help you find your way, and the steps you can take now to prepare yourself and your organization for ethical challenges. I personally think these chapters are so valuable that you might want to read Section 2 first. Then, as you digest the dilemmas, you can integrate what you've learned.

If you're like me, you may feel uncomfortable as you read. You may wonder, "Have I done that?" or "What would I do?" Don't push the feeling away. I've learned that sometimes discomfort is a good thing—it means you are developing moral sensitivity, which is necessary for moral leadership.

I find it helpful to think of dilemmas as opportunities. Opportunities to decide who you are and what you stand for. Opportunities to use your influence to help others. Opportunities to become an ethical guide. Yes, the wilderness is full of hazards. But when you know how to deal with them and keep climbing, the wilderness is also full of amazing views.

We hope our book will help you develop the moral courage to do what is right, habitually. We hope that when you look at your true self in the mirror, it will be an enjoyable experience, not a burden. As you hone your ethical decision-making skills, you will make choices you feel good about, you will minimize regrets, and you will help your organization thrive.

I wish you the best on your journey.
Bill O.

SECTION 1

13 Wilderness Challenges

By Brad Agle and Aaron Miller, with
more stories by Bill O'Rourke

The Business Ethics
FIELD GUIDE

Introduction to the Challenges
By Brad Agle and Aaron Miller

Any cursory online search will reveal thousands of books and articles that try to help you become a better manager or a better leader. According to many of these texts,[1] *managing* involves activities such as budgeting, staffing, and problem solving; while *leading* means establishing direction, motivating and inspiring people, and creating change. In this book, we propose a third set of skills that are often neglected in leadership courses and books but are just as essential for effective leadership: clarifying individual and organizational values and finding a way forward when these values conflict. This book will help you develop those skills and apply them in your organization to become a better leader.

Ethics as a Skill

In our classes, we regularly see our students making a common mistake: they think that being ethical is merely a matter of good intentions. They believe that if you are a good person at heart, then your choices will naturally be ethical. Our students are not the only ones who make this mistake. The challenges that follow will show you that good intentions are simply not enough. Difficult ethical situations require the thoughtful application of particular skills.

These ethical skills are especially necessary for leadership. You need to be more than just a nature lover to lead a party safely through the wilderness. You need the experience and skills of a wilderness guide. In the same sense, wanting to be ethical, even having a love for ethical choices, falls short of the actual ability to guide others through ethically precarious terrain. Ethical intention is a necessary start, but you need ethical ability to be a useful leader.[2]

Your goal as a leader is to hone your ethical *character*, the combination of intention and ability. As you go through each of the thirteen ethical challenges, or dilemmas, pay attention to how these situations root out where you might have bad intentions. But also notice how these dilemmas shine a (sometimes harsh) light on where your ethical skills fall short. Those skills include an ability to recognize ethical dilemmas, balance competing values, and communicate ethical ideas persuasively. We'll discuss these skills here, before you undertake the dilemmas, but a more thorough review of general ethical skills starts in Section 2, after you've had a chance to get these challenges and some initial practice under your belt.

Recognizing Ethical Dilemmas

Not all dilemmas are easy to spot and, as our research shows, not all dilemmas are the same. That's why the chapters to come are so important. If you don't really know what the dilemma is, you're unlikely to come up with a successful solution for it. We found that as the nature of a dilemma changes, the skills and strategies you'll need change as well. For example, how you manage an unethical demand from your boss is very different from how you manage a request for mercy from someone who works for you. As you go through the next thirteen chapters, you'll quickly see what we mean.

Luckily, according to our research, dilemmas do tend to happen in predictable ways. The vast majority of dilemmas you face will fit into one or more of our thirteen categories.

Quickly recognizing the nature of a dilemma requires practice. (We know this just from categorizing the many stories for this book.) But the ability to identify dilemmas is a skill you can develop. With practice, you'll be better able to see to the heart of a problem and understand what values are in competition. That, in turn, will help you design better strategies for resolving your dilemma.

Balancing Right vs. Right

Our book addresses moments when values conflict, situations we call "dilemmas." These situations are particularly difficult because they don't lend themselves to the typical framework of right versus wrong. Instead, the decision maker is asked to choose between two highly prized values: say, keeping one's word to honor confidentiality versus protecting a loyal supplier or friend; avoiding an unfair advantage versus bringing the best value to shareholders.

Whether or not they are recognized as ethical dilemmas, these right-versus-right[3] decisions arise all the time, in every business situation imaginable, for every kind of employee, in every industry. Thus, clarifying values and resolving conflicting values are not tangential tasks but, rather, are central to organizational success. Your ability to hone these essential skills can make or break your organization and your career.

Resolving dilemmas also impacts your personal well-being. The supposed line separating the professional from the personal is largely imaginary. Decisions you make in the workplace affect your character and emotional state just like the decisions you make in any other circumstance. Rarely will you find a husband or wife who hasn't lain in bed late at night trying to help his or her spouse process a difficult and emotionally wrenching decision at work. The good news is that with tools and practice, you can make increasingly sound ethical decisions.

Communicating Persuasively about Ethics

The majority of the time, your ability to bring about the right outcome will hinge on how well you can communicate ethical ideas to others. Rarely are we in situations where we can act on our own to resolve a moral dilemma. (Note how contrary this feels to the image most people have of ethical dilemmas: a lonely soul caught between two choices and left to work it out on his or her own.) Because you'll need the help of other people, you can assume that you'll often need to convince them to help.

As you go through the thirteen challenges, consider practicing or rehearsing what you might tell the other party. We like to do this with our students in class, and it makes a world of difference. It's one thing to describe what you might tell your boss in a tricky situation, and another to actually find the words themselves. You'll quickly realize that persuasive communication about ethics is a skill you can refine.

A Wilderness Guidebook

Like the guidebooks that outdoor adventurers study before a trip and also take along in case of emergency, this reference book can help you whenever you are confronted with an ethical challenge in your organization. And like those books, this one has been developed by experts with special knowledge in the field. Using the *Field Guide*, you can identify the particular issues at stake and find directions for dealing with those issues. Our aim is not to tell you what to do in every circumstance, but instead to help you think through complex situations in order to arrive at solutions you feel good about.

With the help of this guidebook, you will be able to meet ethical dilemmas in the workplace with more confidence and avoid major pitfalls that have snared other professionals. You'll then become the wilderness expert, safely guiding others through ethical dangers.

The Thirteen Challenges

The following chapters contain dozens of real-life scenarios, shared with us by business professionals. Every story is used by permission, although the individuals and their companies have been made anonymous.

We organize these dilemmas into the thirteen most common types you'll face in your career, based on patterns we observed in a five-year study of conflicting-values experiences.[4] For each type of conflict, we provide a sample dilemma, explain how to recognize the dilemma, guide you through questions that can lead to a solution, warn you of common pitfalls, and give tips for avoiding the dilemma in the future.

Each dilemma chapter also contains advice from Bill O'Rourke, whose career is full of pivotal ethical choices. Bill's incredible understanding of the variety of ethical challenges in business, combined with his amazing business acumen, virtuous character, and ethical courage, make him an ideal guide for anyone involved in a business career. Over the past sixteen years we have enjoyed watching as thousands of executives and business students (both graduate students and undergraduates) have been absolutely stunned by his stories, impressed with his wisdom and judgment, inspired by his courage and fortitude in doing what's right, and motivated by his example. His insights appear under the heading "Bill's Experiences," as well as in other observations we make throughout the book.

Choose Your Own Adventure

The final story in each chapter gives you an opportunity to come up with your own solutions. These practice dilemmas resemble the business cases often used in MBA coursework. Your task is to put yourself in the position of the decision maker and explain what you would do. Note that you are not becoming the person in the story; rather, you bring your own experiences, gender, ethnicity, identity, and so on to the decision.[5] As in any true dilemma, you will need to clarify your own values and use your best judgment to create a resolution that rings true for you.

For most readers, this will be difficult, uncomfortable work. You may find it helpful to talk about these situations with mentors you admire, or to discuss them with your colleagues and friends. If you're still in need of help, or if you want to further examine your thinking, you can find additional resources at ethics.byu.edu.

Also refer to Section 2 in the back of the book. This section has time-honored thinking frameworks and other essential information to guide you. In fact, if you're using this book as part of an ethics course, your instructor will likely have you read Section 2 first. In Section 2 we describe the internal and external factors that contribute to unethical behavior—including rationalization processes, organizational structure, and so on. We provide a one-page toolkit that summarizes classical approaches to ethical reasoning, along with the problems and questions that emerge from each approach. Finally, we offer steps for being ethically proactive and give advice for becoming an ethical leader.

We encourage you to keep this guidebook handy and refer to it often. Your efforts to resolve these dilemmas will refine your ability to make ethical decisions, now and in the future. With practice and the assistance of seasoned guides, you can become an ethical leader—one who clarifies organizational values and points the way for others when those values conflict.

Enjoy the climb!

Brad Agle and Aaron Miller

CHAPTER 1

Challenge 1: Standing Up to Power

Someone in power is asking you to do something unethical.

Nathan left Frank's office unsure of what to do. Frank, the managing partner of the firm, had just asked him to file a return for a major client improperly showing zero fines or underpayment penalties. This client was important to the firm, and especially to Frank, who had a longstanding relationship with him.

Nathan had started working in this tax practice only a few months before. The practice belonged to a prominent CPA firm, but the tax office Nathan was working in was fairly small. In the job interview, Frank had told Nathan he planned to prepare him to take over a retiring partner's client load in a few years.

This morning, Frank had asked Nathan to drop by his office. When Nathan arrived, Frank looked up from a stack of returns and said, "I'm reviewing the Bigglesworth return and have a few changes I'd like to run by you before talking it over with the client. I see you have Mr. Bigglesworth paying an underpayment penalty to the state of $50,000. Could you explain this to me?"

"Sure," Nathan said. "Our state doesn't have a safe harbor rule for estimated tax payments like the federal government does. Since Mr. Bigglesworth's company did so well this year, last year's estimated tax payment didn't cover the total taxes he owed, so he is now subject to state underpayment penalties."

Frank furrowed his brow. "Nathan, I understand where you are coming from, but I'm good friends with Mr. Bigglesworth. I advised him what payments to make during the year. He shouldn't have an underpayment penalty."

When Nathan hesitated, Frank continued, "I'm sure the state has a safe harbor rule similar to the federal one. What is he going to think when I hand him a return requiring him to pay an unexpected fine of $50,000, in addition to all the extra tax he'll owe? Fix the return to show zero underpayment penalties."

Nathan knew the safe harbor wasn't the real issue—both he and Frank were licensed CPAs and could easily verify the proper treatment. The issue was the client relationship and Frank's pride. Frank considered it worth the risk of audits and fines to keep Mr. Bigglesworth in the dark about the botched tax planning.

As Nathan returned to his desk, he wondered what he should do. Should he "fix" the return and hope a state tax auditor wouldn't notice?

Explanation

How should you respond when someone in power asks you to do something you don't feel is right? This is one of the most common of all the business-world dilemmas. Everyone has a boss (executives, team leaders, supervisors, clients, and so on). That reality makes the Standing Up to Power dilemma quite frequent, especially for those at the start of their careers.

The option of politely refusing may seem simple enough, but there are some important contours for you to consider.

First, simply having a boss is not all it takes for this dilemma to emerge. This dilemma almost always requires a difference between the powerful person's needs and your needs. In fact, this is the heart of the dilemma. To act unethically puts you at risk for that person's benefit.

That's the case in our dilemma here. Nathan's boss's decision to file an incorrect tax return puts Nathan at risk because he's the one preparing it. Even if the partner is the one making the call, Nathan's the one doing the dirty work. That's a risk to Nathan and his future well-being.

So when your boss is putting you at risk with a request, realize that he or she wouldn't impose the risk if there wasn't something else he or she hoped to accomplish. For example, with Nathan's dilemma, the partner's interest is to preserve a profitable friendship with Mr. Bigglesworth. Understanding your boss's needs will help you devise an effective response to the unethical request. (We'll return to this concept later in the chapter.)

Usually requesters know they are putting you at risk, so they may apply pressure, or even threaten you, to make you more scared of them than you are of the ethical danger or other risks. This pressure can be very subtle, like simply doubting your loyalty. In fact, it's in their interest to make the dangers vague, allowing your imagination to fill in the blanks, since specific threats can be used as evidence against them.

The most common form of pressure is time. Always seek more time, and be sure that the matter is truly urgent before allowing a perceived time crunch to affect your decision. In the dilemma we've described, the return probably doesn't have to be filed right away. Even just a few days could be enough time to craft a better solution. Do all you can to take your time. Research repeatedly shows that quick decisions are usually less ethical.

Even though most people will know the position they're putting you in, don't be too quick to assume ill intent. Sometimes the requester is genuinely unaware of the ethical danger. Even in Nathan's dilemma, the partner may not fully understand the risk of filing an incorrect return. (He didn't seem to know the local tax law very well, after all.) If this is the case, it may affect how you approach your boss when discussing alternatives. It doesn't necessarily make the conversation any easier, though. People, especially those in power, can take criticism poorly. It would undoubtedly be a mistake to simply tell the partner that he's making an unethical choice. Pointing out people's ethical missteps will almost always make them feel like you are questioning their character. You'll need to educate them without scolding them.

Although we've used the example of a supervising partner giving an unethical order, be aware that the directive doesn't have to come from your direct boss. It might not even come from someone with actual organizational authority over you. Perhaps a boss's friend or relative is making the request. The lack of a role above you in the org chart doesn't diminish the person's influence over you.

Questions to Ask

Thinking through the following questions may help you decide whether and how to stand up to power.

1. Does the powerful party have the right to ask me to do what they are asking?

Rights can come from different sources. Let's consider three of them here.

Legal. Following the law is always important, and that makes understanding the law equally important. Knowing the law means you can understand if your boss's request puts you at any legal risk. But legal understanding won't always matter. Sometimes, like with Nathan's tax filing dilemma, the low risk of being caught influences his boss more than following the law for its own sake.

Keep in mind that the boss's request may be legal, but still immoral. The truth is that the law, by itself, is a deficient guide to ethics. US Supreme Court Justice Potter Stewart wisely noted, "Ethics is knowing the difference between what you have a right to do and what is right to do."[1] Be sure not to give in to your boss just because the request is legal.

Contractual. Even if there are no laws governing the boss's command, contractual obligations, including those you have made with other parties, may come into play. But contracts are rarely exhaustive and are often overlooked. For example, there's probably no particular contract provision preventing Nathan's managing partner from asserting his interpretation of the tax law.

One contract worth exploring is your own employment contract. Even if you didn't sign a written contract, employee handbooks or corporate policies can define the employment agreement. It may be that the boss is violating the employment contract with you through his or her request. For example, Nathan's boss may be violating their employment agreement by asking Nathan to violate the CPA code of conduct.

Moral. Could your boss have a moral right to make an immoral request? Possibly. Managers' obligations often come in conflict with each other, forcing them to choose hurting one party to benefit another. Be sure to evaluate your boss's competing interests to be sure that the harm done isn't actually necessary. Nathan's managing partner in the tax office has an obligation to Mr. Bigglesworth that he's trying to uphold. He'll consider that ethically important.

2. Are there others in my organization who agree with me?

Few dilemmas will make you feel more alone than Standing Up to Power. Most likely the boss made the request in confidence. You may feel like disclosing your dilemma will make things worse. But remember that, just like in the wilderness, the best protection is often someone else to help.

In situations like these, you'll probably need to draw on any *social capital*[2] you've developed. This term describes the way you can rely on relationships for help. It's good to have friends and mentors in the office who can stand up for you and guide you through tough situations with your boss. They may have particular insights about his or her personality that could help. They might even go to bat for you, given their more powerful relationship with your boss.

But such relationships take time to build. Social capital accrues through genuine, caring relationships, not through mercenary or manipulative means. Be social and friendly in your workplace. Offer help to others and they will be more likely to help you when a dilemma like this one arises.

3. Is what is being requested of me in accordance with the stated values, or ethics policies, of the organization?

Virtually every large company and many small companies have written value statements, ethics policies, or both. These usually articulate what the company leadership considers important and appropriate behavior from employees. Professional codes of conduct, like those for CPAs, may also apply.

Take the time to learn your company's policies. Knowing what behavior the company and profession expect—especially if it's at odds with what your boss is asking—can give you additional tools for this dilemma. For example, company policy or professional standards could give you a great line of questions for your boss to consider. You might say, "I'm worried about how the CPA board would view this decision. I would have a hard time this early in my career with a disciplinary action brought against me. What do you think might happen to me if they knew?"

You can even draw attention to how your behavior would reflect on the company if it became public. All organizations develop reputations based on how their employees act. An employee violating the company's stated values makes the company look bad. In the case of the accounting firm Nathan works for, it's worth remembering that one of the largest accounting firms in the country, Arthur

Andersen, was destroyed because of the dishonesty of a relatively small number of accountants working with Enron.

Unfortunately, many companies rarely consider or discuss their written values and policies, making it hard to rely on those policies for help. A managing partner like Nathan's may not even be familiar with them. If that's the case where you work, look to the unwritten values in the company that can help you. (Every company culture has dominant values of some kind.) For example, if the company puts profit above everything else, try to explain how the unethical request could hinder profits.

4. Does my company have ethics resources?

In addition to a written policy, many companies also have dedicated staff for addressing and resolving the ethical concerns of employees at any level in the organization. Federal law requires publicly traded companies to have anonymous reporting mechanisms for accounting matters, and most companies have extended the reporting resources to include other ethical concerns.

Like Coca-Cola, Chevron, and New York Life, your organization may have an ombudsman program. If so, the ombudsman in your company serves as your advocate, particularly in matters relating to ethical concerns. Ombudsmen are typically empowered to hear your concerns in confidence and advise you on the best course of action. They also document your concerns, assuring that you can create an official record representing your perspective. If your company doesn't have an ombudsman, a human resources representative usually fills this role. Also, most professional associations have an anonymous hotline to call for advice.

As you consider using company ethics resources, remember that most corporate policies, and in some cases federal law, require the company to investigate and act on the information you provide. This could have serious consequences for the other people involved. Be sure to weigh your decision carefully and to fairly consider what damage could be done to their careers. You don't want to overreact and cause more harm than necessary.

5. What is this person attempting to accomplish through what he or she is asking you to do? Is there a different way of accomplishing it?

Creativity and hard work may be your two most powerful tools for resolving this kind of dilemma. To use them best, you need to understand what your boss is asking of you. You may think the answer is obvious, but it often isn't. Usually, the person in power knows things that you don't. That's why you need to ask really good questions.

For starters, see if you can tactfully figure out the answers to these four questions:

"What's the best outcome my boss is hoping for if I do this?"

"What options has my boss already considered and why were they dismissed?"

"Why did my boss choose me for this request?"

"What are the reasons my boss might want this request kept private?"

The way you ask matters immensely, so your questions shouldn't sound like accusations. Try to get at the information in a way that shows you have an open mind and respect for your boss's position.

6. How can I help my boss save face?

The relationship between a boss and an employee is defined by authority; the kindest, most thoughtful personality can find it hard to have their authority questioned. That is why you need to be careful to frame your response so it does not sound like you are questioning your boss's authority. Even worse, your response may feel like a judgment of your boss's character. No one likes to be called unethical, so you have to tread very lightly. Do all you can to help your boss save face. The following strategies will be helpful.

Try to solve the problem together. Don't come to your boss with a pre-packaged solution that is at odds with the request. To the extent that you have to do some of the thinking on your own, seek feedback so your boss can be a part of the solution. Be sensitive to his or her time, however. For example, Nathan's boss probably manages many accounts and isn't going to have much room to go deep into the problem with him.

Give credit liberally. Getting recognition for good ideas is far less important here than being able to do the right thing. It's important for bosses to feel equal to their role. Giving them credit for solutions reaffirms their confidence.

Be careful to avoid accusing words like "unethical" or "wrong." Even if you direct the language toward yourself, it sounds like an accusation. Saying, "I personally feel like this would be unethical," implies that your boss is unethical. Use much less direct language to express your concerns. Consider something like, "I'm a little uneasy about this."

Finally, don't draw a line in the sand unless you absolutely have to. Always leave open the possibility that you're wrong. This acknowledges the nature of the relationship and your boss's ability to have the last word. If you draw a line in the sand, your boss has to choose between being unethical or being trumped by a subordinate.

The best outcome you can hope for is creating a solution where your boss can do the right thing both ethically and logistically. Here, creativity and hard work are your best approach. If necessary, ask for time to find another solution and put in the work to make it happen. If the two of you can come up with an alternative that is better on all counts, it strips away the ethical dilemma. The best choice becomes obvious, and your boss gets to retain his or her dignity.

Pitfalls

Be aware of these common mistakes as you consider your Standing Up to Power dilemma.

Charging the Hill

Probably one of the most common mistakes when standing up to power is charging the hill; that is, vocally and stridently opposing the request. Ethically, this approach may feel noble, but it isn't the only ethical approach. Strategically, this approach is a potential disaster for you. You should generally consider it a last resort.

Explore all of the indirect approaches that can lead to an ethical outcome. These include using softer language, asking sincere questions, and finding creative alternatives. Some people skip these options, cynically considering them ineffective. The truth is that indirect approaches can have a far greater influence than most people realize.

Acquiescing Too Quickly

On the other extreme, don't acquiesce quickly, assuming the blame will fall on your boss if you're found out. While it may, you can't count on it, and there are other downsides to readily acquiescing to unethical requests. You might be tempted to think that just giving in will allow you to take care of the problem quickly and move on to other things. The danger is that if you do what's being asked, you'll get a reputation for being reliably unethical. Odds are that the person in power will come back to you more often for similar requests. You need to resist in diplomatic, thoughtful ways so that you aren't considered useful in carrying out unethical demands.

Gossiping

Avoid the appearance of gossiping while recruiting help from others. It's almost certain that you don't know all the facts. Be sure to use careful descriptions of your situation that allow the listener to reserve judgment. Instead of saying, "You'll never believe what Frank just asked me to do," say something like, "I could really use your advice with this situation. I'm not sure what to make of it." Gossiping will come back to hurt you, even if it does provide some emotional satisfaction at the time.

Not Protecting Yourself

When it's time to assign the blame, people with more tenure and power in the organization tend to win out. Don't be caught in situations where it's your word against your boss's word. Whenever something seems amiss, it's time to start documenting. You might print out questionable emails and file them at home, keep a daily journal, or try to involve coworkers as witnesses who can support your claims. In serious situations, you might even consider surreptitious audio recording. (Note that local laws about audiotaping without permission vary.)

Assuming Too Much

Finally, don't assume you know all that you need to know. As mentioned before, your boss probably knows more about the situation than you do. An errant assumption will make you look incompetent and may strip away the moral authority you'll need for persuading others to do the right thing. Try to get as much time as you can before giving your answer. Use that time to collect useful information. Just the right insight, like a company policy or a helpful experience of a friend, might be the thing you need to get the best outcome.

Bill's Experiences

Like most people, you will probably face the challenge of an immediate supervisor ordering you to do something that you both know is wrong. It might be to misclassify expenses in the accounting records, suppress data that should legally be disclosed, destroy a written record that is the subject of an ongoing litigation, overbill a customer, lie, or any number of other misdeeds. You can't do it. You just can't. But how do you tactfully let your supervisor know you believe the action is wrong?

One approach that you might find successful—but probably only once—is to look your supervisor in the eye, smile, and say "Ah, this is your way of testing me. Oh no, I won't fall for your test. You won't catch me agreeing to do that." That approach sometimes gets supervisors to come to their senses and drop the matter. Often, though, you'll need to carefully, and tactfully, stand your ground.

Refusing to "Spin"

During my early years at Alcoa, a leading metals company, the CEO asked me to compare the lifecycle of metal to those of glass and plastics. Lifecycle analyses are heavily influenced by recycle rate assumptions. I used current recycling rates and found that lifecycles for all three materials were similar. The CEO had hoped to present results that widely favored metal. He suggested I rerun the analysis using a 100% recycle rate for our metal product and a 0% recycling rate for glass and plastic. These results were much more to his liking. He instructed me to use the new results in our presentation.

Not wanting to directly challenge the CEO, I followed his instructions to the letter. Then, I added back in my original analysis. I made sure both sets of results—and their underlying assumptions—were conspicuously displayed in our presentation. The CEO was not pleased, but he could not fault me for refusing to comply.

In this era of "spinning" all information, we don't have to be a party to the distortions. I believe that full, fair, complete, open, honest communication builds an organization's credibility with all constituents and reaps dividends for years.

Insisting on Severance

Standing Up to Power dilemmas can occur even when you carry an official responsibility that gives you the final say. That's because power in organizations isn't tied to authority alone. Any time you cross someone whose influence matters to you, you need to tread carefully.

When I chaired our company's benefits committee, one of my roles was to advocate for employees who filed benefits-related appeals. In the middle of a layoff, we received an appeal from one hundred employees in our New Hampshire plant. Two weeks before they were notified they would be laid off, the plant had changed its severance policy—from two weeks' pay for every year of service to just one week's *pay for each year of service. For longtime employees, this amounted to a difference of nearly $50,000. With their manufacturing-specific skills in an economy moving toward knowledge work, few of these employees were expected to find alternative employment.*

I first checked with the legal department. I learned that the company had the unilateral right to change certain benefits programs, including the severance policy, at any time. Still, the timing of the change seemed inappropriate.

Next I visited the president of the New Hampshire business unit. I asked him whether the motivation for the policy change was to save money in the impending layoff. He said "no." (But of course he was motivated by the chance to save $5 million!)

I advised the president that the benefits committee was going to reinstate the old severance policy for these newly laid-off employees. The president countered that he was not going to allow that. He reminded me that he was the president and should have the final say. That's when I explained the nuances of the benefits committee. We functioned as a separate entity from the company, with a separate fiduciary obligation to protect employees. He didn't care.

The benefits committee granted the appeal. The employees got two weeks of severance for every year they had worked. That president didn't like me, but I believe I still held his respect.

A Quitting Decision

In cases where the infraction is severe, you may have an obligation to let others in authority know of the circumstances. Hopefully the authorities would not condone such behavior. Be prepared, though, for negative repercussions or for less support from company leaders than you anticipate.

At some point, you may be faced with what I call a "quitting decision," a situation that is so wrong that it must be corrected or you will have to quit. I believe we get three of these in our career. Often these situations will be rectified and you won't have to resign. But if the situation is not corrected,

*you may decide you cannot work for that organization. And
you probably wouldn't want to work for that organization.*

Planning Ahead

Consider these preventative steps to avoid running into Standing
Up to Power dilemmas in the future.

1. Build friendships. Social capital will help you more than
almost anything else in this dilemma—not to mention the many,
many other ways strong relationships will benefit you. Perhaps
the most obvious benefit is that if your boss does make an
unethical request, you'll have the friendship space with him or
her to be frank in your reply.

2. Be ethical in the little things. As we'll point out many times
in this book, nobody ever got a reputation for ethics by being
ethically lazy. The people we admire for their ethics tend to be
assiduous about doing the right thing, even when personally
costly. Think of your ethical reputation as something like armor:
people don't choose the strongest targets first. Your reputation
for being ethical might keep these requests away altogether.

3. Work on creating an ethical culture. If no one is conducting ethics trainings in your company, volunteer to lead them.
Unfortunately, corporate ethics trainings have a bad reputation
for being boring formalities. This is a pity, because there are
so many tools available to teach ethics in engaging, fun ways.
(Just ask our students!) Consider starting with some of the
dilemmas in this book. Whatever your approach, if everyone
around you learns to value ethics, they'll likely do the right
thing before situations drop in your lap.

What Happened

Now we return to the chapter's opening dilemma. Recall that
Nathan was trying to decide whether and how to stand up to his

boss, Frank, who wanted Mr. Bigglesworth's tax document changed to show no underpayment penalties.

Nathan chose to not interfere with the filing of the return. He reasoned that it was Frank's client and Frank's signature on the return, and therefore Frank's decision how he wanted to handle it. This incident was just one of many differences of opinion he had with Frank, however.

Ultimately, Nathan stayed on through the end of that year's busy tax season, then found a new opportunity. He maintains friendships with other coworkers and partners at the firm, but has not had contact with Frank since.

Practice Dilemma

"Just keep doing business the same way you've been doing it. Don't tell them anything has changed." Such were the direct instructions from the new CEO of Nisha's company concerning how she should conduct business with a longtime supplier—a supplier that her company plans to quit using in just a few months.

Nisha is the manager of a bicycle manufacturing business that has annual revenues of $4 million, part of a diversified company with revenues of $100 million. Nisha's new CEO has decided he wants to liquidate Nisha's unit and use the cash from that liquidation for other, more profitable, business opportunities. Right now Nisha's unit has about $2 million in inventory. If consumers learn that her company is discontinuing the bicycle line, they will avoid the bikes and the inventory will immediately lose half of its value. Under the new CEO's plan, Nisha's unit will continue to manufacture bicycles for the next three months, then discontinue manufacturing and only sell bicycles until inventory runs out.

Nisha has been the primary contact with the major supplier of the bicycle parts for over a decade. This supplier, a family-run business, is based in a small town in Brazil. When Nisha started working with the supplier, it employed five people and supplied several companies. Today it employs twenty-eight people and provides the majority of its products to Nisha's company. It generates the majority of wealth for its small village.

It has also been an excellent supplier. When Nisha's unit saw unexpected spikes in demand, the supplier worked hard to meet her needs as quickly as possible. After several of these spikes, and in order to serve her unit better, the supplier began building inventory so it would always be able to respond quickly. In turn, Nisha began providing the supplier with historical sales figures to help it predict coming demand. She and the supplier have been sharing this information for several years.

Nisha feels that she has a responsibility to tell the supplier that she will no longer be buying its bike parts. She knows that if she suddenly stops using this supplier, it will certainly go out of business. On the other hand, if she informs the supplier about the discontinued bike line, it could begin finding new business right away. At the very least, it wouldn't spend all that time and money building worthless inventory. Nisha has explained this to the CEO.

But her CEO said, "We have no legal contract with the company. It's their problem, not ours." He's concerned that if the supplier knew that Nisha would only be using about three more months of inventory, it would immediately stop production and look for others who could use its manufacturing capacity--thus surely tipping off the market to the impending change.

Nisha offered several possible ways to help the supplier while her company makes this change, all of which were rejected by the CEO. He is adamant about his position. Further complicating the issue, Nisha has a non-disclosure agreement with her company, preventing her from disclosing any important company information. She will continue to be the contact with this supplier until all business is completed with them.

Nisha has always thought of herself as a very ethical person. Now she asks herself, "What would an ethical person do in this situation?"

CHAPTER 2

Challenge 2: Made a Promise (and the World Has Changed)

Conflicting commitments force you to choose which to keep.

Susan stared at her computer screen, unable to concentrate on the task at hand. So far, her responsibilities at this nonprofit organization had been fun and engaging, and she found it deeply rewarding to work with people in need. But now a better job opportunity had come her way.

Although she felt indebted to her coworkers for all of their kindness to her, Susan didn't want to stay in this low-salary, low-skills job. Unfortunately, she'd promised to work for the nonprofit for at least six months.

She had been reluctant to accept the nonprofit's job offer in the first place because it wasn't in her field and the title and pay were well below what she would normally demand. But these were extraordinary times—Seattle in 2008. After three months of hunting for work in a frozen job market, Susan began working temporarily at the nonprofit, building strong relationships with the staff and clients. She felt loyal to them and the cause.

When a full-time position became available at the nonprofit, the staff convinced the CEO to meet with her and negotiate a competitive offer. Susan expressed her concerns, including the fact she felt severely over-qualified. The CEO stated he would ask for a commitment of only six months, after which time Susan could leave with his goodwill. He offered a salary that was much higher than the organization would normally pay, as well as a quasi-management position. Susan accepted.

One month later, a visiting consultant recognized Susan's abilities and offered her a job with his consulting firm. The pay was $20,000 more per year and would give Susan the kind of experience she needed to get into the MBA program of her choice. The office was closer to downtown and to her social life, and the work was in line with her training.

Susan's immediate response was to reject the offer on the basis of her promise to stay with the nonprofit. She called her father, who owned a small business, and asked his advice. He insisted that although no documents had been signed, she had made an oral contract and ought to honor it. However, when Susan asked her friends, a group of young and competent professionals, they were all in favor of her taking the new job.

"If there is no legally binding agreement, you are free to follow the better offer," they said. "People of our generation know this."

"Your father's advice is old-school. *Salary* buys loyalty. A verbal agreement doesn't."

"The CEO of the nonprofit should have known better than to hire someone as overqualified as you. Welcome to free markets."

Susan continued to stare at her blank screen. She knew this was a defining moment because the decision she made would either open or close a future of opportunity. Somehow, she worried, it might also define her character.

Explanation

We all make lots of promises. Some of these commitments are casual. We tell our friend we'll go to a movie on Tuesday night, promise our children we will take them to Disneyland next month, or agree to have the report on our boss's desk by Friday. We also make serious long-term commitments, personally and profession-ally. Some of these commitments are so important that they carry with them the weight of law.

Arguably, some of the most important commitments we make involve a great deal of uncertainty. For example, at weddings, promises are often made to love, honor, and cherish in good times and in bad. For some, this vow might involve seeing each other a few times a year and periodically expressing love. For others, it might involve providing significant care all day, every day. When we make a marriage promise, we don't know what exactly will be involved. Similar uncertainty is found in parenthood, acceptance of employment, and taking on religious or community commitments.

Of course, a basic moral principle is that one lives up to one's prom-ises. However, in a world of multiple commitments and uncertainty, conflicts among promises are certain to occur, often in ways never foreseen. In these situations, the question becomes how to prior-itize multiple responsibilities while retaining relationships. Keep these two points in mind:

(1) Breaking some promises will be necessary in order to live a moral life; and

(2) People remember when and under what circumstances promises were fulfilled or broken.

Sometimes, the choice is straightforward. Say, for example you are heading out to mow your neighbor's lawn, as promised, when you receive a phone call about your spouse. There has been a car accident and he or she is being rushed to the hospital. In this situation, your priority is clear and would receive social consensus.

At other times the choice won't be as clear. Some people make the mistake of always prioritizing a promise that is specific over a vague, but potentially more important, promise. Other people don't even notice multiple commitments and make decisions without regard to some of their promises. This chapter offers you an opportunity to think about your own promises—present and future—and how you will prioritize them.

Questions to Ask

1. Can you still keep your promise?

Occasionally the world changes and it becomes completely impossible to fulfill a promise. For example, if you arrange to host a friend's party in your home and then a tornado destroys your roof, you can't fulfill that specific promise. You may be able to do something different to help your friend, but no one would hold you morally responsible for reneging in this circumstance.

Years ago, Brad's son wanted to get scuba certified. Because diving in the frigid October waters of Pennsylvania proved troublesome, Brad offered to take his son with him on an upcoming business trip to Miami, where he could get certified in the warm Atlantic waters. However, walking through the Miami airport, they heard people discussing an incoming hurricane. In his busyness leading up to the conference, Brad had failed to check the weather—and now scuba diving was completely out of the question.

In some situations, you could keep the promise, but at a high price. In Susan's case, nothing was prohibiting her from fulfilling her promise to the nonprofit. However, keeping the commitment would mean losing out on a great personal opportunity.

Richard Maynes, former CEO of a bottling equipment manufacturer, tells the story of meeting a commitment at a high price. His company signed a contract to deliver equipment to a new bottling plant in England on a certain date. A few weeks before the date of delivery, it became clear that the deadline would not be met. The contract called for penalties for failing to deliver the product on time, but the project would still be profitable—which would allow for bonuses at the end of the year. Someone mentioned the company could airlift the equipment from the Western United States to England in order to meet the deadline. Richard chose this path—which forfeited any profit on the deal and cost him and his staff yearly bonuses.[1]

2. Did you predict or could you have predicted the change?

When we make promises, we generally do so with a prediction related to the future. For example, with the prediction of good health, one of our students accepted a job in the boondocks—only to later learn his spouse had cancer and needed to be treated at a major urban center.

As a general rule, if you could have anticipated the change when making the promise, you will not seem to others to be morally free from the promise. Conversely, the more unanticipated the change is, the more moral space you will likely be given to alter the commitment. For example, reneging because your spouse has cancer provides a better moral justification than reneging because the high-salary job offer you had hoped for finally arrives. In Susan's case, the consultant's job offer came out of the blue—she had not anticipated it when she made her promise. Yet she and her boss were well aware that a competing offer might be a possibility—that's why they agreed on a 6-month commitment in the first place.

3. Does the other party still want you to keep your promise?

All parties to a promise have their own particular circumstances. In certain cases, the change you have experienced may also affect the other parties to your promise such that they would prefer you not fulfill the promise. Say a sudden economic panic makes it difficult to fill a customer's order. You may be off the hook if the customer is also dealing with the panic and no longer wants to receive the order. Thus, it may be in everyone's interest for the commitment to change.

In other cases, it is still in the other party's interest for you keep your commitment, but they may be willing to accommodate your need to change. While experience and research reveal that individuals are self-interested, experience and research also reveal that most people are also other-regarding[2] and act in pro-social ways[3]. Under many circumstances, the other party is happy to release you from your promise, and, in some cases, even insists on it. It's hard to know how understanding Susan's boss would be about her new opportunity, but it could be helpful to present the situation and allow him a chance to weigh in.

4. Is there an alternative that would make the promised party as happy as if the original promise were kept?

Sometimes, the changing circumstances that prevent us from keeping our original promise create space for a viable alternative. When Brad couldn't keep the scuba diving promise, his wife helped to arrange another activity that Brad and his son could do together in Florida—a visit to SeaWorld to swim with the dolphins. The disappointment at not being able to scuba dive disappeared.

The concept of moral imagination[4] comes into play here. (No, we don't mean imagining away morality.) Moral imagination is the idea that decisions with moral content do not have just two alternatives. Rather, by using our imagination, we might be able to come up with a creative solution that satisfies the moral obligations of all parties. While moral imagination does not always produce such solutions, most of our students and executive clients are surprised at how often thinking through potential solutions using ethical perspectives allows them to find workable solutions. Going back to Susan, perhaps there are possibilities beyond the two options she sees (quit right away or forgo the new opportunity completely).

5. What will happen to the other promises you've made?

As discussed earlier, when promises suddenly conflict, you may have to decide which promise you will honor. For our student who had accepted a job offer in the boondocks, his wife's cancer diagnosis made it much more difficult to keep the very specific promise to his new employer. Instead, he chose to live up to his vague, but many would argue more important, promise to love, honor, and cherish his wife. He found a new job near a first-rate cancer institute, in a city with family members who were eager to lend support. By contrast, Susan's story doesn't mention other promises that would be put in jeopardy by keeping her original promise to the CEO.

Pitfalls

Assuming the Promise Isn't Important

When the cost of fulfilling a promise rises, it is easy to assume our involvement is not actually important and others are not really counting on us to deliver. Often, the costs to others are greater than we realize.

Here's one story to illustrate. Jim, a promising business student, accepted a full-time offer with the company where he had interned over the summer. Then, one week before he was to start, Jim emailed the company president that he had chosen to take a different job. Jim didn't think this was a big deal. Surely the company would have no trouble finding another eager employee. Of course, Jim's decision had a farther-reaching impact than he anticipated.

One of Jim's classmates happened to be the daughter of that company president. She told one of our colleagues that her father had only recently taken the job of president and had lobbied hard with his co-owners to be able to recruit at his alma matter. When they finally consented, he hired four excellent interns, who impressed all of the co-owners with their initiative, work ethic, and intelligence. However, when Jim reneged on his commitment so soon before he was to start his job, without a good explanation, it left the company in a bit of a lurch and left a sour taste in the co-owners' mouths.

They decided never to recruit at Jim's university again, and they even withheld support from the company president when he was invited to speak at that school.

Deciding Alone

When breaking a promise, it is usually a bad idea to do so without having a conversation with the other party. Indeed, if the circumstances are such that breaking the promise makes sense, the other party is likely to release you from the commitment. In the process, you will have avoided overtly breaking the promise, and you will have allowed the other party to be magnanimous. In addition, discussing the issue allows both of you to act with fuller information, information which might even lead to a better outcome than either of you could have imagined.

Looking for Excuses

Moral duties generally require the fulfillment of promises. In this chapter, we've opened up a discussion of when it is appropriate to break promises. Indeed, sometimes in order to live a moral life, one will, at times, need to break promises. Unfortunately, some individuals will use any reason they can think of to break a promise, whether morally appropriate or not. In the scenario at the beginning of this chapter, Susan's friends argue keeping promises is old-fashioned and not supported by today's culture. Other people, in this situation, are quick to point out how often organizations fail to meet commitments to employees, thus providing the rationale for breaking one's promise.

If you want to develop a reputation as a moral individual, one with integrity and high character, you have to resist this urge. It is easy to find reasons to break a promise—that's one reason most people fail to develop strong reputations as ethical leaders. To the extent you can be creative in keeping or modifying commitments in ways that please the other party, you can be a promise-keeper, even when doing so is difficult.

Imposing on Others

Earlier we talked about the importance of discussing your dilemma with the other party. Now, we need to backtrack a bit on that advice. Asking for release imposes a dilemma on the other party. Don't ignore that imposition.

Even discussing your dilemma with the other party creates a dilemma for them. They must decide whether to honor their values of generosity and accept the consequences, or hold you to your promise. In situations where you don't have a good justification for potentially breaking a promise or have a solution that might actually make the other party happier, you need to be very careful about imposing on the other party. Oftentimes, when the other party finds out you do not want to or cannot fulfill your commitment, they will let you out of it. However, while the other party won't necessarily say anything, they won't be happy about the situation or think well of you. Research has shown most supervisors don't like to give negative feedback, even when doing so is important in an ongoing work relationship. Asking to get out of a commitment for selfish reasons is not a good way to build a strong reputation or social capital.

 ## Bill's Experiences

Promises are vital in your personal and professional life. My experience is that a history of keeping your promises makes it easier for others to support you in the rare occasions when you will need to change or break a promise.

It's the Customer's Call

One of my plants was up against a tight shipping deadline when the quality control equipment broke down. So the plant supervisor shipped the product without doing the quality inspection. "After all," he told me, "we haven't found a single defect in over two years."

This was a breach of our promise. Our contract with the customer specified 100% inspection. But holding on to the product until our equipment was back on line would breach our promised delivery date. I thought it would be best to let the customer decide which promise we would keep. (Of course, if this had been an aircraft component, the decision would not belong to the customer. Some parts require inspection by law.)

So I had the plant manager call them and explain our situation. Would they prefer to accept the product when it arrived, or send it back at our expense to be inspected as soon as possible? They opted to accept the shipment. Often, openness, honesty, and transparency will help resolve competing promises.

Balancing Family and Work

The promises we make often involve relationships with those closest to us. Don't make the mistake of always prioritizing work commitments at the expense of your loved ones. Chances are, you can find a way to fulfill your obligations in both areas.

My wife was diagnosed with breast cancer three times. The third time, she died. When we received the initial diagnosis, I promised her I would be present for every doctor's appointment, surgery, chemotherapy session, and radiation procedure. And true to my promise, I was there every time.

But it wasn't easy. My obligations, meetings, and work assignments were as demanding as ever, and they sometimes conflicted. Thankfully, my employer was willing to let me work evenings and weekends in order to meet my commitments. Looking back, I am so pleased that I was able to be an integral part of my wife's ordeal.

Similar juggling was necessary when I made commitments to coach my children's soccer and Little League teams. I firmly believe that personal and work commitments can be balanced and even balanced well. On reflection, I'm convinced that my deep involvement in my family's life made me better at work, and vice versa.

Job Offer

When young professionals ask my advice about promise keeping, I encourage them to think about the long-term consequences of the decisions they are making today. How will their actions affect others? What kind of reputation do they want to build?

I once acted as a mentor to an undergraduate student at Duquesne University who was looking for a summer internship between his junior and senior year. Chris had a lot to offer in the supply chain area, having already served two summer internships. After interviewing with the University of Pittsburgh Medical Center's (UPMC) procurement organization, he was offered a summer job, which he excitedly accepted.

Chris was all set for the coming summer when his world changed: another employer, Dick's Sporting Goods, offered Chris a summer job. The job offer was appealing, particularly because the pay was higher, and compensation was an important consideration for Chris. He needed to make rent payments on a new apartment, insurance payments for his car, and so on. The higher paying offer made him question whether he should follow through with his commitment to work at UPMC.

When I met with Chris, he had already thought through several rationalizations to justify accepting the Dick's Sporting Goods offer. We talked at length. I acknowledged it would not be "illegal" to renege on his acceptance, but it would certainly call into question his integrity and his word being his bond. Putting himself in the shoes of the prospective employer, how would Chris feel if he extended a job offer to a student—which was accepted—only for the student to change his mind? I also invited him to consider the point of view of the Dick's Sporting Goods manager. If he sees that you are willing to back out of an acceptance with another employer over a few dollars, he might wonder what you might do if another employer were to offer you even more money in the future. You have to be very careful of the reputation you build for yourself.

Chris left my office and later called me saying he would honor his original commitment to UPMC and advise Dick's

Sporting Goods that he had already accepted another offer. The job at UPMC provided Chris with remarkable opportunities and industry exposure. He performed so well that UPMC continued to employ Chris during his senior year of college. He ended up very happy with his decision and the reputation he earned.

Planning Ahead

Because we can predict with certainty that you will frequently face this dilemma, we have some advice for you.

1. Be careful in the promises you make. Understand that life changes in unexpected ways. Indeed, the majority of contracts are written not because of the straightforward aspects of the contract, but because potential changes in the future must be acknowledged and adequately dealt with.

2. Don't overbook yourself. It can be difficult to predict the time required to meet some of the most important commitments in life, such as marriage or parenthood. These promises involve a great deal of uncertainty because you can never predict when you will have to dedicate time or resources to help your spouse, children, or community. Similar uncertainty attends most new projects you might consider taking on. Therefore, it is important not to "overbook" yourself. Say no to new commitments as necessary. Build in time for unpredictable developments you must attend to in order to keep your promises.

3. Build good relationships. By fulfilling normal commitments, and sometimes going above and beyond for colleagues and friends, you build social capital. Social capital can serve you well if you ever have to break or modify a commitment.

What Happened

In this chapter's opening dilemma, Susan had to decide whether to honor her agreement to stay with the nonprofit, or take a better paying offer for a consulting job that matched her interests and training. In the end, Susan took the offer with the consulting firm.

She justified her decision by telling herself that employee loyalty is won by recruiting top talent and paying them what they're worth, rather than by extracting verbal promises. Giving notice to her supervisor was stressful. The supervisor felt betrayed, given all the staff had done to land Susan the job, and her communication was somewhat hostile.

When Susan talked with the CEO, he expressed disappointment but made no mention of her oral agreement as something she should honor—he simply accepted the situation. He then told Susan about the career path he had hoped for her. If she performed well, he had planned to put her directly into management, with a corresponding increase in pay. This surprised Susan. If she had known, she thought she would probably have stayed on. At this point, though, she felt it was too late to change her mind.

The new job at the consulting firm gave her great experience but ironically placed her in another difficult ethical dilemma. She left that firm after just six months.

Practice Dilemma

"I wish the company had announced this acquisition two days ago!" Natalia said to herself. Last week, after a long and unfruitful hiring search, she had offered a critical security job to a marginally qualified candidate, Rajeev. Now, because of the pending acquisition, the person she really wants and needs on her IT team, Brian, has suddenly become available. Should she honor her commitment to Rajeev or use the acquisition as an excuse to let him go?

Natalia works for Fleet Technologies, a large IT vendor, as the technical team leader on a multimillion-dollar enterprise resource project for one of the company's newest clients. This client is a major medical device company, part of a cash-rich industry sector that Fleet has struggled to enter. The project is so important to Fleet and to the client that it is being overseen and closely monitored by vice presidents in both companies.

Due to the project's high profile, Natalia handpicked each member of her team. The medical device industry is highly regulated, and security management is one of the highest risk areas to be met by her technology solution. The application and processes need to conform to a variety of governmental standards and best practices. Brian, a longtime Fleet employee, had initially helped Natalia scope out the security-related activities for her project proposal. Natalia had worked with Brian on several other projects and highly valued his contributions and expertise. But Brian was not available to join her team because of his obligations to another important client.

Fortunately, Natalia was able to hire Nandu, a security expert from outside of her company, to work on the project. However, after a couple of months, Nandu decided he could no longer continue on the project because of family demands and had recently given his two-week's notice. Natalia's plan was to get someone in place immediately so that the new person could transition with Nandu before he left.

Natalia again checked with Brian's director and was told that Brian was unavailable. His current project was in a critical state. After searching exhaustively to find a replacement for Nandu, she found Rajeev. Rajeev lacked the ability of Nandu or Brian and would be unable to handle the second and third phases of the project. However, he could probably manage the first. She hoped that between her tutelage and some part-time consulting help from Brian, Rajeev might be able to grow into his role in time for the second phase.

On Thursday, Natalia had called Rajeev with an offer and asked him to report to the office on Tuesday for the onboarding process. He accepted. She then asked him to contact Nandu immediately to begin the transition.

On Monday, the office was buzzing with the news that Fleet was acquiring one of its biggest competitors. Brian called Natalia that afternoon to inform her that due to the competencies of the acquired company, his project was seen as redundant and had been cancelled. He was now available and eager to join Natalia's team.

Brian is everything Natalia needs for her project. Beyond his expertise and vision, he has been working on the hardware platform her client currently uses, and thus could provide even greater value to her client.

What should Natalia do? Her project is already slightly over budget and just barely on schedule. It is a slow time in the IT industry. Because of the acquisition, downsizing and layoffs in her company are inevitable. If Brian is laid off, Natalia doesn't know how Rajeev could possibly succeed during the second phase of the project. However, Natalia has already given her word to Rajeev and presumes he has already contacted Nandu to begin working on the project.

Meanwhile, she wonders which employee has a greater right to the job: the one who is highly qualified and has been working at the company for several years, or the one who is marginally qualified and only recently accepted an offer. Rajeev is scheduled to come in tomorrow morning. Natalia has a few hours to decide what to do.

CHAPTER 3

Challenge 3: Intervention

You see something wrong and you're not sure how to proceed.

Eric thumbed through the patient files to take another look at Mr. Bell's MRI results. As the office manager of the physical therapy practice, Eric didn't know a lot about medical imaging. But even to his untrained eye, it was clear that Mr. Bell would need knee surgery. Unfortunately, Jason, the lead physical therapist, had no intention of telling Mr. Bell until they had maxed out his insurance benefits.

When he pulled Mr. Bell's MRI results off the fax machine, Eric thought it was strange to be receiving them. Results were usually sent to the surgeon or primary care physician. Eric assumed the fax was a mistake and simply filed it in Mr. Bell's records. Later, Eric asked Jason if the test results needed to be forwarded to Mr. Bell's regular doctor.

Jason said Mr. Bell didn't like his regular doctor, so Jason had volunteered to take a look at the results and make a recommendation. After all, Mr. Bell was Jason's neighbor and also the general contractor whom Jason had hired to build a new home.

Eric didn't think much about the circumstances until he overheard a resident and an assistant discussing the severity of Mr. Bell's injury. They seemed surprised that Mr. Bell was coming in for treatments instead of opting for surgery first.

The next time Eric met with Jason, he asked if Mr. Bell would need surgery. Jason, in turn, asked Eric how many visits were approved per calendar year by Mr. Bell's insurance. When Eric told him the policy approved 12 visits, Jason responded that Mr. Bell would need surgery, but not right away. When Eric asked about the reason for the delay, Jason admitted he was hoping Mr. Bell would use up his insurance-paid visits prior to surgery. With the additional physical therapy that would be needed post-surgery, Mr. Bell would owe the clinic several thousand dollars, which Jason hoped to use as a credit on his house.

Jason sounded proud of his clever plan. Eric carefully suggested that this approach might not be in Mr. Bell's best interest. Jason pointed out that physical therapy was making the leg considerably stronger, so the eventual surgery would go much better.

Unconvinced, Eric asked the resident and the assistant how they felt about the plan. While they both disagreed with Jason's choice to withhold information, they admitted that the current therapy was not harming Mr. Bell. In fact, they concurred with Jason that patients who do strengthening exercises before surgery have smoother recoveries with more lasting results. They also explained to Eric that pre-surgery physical therapy is not common simply because of insurance limits. Neither offered to confront Jason or to tell Mr. Bell.

Eventually Eric suggested again to Jason that Mr. Bell should be informed of his test results, as well as the benefits of pre-surgical treatment, so he could make his own choice about therapy. Jason responded that the clinic couldn't tell him now without looking bad. Eric didn't know what to do.

Explanation

Uncle Ben famously told his nephew, Peter Parker (a.k.a. "Spider-man"), "With great power, comes great responsibility." This one insight describes the essence of the intervention dilemma. This dilemma is one of the most common revealed by our research, so Uncle Ben's advice is far-reaching.

The Intervention dilemma occurs when you see something wrong, but are not sure how to proceed. This can be especially complicated when you feel that acting will be risky.

To be clear, not acting is also an act. Withholding whatever resources or influence or knowledge you have is as much a choice as intervening is. Eric, for example, may be tempted to think keeping silent means he is not responsible for what happens to Mr. Bell. But not speaking out has moral significance, even if it keeps Eric out of trouble. That's what creates this dilemma.

Once you understand that non-action is a morally significant choice, you have to evaluate whether restraint or intervention is morally superior. Because intervention often imposes personal risk, it can be very hard to know whether the situation is so bad that you need to take that risk. The questions in the next section will help you determine your threshold.

Going further, your intervention might impose risk on others. For example, Eric could get the resident and assistant in trouble if he tries to help Mr. Bell. You might think you are saving the day by intervening, when really you are meddling. Be careful not to make things worse.

Whistleblowing, a dramatic and difficult choice, is one type of intervention. Publicizing something wrongdoers (often coordinated ones) want to keep private takes particular courage and willpower. It also requires a great deal of preparation. If your intervention means accusing people, expect to be accused in retaliation. Do all you can to document your accusations with strong evidence. Be sure to remove any potential conflicts of interest that might impugn your motives. Be ready for others to doubt your integrity. Be aware that whistleblowers usually bear significant personal costs.

Fortunately, there are other, less dramatic ways to respond to wrongdoing. You might be able to intervene without actually accusing anyone. That's what Eric might do in his dilemma. Rather than revealing the whole scheme to Mr. Bell, he could simply encourage Mr. Bell to get a surgeon's opinion. Jason's nefarious purposes don't need to be revealed. If the situation does not need to be reported to civil authorities and is unlikely to arise again, you may be able to protect the innocent without calling out the wrongdoer.

Recognize that some interventions take time and patience. Rarely can you dispense with such problems through a single, dramatic gesture. Wrongdoing can be deeply entrenched in some organizations, even institutional. Don't lose hope if this is the case. You may not be able to solve the problem at once, but you can move the needle in the right direction. It may still be right for you to act.

Whatever you do, don't assume you can avoid this dilemma. The more friendships, relationships, and professional connections you develop—the more involved you are with the world around you—the more frequently you'll encounter this dilemma.

Questions to Ask

1. Are you the right person to intervene?

Before you decide the right way to act, make sure you're the right person to act. In many organizations, someone is probably assigned to deal with the very problem you want to stop. Your best approach may be nothing more than reporting the situation.

Even with such a person in your organization, though, you might still need to intervene. You might be in a position of special influence, have a better relationship with the parties involved, or possess a special set of skills for fixing the problem. In these situations, you'll need to figure out how to best proceed.

2. Can you recruit help?

Just because you're the right person doesn't mean you need to act alone. Consider recruiting others to your cause. Allies can help you craft a better strategy for intervention. They can join you in confronting the wrongdoer. As is true for most dilemmas, you're likely better off with help than going it alone.

3. Do the urgency and potential impact require you to act now?

For the great majority of dilemmas, our advice is to wait, observe, and consider. You may not have that luxury here. Consider using the standard that courts of law use for making decisions like this (otherwise known as injunctions): quick intervention is probably needed if you believe the situation may lead to serious and irreparable harm. In situations like this, find the least invasive thing you can do to prevent that harm, then do it as soon as you can.

If you fill a formal leadership position in your organization, you probably need to respond right away. Coaching employees as soon as you notice poor behavior can help them recognize their mistakes and change their ways. If you allow poor behavior to continue, even for a short time, you send a message that behaving poorly is okay.

4. Does your intervention plan require you to act unethically?

Sometimes we are privy to wrongdoing because of a special responsibility we have. Your dilemma might relate to promises you made, duties you assumed, or trust others placed in you. To intervene might violate an obligation you owe someone. For example, Eric has an obligation to keep his employer's confidences. If you find you have to lie, break a promise, hurt innocent people, or benefit unfairly when intervening, weigh the ethical consequences very carefully.

Your own abilities or expertise might pose another problem. Eric, for example, needs to be careful of making a medical diagnosis without sufficient training. Acting beyond your abilities could make things worse and would also be unethical.

5. Does your intervention create a permanent solution or a temporary fix?

Ideally, you will intervene in a way that prevents both the current problem and also any future problems like it. Your intervention could set a precedent for everyone else you manage. But urgent circumstances or limited options may mean that a momentary fix is the best you can get.

6. What are your own motives?

If the wrongdoer has any complaints against you, the most damaging objection will be calling your integrity into question. Intervening out of personal interest, instead of purer motives, will hamstring your ability to get things done. Intervention often requires the trust of decision makers. Be careful that they have good reasons to trust you.

If you happen to benefit from the intervention, but actually believe you have pure motives, try to recruit an unbiased party to help. He or she can champion the cause where you appear compromised. In seeking help, be sure to be transparent with the person about your situation. You'll lose their trust quickly if you're not honest about your personal involvement.

7. Is the problem the result of one person's behavior or a systematic failure?

Often, people get hurt because of the way multiple decisions by different parties just happen to combine. For example, a longstanding but small client might be left behind by a series of decisions about your product's direction. Multiple departments might play a role in an outcome that breaks promises. These systematic failures won't go away by singling out a solitary actor and making a scapegoat of that person. You'll need to address the problem at a much higher level and create guiding principles to avoid the problem in the future.

8. Does your intervention require one act of intervention or sustained, regular effort?

Are you in this for the long-haul? You may need to be. Sometimes interventions, especially those involving accusations, can be drawn out by inquiries and deliberation. You may need to reach out multiple times to the people who can help. The right way to intervene might be through tireless lobbying. Alternatively, your intervention may have stopped the problem, but now you and others will need to be extra vigilant to make sure the same problem doesn't happen again. The point is that whatever problem you are helping to fix, you will probably need to give more effort than one bold gesture.

9. How can you create the least harm to everyone involved?

Don't forget that the situation involves more parties than just the wrongdoer, the victim, and you. However you act is likely to have cascading consequences. You can't perfectly predict the future, but you can consider how your intervention will help or hurt others. Clearly, you want the best outcome you can get—for everyone.

Also, remember that the wrongdoer doesn't deserve unlimited punishment or suffering. Fairness requires thoughtful consequences. It's very easy to overreact in the process of protecting the innocent. Moreover, the victim may not be as blameless as you first thought. Try not to be excessive or zealous in your intervention. A measured response could be more effective.

Pitfalls

Steer clear of these poor alternatives as you decide when and how to intervene.

Signaling Acceptance

As noted in the beginning of this chapter, not acting is still a morally significant choice. You set a standard by not intervening, signaling the behavior is okay. Even if the current instance isn't a big deal, your silence now could endorse every similar situation to come.

Acting without Information

Don't confuse an Intervention dilemma with a Suspicions Without Enough Evidence dilemma. The latter requires a very different approach to solving the problem. Acting without the right information leads to potentially disastrous consequences. You don't want to falsely accuse anyone or hurt a third-party you hadn't considered. Be sure you understand the situation accurately before you intervene.

Communicating Harshly

As with most dilemmas, style matters. Avoid needlessly combative language. Be a good listener as people respond to you. Accurately communicate any uncertainty on your part and express a willingness to work for the best solution for all involved. Don't draw a line in the sand if you don't need one. Remember, your goal is fixing the problem, not being "right" or looking better than those around you.

Demonizing Wrongdoers

Although wrongdoers often need to be punished, don't overdo it. Overzealousness can be as bad, or worse, than silence. Keep a goal in mind for a fair outcome and ask yourself if how you are intervening helps you get that outcome.

It is easy to get caught up in demonizing wrongdoers. Remember they are people too and might simply be making a mistake. Of course, wrongdoers might need to be removed from the opportunity to hurt others in the future, but that doesn't mean you should destroy their lives altogether.

Discounting Culture

Before you choose to intervene or keep silent, remember that culture matters. Are you seeing wrongdoing where everyone else sees acceptable behavior? If so, you might misunderstand everyone's expectations and it could be that within this context, the wrongdoing isn't really wrong. For example, you might be applying rules from your previous company that your present company doesn't have. Norms can vary considerably between different industries or locations. Alternatively, you might find that everyone has come to accept behavior that really is bad. In either case, culture will make intervention especially difficult. Don't ignore or underestimate it.

Ignoring Expertise

Finally, let the right people handle the right problems. There are likely people in your company who have better training and more extensive experience than you do. They know the broader context in which the problem matters, and they may have authority to decide what to do. When they make a decision, consider their expertise before you criticize. You can advise and consult them, but you need to acknowledge that you don't know everything that they know.

Bill's Experiences

The most common risk when intervening is that others will not look kindly to your actions and could retaliate in some way. Despite the risk, those in a leadership position have a duty and responsibility to intervene.

A Leader's Duty

A leader actually has a license to intervene. Common situations that call for intervention include off-color jokes, the use of profanity, rudeness, bigotry, and discrimination of all kinds. Employees at every level should take a stand when they see colleagues being mistreated. But when you become the boss, you have an obligation to confront these inappropriate behaviors and to set the example for your organization. As the leader, you are the person responsible to assure dignity and respect in the workplace.

When leaders need to intervene, immediate action is often the best. Allowing questionable behavior to persist can result in confusion, lost productivity, retaliation, or anger.

Addressing Favoritism

Supervisors show favoritism. It's natural. If special treatment is based on work performance and is applied fairly, this could create a positive work environment where all employees are motivated to perform. If an employee is given a flexible work schedule so she can attend her husband's surgery and that same special flexibility is allowed to all in similar circumstances, that's fair. But when the favoritism is arbitrary, that is inappropriate.

If you see this type of unfair favoritism and it is frequent or egregious, it is wise to say something about it. Given the right culture in an organization, you might approach the supervisor directly with your concern. However, without the right culture, it might be necessary to report the situation to a human resources professional, to the supervisor's supervisor, or to an anonymous hot line. If you are a peer and see favoritism, let it be known. If you are the supervisor's supervisor and you notice it, stop it. These situations require facts and tact, but my recommendation is to address them and they will improve.

The Confederate Flag

At Alcoa, I frequently consulted with managers who wondered whether and how they should respond to inappropriate behavior. In turn, I sometimes turned to experts for advice.

For example, one morning a union worker at our 600-person manufacturing plant in North Carolina drove onto the company parking lot with a four-foot by eight-foot Confederate flag flying from his pickup truck. The black workers at the plant, who comprised 37% of the workforce, complained to the human resources manager that they didn't like it. The HR Manager met the plant manager when he arrived at *work that morning and explained the situation. Should the plant manager intervene?*

The plant manager grew up outside the United States and had no sense of the history surrounding the Confederate flag. He called me and asked if I saw any issues. I admitted that I was the wrong person to ask. Because I was raised in the northern part of the United States, I really didn't have an appreciation of the flag's significance, either.

So I met with my friend, Harold, a black coworker who was raised in the South. Harold explained how, to many people, that flag represents slavery, bigotry, and racism. He told me that beyond the flag's origin in the Civil War, it was often used in protests against civil rights and school integration. I also called my friend Brad, an ethics professor at a nearby university (and also a coauthor on this book). Brad confirmed Harold's assessment and recommended I resolve the situation right away—both to show support for our workers and to avoid bad press. Apparently, there was a lot of controversy around the common, and sometimes even state-sponsored, use of the Confederate flag.

I called the plant manager and relayed what I had learned. We discussed the situation at length. We considered the option of doing nothing and letting the situation blow over. We weighed the importance of freedom of speech, the right employees have to express their opinion, against the right of property owners (here, the company leaders) to restrict what happens on their own property. We also talked about the precedent our action—or inaction—would be setting. Did we want employees to continue to speak up when they felt discriminated against or offended? We agreed this would be a positive culture to establish.

The plant manager decided to tell the worker that same day that he was free to fly the Confederate flag on his truck, but not on company property. He would need to park his truck elsewhere. In effect, the plant manager took the position that he and the company would not condone that behavior.

Most of the issues that arise in the daily operations of a manufacturing plant are minor and localized. Sometimes they are not. In this case, the Wall Street Journal *reported our story on the front page of the newspaper a few days later.*

The plant manager looked very good under public scrutiny and was complimented for his quick, decisive action.

Planning Ahead

The following ideas can help you prepare for the next Intervention dilemma that comes your way.

1. Practice leadership. As a manager or leader, people will come to you with complaints about coworkers. You'll also see those you manage making bad choices and you will need to step in. If you are not yet in a leadership position, take the time to practice managing this kind of dilemma by intervening in small ways, such as when you see a coworker being inadvertently belittled. Do your best to approach each situation with care and tact. As you rise in influence, you will need to intervene more often. Plan on it.

2. Rely on relationships. Intervention almost always means persuading others to help fix the problem. Rarely can you fix it on your own. Make an effort now to build strong social capital with others. If your coworkers like you and respect you, they will be more willing to assume the risk that comes with helping you. They can also help you avoid mistakes and will be more forgiving when you mess up.

3. Be prepared to sacrifice. Some interventions will cost you personally, but are still the right thing to do. As a person of integrity, be ready to make sacrifices. Unfortunately, as much as we honor some prominent whistleblowers, most suffer great personal costs for their actions. Keep your personal finances in order. Be prepared for the worst so you can weather the storm.

4. Live your values now. It's hard to suddenly be a white knight if you've previously had a lower standard for yourself and others. Your critics will jump on any hypocrisy or inconsistent behavior. The reputation you built before intervening can't be changed easily or dramatically now that you have to act. Don't let your virtue be a surprise.

What Happened

At the beginning of this chapter, Eric was trying to decide whether and how to intervene. The lead physical therapist, Jason, had not been honest with Mr. Bell about the probable need for surgery.

Uncomfortable with Jason's deception, Eric decided that he had a moral obligation to tell Mr. Bell about his knee. Wisely thinking ahead, Eric also realized that the next difficult decision was whether to tell Jason that he had told Mr. Bell. "Ultimately," Eric told us, "I determined that if I knew telling the patient was right, I should be willing to risk my job over it."

Before Mr. Bell's next visit, Eric made a photocopy of the MRI results. Handing them over, he explained that they needed to be looked at by a surgeon or primary care physician. When Mr. Bell protested that Jason had already ruled out the need for surgery, Eric again insisted that he should get a second opinion. Detecting Eric's nervousness, Mr. Bell suddenly understood that his physical therapist's diagnosis might have been swayed by self-interest.

When Eric told Jason what he had done and why, Jason was very upset. He reminded Eric that he was in charge and that he signed Eric's paychecks. Eric responded (perhaps a bit too zealously) that no paycheck was worth violating his conscience. The conversation did not end well, and Eric ended up quitting a few months later.

Practice Dilemma

Andrea scrolls back through the privacy and security questionnaire her CEO just sent to their client. No, these are not the answers Andrea supplied when she prepared this document. Clearly the CEO has altered her statements to enhance the perception of compliance. Whether the new answers are flat-out false, Andrea can't determine. But they certainly seem deceptive. Andrea is a new employee with two small kids to support. Can she let this misinformation slide?

Andrea works for a digital security company as a compliance analyst. When Andrea joined the organization a couple months ago, she quickly sensed the authoritarian culture that had been created by the CEO.

One of Andrea's primary responsibilities is responding to client information security and privacy questionnaires. Her company analyzes and stores sensitive data, and clients routinely assess the company's policies and procedures to ensure they are meeting industry-standard laws and regulations. If the company seems not to be following best practices, clients will likely move to a competitor, so there are millions of dollars at stake. Andrea's responses to the questionnaire are critical to keep existing clients happy and to win new clients.

Last week, Andrea's supervisor, also new to the organization, called her into his office and explained how the client questionnaire process had worked in the past. He mentioned that a questionnaire from an important client had just come in, and he handed Andrea a copy of the client's questionnaire from the previous year, which had been reviewed and approved by the CEO. The supervisor asked Andrea to leverage the old questionnaire to fill out this year's new request.

After spending a few days reviewing the questionnaire and following up with various departments for insight, Andrea felt confident that last year's questionnaire was not filled out correctly. Many questions she believed should have been answered as "no" (or out of compliance) were answered as "yes" (in compliance).

Andrea scheduled a meeting with her boss to discuss her findings, eager to make him aware of the gaps she had identified. Upon reviewing the responses in question, he took notes and scheduled a meeting with the CEO.

The next day the boss called Andrea into his office again. He explained, "For a lot of questions the client was not specific enough, so we can interpret those to our advantage."

Andrea agreed that many of the questions were vague and open to interpretation. But, she pointed out, "We know what principle of compliance they are referring to and why they are asking about it, regardless of how the questions are worded."

Andrea and her boss ended up incorporating a meet-in-the-middle approach, arriving at answers they both felt comfortable with. Then they passed the questionnaire on to the CEO.

A few days later, Andrea received the final copy of the questionnaire, which had already been submitted to the client. As a junior compliance analyst, she understands the intent of the questions being asked, but has limited understanding in some of the more technical areas. Still, she's pretty sure that many of the CEO's changes did not reflect the truth. What should she do?

CHAPTER 4

Challenge 4: Conflicts of Interest

Multiple roles put you (or your company) at cross purposes.

It's Abed's last day at TerroTech and he's in the exit interview, returning confidential materials. While retrieving the next document from his bag, he notices that one side has proprietary TerroTech content and the other has highly sensitive handwritten notes about StartNet, Abed's new start-up. Abed had completely forgotten about the notes, and if he turns them over now it could seriously endanger the future of his new company. Does he return the document to comply with the employment agreement, or does he withhold it to protect StartNet?

Abed and his co-founder, Dave (TerroTech's current VP of Operations), had been extremely cautious in starting StartNet. Four months ago, TerroTech adjusted its strategy and decided to liquidate an old product line. The CEO asked Dave to explore selling the product to TerroTech's contract manufacturer and asked

Abed to sell the supporting R&D team. When Abed pitched the offer to the contract manufacturer's venture capitalists, they were impressed with his presentation but decided not to acquire the product or team. Instead, they recruited Abed and Dave together to found StartNet. To avoid conflicts of interest and confidentiality issues while employed by TerroTech, they both deferred any new product development until after they left the company.

The origin of the incriminating notes is harmless; they are merely the result of a long-past academic conversation. Years earlier, a coworker had asked Abed about a business school homework question: "If you were to start a new company, how would you staff it and in what order would you recruit the employees?" After thinking for a while, Abed began to draw a hypothetical org chart, using generic titles. When the coworker struggled to understand his strategy, Abed added the names of people they knew at TerroTech.

Now Abed is concerned that the handwritten notes will be seen by the exit committee as a plan to systematically recruit TerroTech's key employees to staff his new company. To make matters worse, Dave, his co-founder, happens to be the first name on the list.

TerroTech's VP of Engineering and legal counsel are attending Abed's exit interview. As a senior R&D manager, Abed has contributed significantly to TerroTech's business-critical development plans and strategies, and the role of the exit committee is to ensure he won't steal key talent or information during his departure.

Abed fully intends to honor TerroTech's non-recruit and non-compete clauses. He also fully intends to return all of TerroTech's confidential information. He has a contractual duty, it's the honest thing to do, and his integrity demands it.

But Abed also has obligations to StartNet's stockholders, employees, and future stakeholders, as well as responsibilities to their families and to his own future. Any allegations against StartNet—even if proven groundless—could cause the venture capitalists to back out or make future funding more difficult. Further, even if TerroTech considers the notes to be inconsequential now, they may choose to use them once StartNet succeeds, threatening StartNet and its stakeholders.

For now, no one has seen inside Abed's bag. He could pull out a different document and pretend the handwritten notes don't exist. On the other hand, if he doesn't reveal the document himself, TerroTech might search his bag and discover it. How should he handle this conflict of interest?

Explanation

Perhaps the most important observation about conflicts of interest is that they are the most frequently excused dilemma in the business world. More than any other dilemma, this one invokes the argument, "That's just how business is done." A true statement, for sure, but not one that actually makes an ethical argument.

Sometimes you're faced with the choice of abandoning a commitment, or interest, because doing so will force you to compromise another commitment you have made. This is the classic Conflict of Interest dilemma, which we define as "a structural situation in which one person occupies multiple roles that have the potential to be at odds with one another."

Think for a moment about the many different ways important interests are sacrificed or compromised every day. For example, vendors often seek to earn the loyalty of their customers' employees by offering them gifts, perks, trips, or meals. The hope is that those employees will favor them when it comes time to spend the company's money. This technique places the employees in a conflict of interest, because they must choose between honoring the reciprocity and good will they feel toward these vendors and making purchasing choices that may be best for their company.

A conflict of interest likewise occurs when an employee uses company information or resources to leverage a better job offer outside the company. It can be hard to draw the line between your own abilities, skills, or expertise and the resources provided by your employer. But some things, like client lists, processes, or even your work time don't belong to you.

The most tempting competing interest—and the most common—is personal benefit. A position of influence or power almost always comes with the opportunity for inappropriate gain. Remember, though, that this competing interest is also the least tolerated. You will impugn your reputation more quickly by abusing power for your own benefit than by any other way. Conversely, forthrightness in appropriately managing conflicts of interest is one of your best opportunities for developing a stellar reputation for ethical behavior.

Many high profile cases demonstrate the necessity of vigilance in identifying and effectively managing conflicts of interest. For example, the board of directors at Enron voted to override the conflict of interest provision of its own code of conduct to allow their chief financial officer, Andy Fastow, to also be the president of the off-balance-sheet special entities he was creating. Having one person fill both roles made it impossible to maintain accounting standards that required an arms-length transaction between the organizations. Of course, all of this ended very badly with the demise of Enron and the incarceration of Andy Fastow, among other Enron officials.

In another high-profile case involving conflicts of interest, Darleen Druyun, the principal deputy undersecretary of the U.S. Air Force for acquisition, and Michael Sears, chief financial officer of Boeing, both went to prison. Ignoring rules that forbade organizations doing business with the federal government from discussing post-retirement employment positions with those government officials, Darleen and Michael met at a private airport in Florida to discuss a job for her at Boeing after her retirement. They were at the time in the middle of negotiating a multi-billion-dollar contract for the Air Force to lease Boeing 767s as air-refueling tankers. Darleen later admitted to inflating the bidding price to benefit her future employer and to sharing information with Boeing from the bid of a competitor.

Similarly, numerous cases document the harm that accrues through the perverse incentive structures that exist in many professions. Examples include performance of unnecessary surgeries and tests, utilization of inferior medical devices, employment of inferior building materials and designs, and use of shortcuts in buildings, bridges, and roads. Finally, in the 2016 voting cycle there were a number of voters in the United States wondering how U.S. presidential candidate Hillary Clinton could act with adequate objectivity as president when she and her husband had accepted so much money from companies and foreign governments for their own personal bank accounts, as well as for their foundation. Similarly, voters wondered if they could choose a presidential candidate like Donald Trump, who even during his campaign seemed more concerned about how well his company was doing financially than he was about how well the country was faring.

Whatever the conflict, the underlying principles are those of priority and balance. Some obligations and commitments rank higher than others because of what you get in return. For example, your employer bargained for your time, ability, and loyalty; you agreed to the bargain by taking the job in exchange for pay, benefits, and professional development. Many other important commitments, like marriage or citizenship, also include reciprocal benefits and require high prioritization. Further, when you have obligations to multiple entities—even obligations that don't involve personal gain—you need to be able to balance those obligations.

For example, while Brad was chairing the Pittsburgh Business Ethics Awards program, he visited with several finalist organizations to help determine the winner. While meeting the executive director of the Pittsburgh Symphony Orchestra, Brad mentioned that he was the vice president of a local high school band booster organization. The executive director mentioned that they often provided pro-bono mini-concerts as fundraisers for local high schools. Would Brad be interested in having these world-class musicians come to his children's high school?

In this instance, Brad needed to balance the importance of being completely objective in determining who won the award with his desire to help the local high school band. As lucrative and educational as the mini-concert might be, Brad felt it would look suspicious—and even cloud his judgment—if the Pittsburgh Symphony Orchestra began to be involved with his fundraising while he was considering them for the Ethics Award. Because his assignment to chair the awards program had facilitated his contact with the symphony in the first place and was closely related to his reputation as a professional and scholar, he chose to honor that commitment. Brad thanked the executive director for his generosity and said he would pass along the information to the booster organization—for consideration in future years.

Whatever your particular conflict, you'll resolve this dilemma best by recognizing the most important obligations and giving them the priority they deserve.

Questions to Ask

When multiple roles create an ethical conflict, you may find a way forward by considering these questions.

1. Are there any clear rules (organizational or otherwise) you should be following?

Many organizations have developed policies or guidelines to help employees and vendors deal with conflicts of interest. Policies around gifts often vary by organization. For example, while most businesses allow for "nominal" gifts, the U.S. government has a zero tolerance policy, not allowing its employees to accept any gifts. Policies around time use also vary. For instance, because university faculty members are often called upon to use their expertise for organizations outside of the university, many universities have a policy that allows faculty members to work one day a week on behalf of entities other than the university, even when that work is financially compensated. Other organizations prohibit employees from spending even non-work hours on projects that might conflict with the primary employer's interests.

In addition to being helpful personally, policies also help employees and managers speak up when they see others in conflicts-of-interest situations. In the TerroTech dilemma, there was a clear rule: Abed needed to return the confidential information. However, the two-sided piece of paper made compliance to the rule complex.

2. Would your actions cause others to question your motives?

Probably more than any other dilemma, the perception of wrongdoing in this dilemma is just as important as any actual malfeasance. Many wonder why they should care what others think when it comes to ethics. While it is true that you wouldn't necessarily want to determine your ethics based on the opinions of others, in the real world, your reputation will certainly help determine your upward mobility and opportunities to be a good influence in the future. Many a career has been derailed because an individual did not understand the importance of being above any appearance of evil. In this case, if Abed had not revealed that he had the confidential document, the other party may have never known. At the same time, allowing them to see the other side of the paper could inappropriately make them question his motives. However, if they had asked to look through his briefcase and he had demurred in any way, they would have questioned his motives even more. The difficulty of this question reveals the need for moral imagination in resolving dilemmas. Moral imagination has been defined as "the ability to think outside the box and envision ways to be both ethical and successful." [1]

3. Who has a right to know the details, and have you let them know?

Probably more than for any other dilemma, openness or "sunshine" is often the easiest solution to conflicts of interest. When we have potential conflicts of interest, it is critical that those who might be affected negatively understand the conflicts. Your disclosure can do more than just alert them to be on guard; it can also invite them to help you minimize the conflict. In the TerroTech situation, it would be important for Abed to reveal the situation to both TerroTech and to StartNet, his new company.

4. Is there a way to remove yourself from the conflict of loyalties?

Sometimes there are simple ways to avoid a conflict of interest. For example, you can let those prone to give you gifts know that you do not accept gifts. One of the things that makes the TerroTech situation so difficult is that there is no way for Abed to avoid the conflict of loyalties as he transitions between firms. Waiting to begin StartNet product development until he exited TerroTech was a good move. Properly conducting the transition process, itself, could also help him avoid conflicting loyalties in the future.

5. Have the other parties done, or could they do, anything to free you from your obligation to them?

In many cases, a party might be willing—or even grateful—to free you from your obligation if you explain why it puts you in an ethically difficult situation. However, in Abed's case, it is not at all likely that either party would release him from his duties.

6. Is there any way to uphold both of your obligations?

This is another place where moral imagination can save the day. It is really critical that Abed uphold his obligations to both parties—meaning he must return the confidential information on the TerroTech side of the piece of paper while not divulging his notes on the other side. In "What Happened," we will see Abed's innovative way of doing this.

Pitfalls

Watch for these common conflict-of-interest pitfalls, so you don't accidentally fall prey.

Not Recognizing the Conflict

We find that people often don't notice conflicts of interest. Because they are so common and because others don't recognize or manage them well, we simply don't see them. Also, because of the negative connotation of "conflicts of interest" and because dealing with them generally means work, our subconscious minds avoid labeling these issues.

Also, we sometimes don't recognize new conflicts of interest arising when things in our world change. For example, it is not necessarily inappropriate for the sole owner of a company to accept extravagant gifts from a supplier. While it is probably not a good practice from a leadership perspective, making a poor purchasing decision when you're the sole owner of the company primarily hurts you. However, we've seen examples of owners who sell a minority interest in their company and then continue to accept those same gifts from suppliers, not recognizing that they now also have a fiduciary responsibility to their minority owners that they didn't have before.

Running from or Hiding the Conflict

When we do recognize a conflict of interest, we often want to run from it or hide it. We may even go to great lengths to avoid dealing with it. Realize that conflict of interest situations will generally be revealed, so running or hiding will only make the situation worse in the long run.

Assuming Disclosure is Enough

We said that one of the best ways of dealing with a conflict of interest is disclosure. Now we need to warn you that disclosure has a dark side. Research has found that when salespeople disclose their conflicts of interest to a client, they oftentimes will then assume that it is the buyer's responsibility not to be taken, so they actually end up taking more advantage of the client. In fact, they may have an easier time fleecing the client, because the act of disclosure signals to the client that the salespeople are trustworthy.[2] All who are in a conflicted position need to be proactive in making sure that others' interests are protected.

Pretending Objectivity

We all like to see ourselves in a positive light. Consequently, we have a tendency to believe that we can be objective even when our self-interest is at play. However, social science findings clearly demonstrate that we are not completely objective. In fact, it's fair to say that we are never really objective at all. Our values, experiences, and interests all color what we notice, how we interpret what we do notice, and how we respond to our interpretations. No matter how pure your intent, you can't simply outsmart or dodge bias created by your own perceptions. Beyond this problem, even if you could be above the influences of a conflict of interest, others would not believe that you are. The best bet—for you and your organization—is to acknowledge that you're human and attempt to resolve your conflicting interests.

Bill's Experience

Conflicts of interest arise all the time in business. I have found that a little thinking ahead can save your integrity and your reputation.

Relationship Advice

Do friendship and business mix well? Professional relationships can be complicated when a close relationship already exists between the parties. I have seen this in my career with both familial and personal relationships.

One day, back when I was heading a large procurement organization, the buyer of rubber products came to my office and told me that his son, a recent college graduate, had just accepted a job as a rubber salesman at one of our largest suppliers. The buyer readily disclosed that his son would be calling on him and that he was fully aware of the need to be open, transparent and fair. He wanted me to be aware of the situation, but gave his guarantee that he would handle the relationship fairly. While I appreciated his openness, I was skeptical of the arrangement. I explained that no matter how fairly, honestly and openly he conducted his business, this situation both looked and felt wrong. I knew him to be an excellent buyer, but that didn't matter. I suggested that our organization was sufficiently large that we could swap commodities so that another buyer would handle the rubber commodities. He agreed to the arrangement, and the potential appearance of impropriety was avoided. From this experience, I learned that even when potential conflicts of interest are fully communicated and transparent, it's often best to avoid them altogether.

I believe friendships in business are good. They build rapport, trust, and loyalty. But there are also risks of favoritism, back-scratching, and exclusion of others. These risks must be faced with openness, honesty and transparency.

Gift Giving

Another complicating aspect of mixing friendship and business is the exchange of gifts or favors. Gifting persists everywhere in most organizations, which often leads to ethical issues and the need for greater awareness and guidelines. Most procurement and sales organizations—where gifting is most prevalent—do a very good job of educating their buyers and sales professionals about policies on giving and receiving gifts. However, even the most ethically mature employees are sometimes unaware of the ethical issues that could be involved.

Our corporate medical director at Alcoa, an MD, got married during the time he was reporting to me. Upon returning from his honeymoon, he told me that two of his doctor friends had gone to his wedding and presented him with cash gifts of $2,000 each. These same friends were medical consultants to Alcoa, receiving annual fees of about $80,000 a year under contracts authorized by the corporate medical director. I explained to him that some people might *interpret what had happened as him inviting his suppliers to his wedding in exchange for kickbacks.*

Of course, he protested by saying that it was nothing of the sort; these gentlemen were real friends of his, and they had given him the gifts out of the goodness of their hearts. We discussed the situation at length, and I explained that regardless of what the facts were, he needed to be aware of how the situation would be perceived by others. The fact that the gift amount was identical for each doctor suggested that they must have discussed the situation beforehand. The fact that they gave these gifts in cash raised another red flag. After an hour of discussing the issue, he agreed to return the money.

This situation could have and should have been avoided. For example, the medical director could have invited the doctors to his wedding, but written on the invitation, "Given our business relationship, gifts would be inappropriate. I hope you can attend the wedding." A lesson learned: even the best people don't always recognize ethical dilemmas.

Giving or receiving gifts in a business situation is always fraught with ethical risk, so be careful! A good first step is to review your organization's policy. Most policies say that it is inappropriate to give or receive gifts that exceed a "nominal" value. Then gather cultural information by discussing with your boss, your coworkers and others the question, "What is nominal?" It can also be helpful to watch the behavior of your coworkers and ask them about it. If your peers go to a professional sporting event as their business client's guest, ask them how they reconcile that with the "nominal" policy. You might learn that there was a clear business purpose, or that the event was disclosed to the manager and permission to attend was obtained prior to the event. By asking, you might also make them aware of the policy and of the fact that others are watching how they behave, motivating them to be better in the process.

Personally, I like the policy of the U.S. government: it is inappropriate to give or accept anything from those with whom you do business. Several governments have the same policy. Government officials will not let you buy them a beverage, a snack or a meal. They will not accept even small token gifts like notepads or pens. They have a clear line that is easy to see. By contrast, the "nominal" guideline will require personal judgment. Judge wisely!

As the leader of a procurement organization I was offered many gifts. The more lavish offers included week-long golf trips to California and Hawaii on the supplier's company plane and trips to major sporting events like the Super Bowl, college football bowl games, a heavyweight championship boxing match, and even the Olympics. Once I was offered a ski trip—again on the supplier's company plane—to Aspen, Colorado, along with the use of a chalet and lift tickets for a week. Not only did I never accept any of these trips, but I also let my organization know about the offers. I wanted to ensure awareness and also help others learn from my scrutiny and behavior.

With regard to meals, I always had two general rules. First, there had to be a clear business purpose for me to accept a meal. And second, for every meal that I accepted from others, I would buy them a meal as well.

One argument I often hear is that refusing a gift is rude in some cultures, particularly in areas like Asia or the Middle East. However, there is a way to navigate such situations. Whenever I began a relationship that involved a negotiation of some kind, I explained that we would forego the customary gift exchange at the end of the negotiating process. This clarification was always accepted and appreciated. As a substitute for gifts, I would often suggest that we have a meal at the beginning of the negotiation for the entire negotiation team, which I would buy, and another meal at the end of the negotiation, which my counterpart could buy. By establishing expectations early on, potential gift-giving dilemmas can usually be avoided entirely.

Bribes as Conflicts of Interest

It is very common in certain jurisdictions of the world that payments to officials are required to do business there. One problem with the practice of paying bribes is that they create immediate conflicts of interest. My approach at Alcoa was to never, ever bribe my way into getting things done. This was not always easy.

For example, to help us navigate an unfamiliar business territory in the Middle East, our company hired a consultant. Early on, the consultant explained that we would be required to make "extra" payments to certain government officials. He even proposed a special arrangement with an "agent" who could handle all of the necessary payments for us. Our accounting records would show payments to a registered agent, such that our company could avoid any appearance of making payments to government officials. Incredible! It was hard for me to believe that governments, consultants, agents, and business leaders would routinely collude through such elaborate schemes to create the appearance of legitimacy. We did not follow the agent's advice. Honest and respectable companies do not play that game.

In fact, when we did make payments to certain entities, we went out of our way to demonstrate real legitimacy. While I was working in Russia, our corporate foundation wanted to make a sizeable donation to a Russian school. Because Russia was known for its corruption, the foundation chose a third party to handle the transaction. We hired an organization from England, who certified the transaction and verified that the money was delivered to the proper organization—not into the hands of bureaucrats. The cost of this service was 25% of the donation. I found that rather excessive. In fact, if we had transferred the money without the third-party service, my guess was that the corrupt system would have taken far less than 25%. The cost of legitimacy is often unfair. Then again, it's hard to place a numeric value on maintaining your company's integrity.

Planning Ahead

Although conflicts of interest are inevitable, getting side-swiped by them is not. Take these steps to minimize the impact of future conflicts.

1. Recognize the obligations you owe. Conflicts of interest often surprise people. It is important to think about the obligations you have to others and consider how those obligations might potentially come into conflict. You should also consider how others might attempt to get you to compromise your duties for their benefit. This is a particularly important process to go through when accepting any new obligation. Recognizing your potential conflicts of interest helps to ensure that you will handle them well.

2. Give yourself some credit. Remember that having a conflict of interest often says something positive about you. The only people who have no conflicts of interest are people who have no friends, no family, and are not involved in anything. Therefore, think of the process of identifying your potential conflicts of interest not as an exercise in seeing how bad you are, but rather as a process of seeing how important you've become. This perspective will help you look more honestly at yourself and your commitments.

3. Watch out for nepotism. Nepotism is a particularly clear conflict of interest. While hiring or working with relatives is oftentimes absolutely appropriate (for example, in a 100% privately owned firm), such appropriateness needs to be demonstrated to those who may be affected. For example, when propriety dictates that an individual report to someone other than a relative, make sure everyone knows about this reporting plan. Clear communication can minimize suspicions of these conflicts. Still, because of financial bundling, marital relationships in organizational and community life are particularly tricky and need to be carefully managed.

4. Acknowledge trade-offs. You will never be able to eliminate conflicts of interest completely. For example, the smaller a community (say, a city, company, or civic organization) the more likely you are to experience conflicts. It is not unusual in a small town for a company leader to also be a government leader. Teachers and police officers likely have close relationships with many of the people they serve.

A similar phenomenon emerges in niche fields, where the pool of prospective candidates is small. For example, through Brad's service on the ethics committee of USA Synchro (the U.S.

Olympic Committee member organization for Synchronized Swimming), he noted this problem in vetting potential judges who would choose the national team. Because synchronized swimming is a small community, virtually every potential judge had some level of conflict of interest. The organization determined that if they wanted to have qualified judges, they would need to allow minor conflicts of interest. For instance, one judge had coached one of the finalists when she was in the fourth grade. Sometimes trade-offs like this have to be made.

5. Develop a system of training and reporting. When you are in an organizational leadership position, it is critical that you develop conflicts of interest policies, train people on these policies, and create systems for reporting and effectively managing these conflicts. In our experience, people deal with these issues much better when they've been educated on them, particularly with training examples germane to their work situations. Systems that remind all employees to examine their conflicts of interest also help. For instance, some organizations include a note on meeting agendas, reminding individuals to disclose any conflicts of interest they may have with any item on the agenda. Regular practices of disclosure, ideally initiated by company leaders, sends the message that conflicts of interest are a normal part of organizational life that need to be managed, but not feared. It is also important to remember that people will change behavior in relationship to policies. Follow up on the outcomes of policy changes to make sure they are meeting your original objectives.

What Happened

In this chapter's opening story, Abed decided that handing in the TerroTech confidential material was the right thing to do. He disclosed his dilemma to TerroTech's legal counsel: He felt that in good conscience, he could not withhold the document from them, take it with him, or destroy it, but he didn't want the notes on the back to be misconstrued as an intent to violate the non-recruit clause or to steal TerroTech's ideas.

Abed proposed that they copy the TerroTech side and then shred the original. The counselor instead suggested that they make a copy of the TerroTech side, put it in the disclosure file, and then seal the original document in an envelope. The envelope was to be placed in escrow with a third party in the event that it should ever be needed as evidence.

Abed agreed to the counselor's proposal. Together they made a copy for the file, put the original in a sealed envelope, and delivered the envelope to a mutually trusted party for safe-keeping.

However, when the counselor copied the document, he pretended to have trouble with the copier's contrast settings. He asserted that the first copy was too dark and quickly put it in the shred bin before making a second copy. Abed requested that it be shredded immediately, but the counselor claimed that it couldn't be retrieved because the shredding company had the only key to the bin. It wasn't until later that Abed found out he had been deceived.

TerroTech was soon acquired, and the acquiring company used the notes against StartNet after they launched their first product. The copy that was allegedly "too dark" had been retrieved from the shredding bin after Abed left. TerroTech used the document as legal leverage to force StartNet to buy a "license" for a modest sum of cash, despite the fact that StartNet never recruited any TerroTech employees. Abed was even presented with a copy of the notes during the legal posturing. Afterwards, he inquired of the escrow party to discover if he had shared the original document with TerroTech. He presented the document to Abed in the sealed envelope, which he still possesses unopened.

Practice Dilemma

The partially opened gift stares at Clyde from his kitchen table. It's a baby present from a key supplier, a sign of goodwill after Clyde worked hard to improve their unstable relationship with his company. Clyde knows that his organization forbids employees from accepting gifts of any kind from suppliers, but he also knows that his boss accepted a similar gift just two weeks ago. "If I keep the gift, nobody will know," he thinks to himself. "But if I send it back, I'll probably hurt someone's feelings."

Clyde started his career with a large national department store and has just been promoted to being a buyer. He loves his work, and his company has been good to him and his young family. Clyde is now in charge of purchasing knives, forks and spoons for the floundering flatware department, which has not even come close to meeting sales forecasts for the last three years. The expectations in the office are low, but he knows that if he can turn around the department's performance, he will look like a hero and his future at the company will be bright.

The previous flatware buyers had not stayed with the company for long. This weakened the company's relationship with one of the major flatware suppliers. If the relationship did not improve quickly, Clyde feared he might lose the biggest flatware brand on his floor. As a result, he worked tirelessly to earn the confidence of the supplier by planning advertising and pricing promotions and communicating often.

Five months into his new role, Clyde told several suppliers that he would be unavailable during the following week, due to the arrival of his first baby. Clyde received many congratulatory emails, but no gifts until now. Then his biggest flatware supplier sent a thoughtful card and a baby flatware set for his new child. The flatware set is small and inexpensive, worth about $25, and was sent directly to Clyde's home, meaning that nobody at work will know about it. He feels honored by the supplier's kindly gesture, especially considering their rocky history with Clyde's company. He's worried that he might offend them if he returns the gift, thereby erasing all of the work he has done to stabilize the relationship.

The retailer's no-gifts policy should make Clyde's decision easy, but the situation is complicated by the knowledge that his boss had accepted a very similar gift from the same company just two weeks earlier. This creates an expectation—for suppliers and buyers—that it may actually be permissible to accept some gifts. If Clyde returns the gift, he risks making his own boss look dishonest for accepting the gift sent to him. Perhaps the supplier will question the integrity of the people who work at Clyde's company, given the inconsistency around this policy.

Clyde knows his wife will love the baby flatware set. No one needs to know if he decides to keep the gift, but many people will probably find out if he returns it. "It is just a kind gesture from a new friend," he reasons with himself. "Sending it back will do more harm than good." Clyde looks at the newly opened flatware set, wondering what to do next.

CHAPTER 5

Challenge 5: Suspicions Without Enough Evidence

You believe that something wrong is going on, but you're not sure.

"Don't worry, I took care of it." Cindy didn't seem willing to give much more detail than that.

This was a critical project for Marco's internship, and deadlines were tight. So when he learned that a major shipment was being rejected by the export authorities in China and would be sent back to the factory, he was more than a little concerned.

Marco felt fortunate, as a college sophomore, to be trusted with this product, a breakthrough in the crafting industry. With $1.3 million in new revenues and an operating profit margin well over 50%, it was a major revenue stream for a very important client.

Cindy is a Chinese national who is responsible for external logistics in the factory. Marco met her during a visit to China several months ago. She is charismatic and likeable. Her reputation at the company is strong: "If you *really* need something to get done, you go to Cindy." She seems willing to do whatever it takes to get results.

Marco and Cindy were on a compressed product launch schedule. What would normally take about eight months, they had to complete in four months in order to ensure that Walmart would receive the shipment in time for Black Friday. After working extra hours to resolve several quality problems, they were barely on track to hit their manufacturing deadlines.

Marco reread the email that was all too brief—written while he was sleeping—to inform him that his shipment from the factory had just been rejected. The Chinese export authorities were claiming that the pallets were 30% overweight, even though Marco had asked the engineers to personally weigh the products to prevent these types of problems. Procedure stated that overweight shipments must be returned to the factory for resubmission.

Marco spent the day determining how much this would delay the project and trying to find the problem's root cause. Around 5 p.m. his time, when the Chinese offices were just opening, he called Cindy. She quickly brushed aside the issue, saying she had already resolved it.

When Marco persisted, she vaguely responded, "I paid a fine so they would not have to return the shipment to the factory. It was shipped to you last night. It's taken care of."

As far as Marco knew, paying a fine was not a normal option in the procedure. Was this actually a bribe?

He could try to investigate, but he was only an intern. Besides, language, cultural, and time zone barriers made it extremely difficult to get many details from the factory. Was it his job to ensure that Cindy did her duties ethically? What could he do about it, anyway, if the shipment has already been sent?

Explanation

At first, this dilemma may seem like an Intervention dilemma, which you read about in Chapter 3. But it differs in one very important way: this dilemma isn't about how you stop something, but how you find out if there is something to stop.

Suspicions Without Enough Evidence is a dilemma because the way you investigate matters. Looking into any wrongdoing usually appears like an outright accusation. "After all," people will ask, "if everything were fine, why the need to investigate?" Depending on how you address the situation, people may fill in the blanks before you've found any answers.

You may not be the best person to investigate the problem. If not, make sure the investigator is appropriately chosen, especially if the investigation needs to be public. Make sure the person is even-handed and has a strong reputation for fairness. But don't think you wash your hands of responsibility just by giving the task to someone else. You will be responsible for the investigator's conclusions. Be ready to shoulder the results.

Whether you are investigating or asking someone else to do it in your place, it's essential that you avoid undue bias—and even the appearance of bias. Others will scrutinize whatever conclusion you reach, even if they don't have all the information you have. You have an obligation not just to follow a fair process, but to make sure the process is clear for all involved.

These dilemmas can be time sensitive, since negative consequences may follow if you act too slowly. For example, Marco's dilemma cannot wait if it means the product timeline is at risk.

Circumstances surrounding Suspicions Without Enough Evidence often require confidentiality. Be sure to consider what is appropriately confidential and what others have a right to know. Even an entirely ethical investigation can have unethical consequences if (1) people don't get the information to which they're entitled, or (2) private information is shared with the wrong people. Be assiduous about knowing the difference.

Questions to Ask

Consider the following questions as you decide how to handle Suspicions Without Enough Evidence.

1. Who is accountable for solving the problem and how do you best inform them?

Before you start to investigate, be sure to determine whether you are even the person who should. Being the wrong person and investigating anyway puts the involved parties at risk. It also puts you at risk. You could lack the knowledge or power needed to find the truth. Mistaken accusations could harm your relationships and career. Be sure that you are the right person to act.

If you decide that someone else needs to investigate, you next need to consider how to inform the right people. If you frame the problem in the wrong way, you might be reaching a conclusion for them. Provide all the information you have. Measure your words carefully to avoid undue influence. For example, Marco might tell his boss or Cindy's boss about what he observed, but he will need to do it without passing undue judgment.

2. What will happen if you act on the allegations and they are false?

Because claims of wrongdoing can carry serious consequences, remember that you have an obligation to the accused just as much as to the accuser. You have the power to ruin someone's life by putting too much stock in a false accusation. Think through the unrecoverable outcomes: loss of reputation, damaged relationships, the emotional toll. Even when people are exonerated, these costs can burden them for years.

If Marco acts rashly, he could damage Cindy's standing in the company. Clearly, Marco needs to be very careful about how he handles his suspicions.

3. What will happen if the suspicions are true and you do nothing?

You probably asked this question first. Once we hear an accusation, we naturally consider all the consequences of its being true. We think of the people who might be hurt. We think of the mess that will need to be cleaned up. In fact, we usually think about worst-case scenarios.

But all that doom and gloom may not really be answering the question, because emotionally charged "what ifs" make us think in sloppy ways. It's important to approach this question methodically. Think through what the real consequences of your inaction will be. What are the risks to you, to those in your workplace, or to those outside of work? Are there legal ramifications? How long can the alleged behavior go on? Does inaction make you complicit?

Just as Marco needs to imagine what would happen if he accused Cindy of things she didn't do, Marco must consider what would happen if Cindy is in fact a risk to the company by paying bribes to Chinese officials. Whether you discover that things may not be as bad as you originally thought, or you realize that they're actually worse, be thorough in thinking through this question to be sure you consider all the possible outcomes.

4. Considering what might happen, does the quality of your information justify action?

Solid accusations or suspicions have two attributes: reliability and sufficiency.

Reliable accusations and suspicions come from trustworthy sources—ideally from individuals who don't stand to gain from their claims proving true. Reliable allegations will survive your scrutiny of the details and will be consistent in the retelling. Don't let the accusers put their claims above reproach. It may be unpleasant for them, and for you, to validate their claims, but if the accusations seem unreliable, you need to be sure.

Even if an allegation or suspicion is accurate, it may not tell the whole story. Sufficient accusations don't leave out critical details. Be very uncomfortable with acting if you find yourself needing to fill in the gaps with suppositions. When accusations or suspicions are insufficiently detailed, thoroughly consider all the possible explanations for what you've been told. For example, Cindy might just know the export process better than Marco and might have acted entirely ethically.

5. Does your bias push you to believe or dismiss too quickly?

Notice that this question assumes that you are biased. Really, it's naive to think that anyone isn't. We all constantly judge information based on our experience, so avoiding bias completely is essentially impossible. That's why we don't advise you to "be unbiased" when investigating a problem. Instead, our advice is to manage your biases. Recognize them and do your best to balance them with patience and wisdom.

The most important way to balance your biases is to take time in reaching conclusions. You will invariably have assumptions about the situation, so be sure to reflect so you can consider possibilities beyond your assumptions.

Notice in the opening dilemma how Marco immediately jumped to the possibility of a bribe. That response probably came partly from his natural biases. Doing business in China comes with a reputation for occasional or even frequent bribe demands. Because Cindy is a Chinese national, Marco's suspicion of a bribe could be heightened because he knows that she understands the culture well. Marco needs to recognize that his suspicion is coming at least partly from some kind of preformed bias.

6. Who deserves the most protection?

No matter how well you investigate, there's a pretty good chance you won't find out all that you need to know. When that's the case, consider who needs to come first and be sure that you protect that party. Here, Marco owes an important duty is to his employer. If bribery was happening, the publicity of this information could be a huge problem for his company and its shareholders. But bribes also hurt a well-functioning society, imposing a cost on the least powerful. Be sure that you protect those who deserve protection.

Pitfalls

When you suspect something is wrong but don't have enough evidence, be careful of the following traps.

Acting Hastily

Acting too quickly is a common mistake. Remember that accusers aren't just trying to involve you, but to recruit you. They may have ulterior motives for what they're telling you. Or they may not have the power they need to act on their own. Don't be a tool for their mischief by jumping in before you know they raise a valid concern.

Delaying Action

On the other hand, don't act too slowly. If the situation is especially unpleasant, it can be easy to find yourself hoping that it will simply go away. Don't wait to investigate until you are forced by a crisis to do so. That time may come too late.

Appearing Overly Biased

When you investigate a potential problem, appearances matter. Take care to avoid appearing unduly biased. If you seem to have an agenda, your apparent bias will make others question the accuracy of the information you reveal. Use careful language to both describe and investigate the problem. Always clearly acknowledge that more than one possible explanation exists. When you explain your reasoning, be quick to point out where your conclusions have weaknesses.

Not Gathering Sufficient Information

To maintain your credibility, avoid being sloppy with information. Take careful notes. Protect the documentation you gather. Try to corroborate the truth with multiple sources. Ask good questions that invite detailed explanations. Remember that in the end, you may be making very serious accusations. The quality of your evidence will protect you from accusations of bias or dishonesty.

Remember that the law prohibits defamation, which is a false claim about someone else. If you aren't thoughtful and deliberate in how you approach this dilemma, you could face personal liability for slandering another person.

Not Reporting Appropriately

Finally, be familiar with reporting requirements. There's always a chance that policies or laws require certain kinds of actions to be reported to higher authorities. Reportable issues usually involve financial malfeasance, risk to children, or danger to the health and safety of others. You might think this is a problem you can handle on your own, when in reality, better trained and more capable people are meant to address the situation. Find out what disclosure rules and laws relate to the suspicions you're investigating.

 ## Bill's Experiences

One rule guides my approach to Suspicions Without Enough Evidence. When confronted with allegations, investigate fast; when the facts are gathered, act fast.

"He Fired Himself"

An anonymous allegation was made on the company's compliance telephone line that the plant manager of a factory in Australia was instructing employees to "spin" the safety results. Our company typically received about 1,200 complaints on the company compliance line each year, about 90% of which had little to no substance or were petty personal complaints about a boss or coworker. Yet despite the low likelihood of discovering actual compliance issues, we fully investigated every complaint.

At the time, I was responsible for corporate safety, and so this specific complaint was referred to me. I chose as the investigator a safety professional from our Tennessee location who had an impeccable reputation for knowing the details about safety record keeping. She traveled to Australia to investigate the report firsthand.

A week later, she called and said that she found 50 unreported safety incidents. Most were minor medical treatment cases, but a few were recordable incidents—safety issues serious enough to endanger our employees. Upon interviewing the victims and the safety manager, she learned that the plant manager had instructed them not to report these incidents. This same plant manager was performing very well in other areas: quality, inventory reduction, revenue, and employee engagement. In fact, he was being groomed to be promoted as a business unit president.

We then confronted the plant manager about the unreported incidents. He denied the allegations but was unconvincing. We invited him to provide refuting evidence, but he had none.

Safety is an essential part of the culture at Alcoa, and the reporting of incidents is integral to safety. Reporting can prevent similar problems in other locations. This plant manager had attended plant manager training, where we stress the importance of safety and how to properly report incidents. We concluded that he simply chose not to follow our rules so that he could look like a better plant manager.

We wrote up the allegation and the results of our investigation in a report that we delivered to the business unit president (the plant manager's boss) and the group president (the business unit president's boss). They invited me to a meeting in New York, where they asked, "Do we have to fire him?"

My response was, "No, he's already fired himself. Now 60,000 employees are watching you to see what you will do."

In the end, the plant manager was terminated. And, of course, all the other employees noticed. Informal communication networks in corporations work quite well. In fact, the two leaders who made the final decision now have an enhanced reputation for supporting the safety value of the company. By acting appropriately, this situation served to reinforce key values instead of jeopardizing them.

No Kickbacks Allowed

In 2005, Alcoa acquired two very large aluminum manufacturing plants in Russia, and I was tapped to be the President of Alcoa-Russia. The Russian plants were very inefficient, so we knew in advance that many employees would be laid off. In fact, during the three years of my tenure, the total number of employees would be reduced from over 15,000 to under 8,000.

In preparing for the layoffs, we went to review the company's severance policy, only to discover that there was none! Under Russian law, employees were entitled to three weeks' pay if they lost their job. Under Alcoa's compensation policy, we decided that three months' pay was more fair to these employees.

The HR manager said that she would handle the layoffs. It wasn't until later that I found out the way she handled it. She would call employees to her office and advise them that their job was being eliminated. Then she would explain that they could get either three weeks' pay or three months' pay, and that the decision was up to her. If they wanted to receive three months' pay, then she expected a kickback. Preposterous!

I only discovered the malpractice because a young, English-speaking HR clerk came to my office and told me what was happening. I was completely floored. If she was telling the truth, then we were extorting our own employees.

I investigated, verified that this was indeed happening, and promptly released the HR manager. Needless to say, she didn't get three weeks' or three months' pay.

I asked our general counsel if we should bring an action against the HR manager, as we would do in the U.S. He advised against it, explaining that no judge or jury would find much wrong with what she had done. That was an indication of just how deep-rooted the corruption culture was in Russia.

We sought to make amends by asking our former employees if they had been extorted. We knew the HR manager had not extorted every employee, but all of the employees said they had been extorted. Again, that was the culture.

Safety vs. Saving Face

Once, during an annual shareholder's meeting, a Benedictine nun made a public allegation that Alcoa was hurting employees in Mexico. The CEO, who had built a strong culture of safety including quick, open reporting of safety incidents, said that the allegations could not be true. But still, he investigated—that's what all enlightened leaders do when faced with allegations. He sent a team of us to Mexico the very next day to gather the facts.

As it turned out, there had been an inversion around the large manufacturing facility one day, and 170 employees had been overcome with carbon monoxide poisoning from the exhausts of the fork lift trucks in the plant. While no employees were seriously injured, they did need medical treatment, and the event had not been reported. The business unit president, whose office was hundreds of miles from the Mexican factory, was deemed to have been responsible for obfuscating the situation, at the very least, and was promptly terminated by the CEO. Remember that the selection of the fact gatherer is an important step in the process. Proper investigators must have the education and training necessary to be thorough and complete in the fact gathering process. Their investigation must be able to withstand the scrutiny that is sure to come.

Artful Auditing

I was the corporate auditor when an anonymous allegation arrived on my desk. According to the note, the general manager of a business unit was purchasing expensive art from his own son for the new business headquarters office. If the allegation was true, the situation would have been most inappropriate, so I decided to investigate.

I called the regional audit manager in the geographic area where the headquarters was located. He had access to all books and records. This audit manager was an excellent investigator. I told him about the allegation and suggested that we keep the investigation confidential for now. He agreed to conduct the investigation that weekend and report his findings on Monday.

He went to the new office building on Saturday morning and took an inventory of all the art (paintings, sculptures, even decorative fish tanks). Where possible, he listed the artists' names. He then examined the purchase orders for each piece, identifying the name of the supplier, the amount of the purchase, and the date of purchase. Expense accounts were also reviewed to assure that art was not purchased that way.

The regional audit manager was able to match each piece of art to a purchase order—except for one large painting that sat on a wall behind the general manager's desk. There was no purchase order for that piece. It appeared that all other art was purchased legitimately under corporate buying protocols and procedures, and that the general manager's son was not the artist of any of the pieces.

However, it was still necessary to get information on the final piece of art in the general manager's office. We decided to do that by meeting with the general manager, telling him about the allegation and the investigation results, and then asking about the piece in his office.

The general manager said he wished that we had come to him initially, but he was pleased that the investigation was concluded so quickly and that the details had been kept confidential. He informed us that the art in his office was indeed a painting by his son. It was a gift from his son, and the general manager had hung it in his office with pride. He planned to take this piece of art with him when he retired.

The conclusion of the investigation was that there was no impropriety in procuring art for the office; supplier selection was appropriate, and proper procedures were followed. By the way, some of the prices for the art did seem to be extreme, but that was not within the scope of our investigation.

In this case, there was no way to communicate to the person making the allegation, because he or she had made an anonymous claim, but we did communicate through our regular reports that an audit of the new building—including furniture, fixtures and art work—was conducted and no deficiencies were noted. Hopefully the person making the allegation learned. No further allegations were made in this regard.

As corporate auditor, I reported to the CEO, CFO and the audit committee of the board of directors. It was my personal policy to disclose all audit activity, not just the audits that unearthed fraud. So I included the results of this investigation in my reports, despite the general manager's request not to do so. Confidentiality was no longer necessary, and I felt that full transparency was essential to doing my job. From my experiences, I have deduced a few principles. First of all, even unsubstantiated allegations should be investigated. Second, the selection of the investigator is always important. Once the investigator has been chosen, investigate quickly, report the results quickly, and maintain appropriate confidentiality during the investigation.

Planning Ahead

Consider the following ways to be better prepared for Suspicions Without Enough Evidence.

1. Establish reporting channels. Create and publicize a process for handling complaints or suspicions. Make sure this process anticipates all of the issues covered in this chapter, like the need for documentation and avoiding undue bias. A multi-layered process is best, one that involves the expertise and insight of multiple trustworthy parties. Make sure your process is widely understood in the organization. When everyone knows the right way to raise a concern, the wrong people are less likely to get involved. An established process also encourages thoughtful and accurate reporting.

2. Build a culture of fairness. On the one hand, don't engage in whitewashing someone's wrongdoing or hiding the truth because you think you can get away with it. As important as key employees can be, they aren't worth more than the health of the organization itself. On the other hand, avoid jumping to harsh, unyielding conclusions. People have a right to a just process. The culture of your organization can reflect and support that.

3. Anticipate allegations. This dilemma is unavoidable for bosses, so expect it. There will always be occasions to question an employee's work or decision making. As sophisticated as employee monitoring has become, workers still have ways of hiding things. To make matters worse, rivalries or competition at work can inspire false allegations.

Anticipate misunderstandings as well. Some people simply don't understand how their behavior appears. Others are too quick to assume the worst of people. Whatever happens, since you are seen as the person with the power to act, people will report their suspicions to you, and you'll need to know what to do.

What Happened

In the story at the beginning of this chapter, Marco suspected that his coworker, Cindy, had bribed Chinese export officials in order to avoid a potentially disastrous delay. Marco didn't feel that as an intern he could do much to explore his suspicions in a meaningful way, especially because the shipment had already gone out. But he still felt uncomfortable with the situation.

Luckily, Marco had a boss he trusted, one with whom he could safely share his concerns. The boss assured Marco that Cindy's actions, under the circumstances, were acceptable enough. With only a few months left in his role, Marco decided to let the issue go.

Practice Dilemma

Craig was a high school administrator at a small private school. One morning he was going about his usual tasks when three sophomore girls asked if they could speak to him. Noticing they were visibly worked up over something, he welcomed them into his office and asked what was the matter.

"It's Mr. Francis," said one of the girls. "He is kind of giving me the creeps. I want out of his class."

"Me, too," another chimed in. "I hadn't really noticed it until Ashley said something to me about it, but now I totally see how creepy he is."

"There's no way I'm staying in that class if my friends aren't there to protect me," said the third.

Knowing that exaggeration came easily to high school students, in general—and to these three, in particular—Craig asked for clarification.

"It's the way he looks at me," Ashley said. "Like the other day, I was working on a math assignment in class. He came up and asked if I needed help. I said I was okay. But he kept standing right next to my desk. Then he said, 'Ashley, you look really good today.' The way he said it just really freaked me out."

The second student nodded in agreement. "I stopped by his classroom after school to drop off some homework, and he totally did the same thing to me—saying I looked good and giving me that weird look." She made a face. "He touched me on my shoulder, and it gave me the creeps. I don't feel safe around him anymore."

"I don't want to be in there with a creeper," insisted the third. "There's no way we can still be in his class, and I don't know if you should leave any of the other girls in there, either."

Craig asked a few more questions and thanked the students for coming to talk to him. Then he asked them to wait outside his office for a moment. He needed time to think.

Craig thought back over his brief interactions with Mr. Francis, who was filling in as a long-term substitute for a teacher on maternity leave. With math teachers in high demand, finding a qualified and experienced person to fill the position had been extremely difficult. Mr. Francis had seemed like a godsend. Granted, the hiring process had been unusually quick. Craig hadn't personally talked to anyone from Mr. Francis's previous school.

On a whim, Craig pulled up the three girls' records and grades. In math, their attendance was spotty at best. In fact, all three were hanging right around the pass-fail line. None of the girls had ever had any disciplinary problems, and their grades in their other classes were fairly high. At the same time, it was easy for Craig to imagine them as front-and-center in the usual high school drama.

Craig leaned back in his chair and sighed. The administration emphasized safety as a top priority, and the school had never had an allegation of faculty impropriety. Craig worried about the inevitable gossip that would spread around school, surely influenced by how he chose to handle this situation.

He also worried about setting off a wave of potentially exaggerated complaints. It was already past the deadline for schedule changes; if he moved these three out of the class, how many other marginally performing students might ask for a transfer?

Worst of all: What if Mr. Francis really was dangerous to the kids?

CHAPTER 6

Challenge 6: Playing Dirty

You could achieve justice by doing something that is normally considered unethical.

David hung up the phone, relieved. His whole team could start work with their company's competitor right away. No more waiting around for paychecks that wouldn't come through. No more assuring each other that everything was going to be okay, while headquarters hoarded their hard-earned commissions due to some "software fluke."

"Now what?" he asked himself. They could all switch jobs tomorrow. Or they could stick around for a while and try to trick the CEO into paying up.

A few years ago, David took a job selling home security systems with a startup company. He excelled in door-to-door sales and worked his way into management quickly. He was now a regional sales manager over one hundred sales reps in four territories, and he reported directly to the CEO. Many of David's area managers had started as sales reps with him during his first year and were dear friends. Things couldn't have been going better.

Then, just before the summer sales season, the company changed its compensation structure. At first, the changes sounded positive. In previous years, sales reps had been paid at the time the security system was installed, after which the company would sell the contract to earn revenue. At the end of the summer, if there were cancellations or accounts that were otherwise unable to be sold, the sales reps would be charged back. Under the new commission plan, the company would only pay sales reps after the account was sold off and fully funded.

David explained to his reps that this was a better plan because they wouldn't have to worry about chargebacks at the end of the summer. He told them that paychecks would be delayed about two weeks at the beginning of the season, but that once accounts were funded, paychecks would be flowing in weekly. Everyone seemed to accept the plan.

About three weeks into the summer, they ran into a snag: nobody had received a paycheck yet. David reassured everyone that things would be okay and that he would get to the bottom of the problem.

He was told that the funding process for the company was taking longer than expected. The owners told David to keep spirits high while they worked on getting everyone paid. At the time, David had full faith that the company would make everything right. Meanwhile, most of his offices continued to work hard and bring in sales.

After one month, paychecks finally started to come in, but none of them were accurate. The CEO told David that there must be some issues with the new payroll system. David explained that he would not be able to keep the employees happy for much longer. The reps were losing faith in the company and would soon lose all motivation to sell.

Despite the situation, David continued to defend the company and told everyone that money was on its way. He even covered basic expenses for some employees out of his own pocket.

By midsummer, things were still not fixed. Sales reps were receiving paychecks for random amounts and had no way to verify for which accounts they were getting paid. The CEO still blamed it all on the new payroll software. Several of David's close friends quit and went home. Although they stayed friends, they blamed him for defending the company while it was not paying them honestly.

David decided he needed to advocate more on the employee side. He did not feel right leading his friends on with hope that the company would come through. So he did a little reconnaissance. At the time, he happened to be engaged to the CEO's executive assistant. She was not in charge of payroll, but she had access to the new payroll system and records. David asked her to look into several accounts that were still pending payment. She investigated and got back to him right away.

David was shocked with what she found. According to the payroll system, there had been no significant delay in funding the sold-off accounts. In fact, hundreds of accounts had been sold off right away and funded right away—with no commissions paid at all. David felt irate and also betrayed. He would not keep working for people he couldn't trust.

Luckily, a competing sales company was glad to hire David and anyone who wanted to follow him. Now he wondered how far he should go to ensure justice for his team. By keeping the CEO in the dark about their plans to quit, they might be able to get him to pay what he owed. Then they could all walk off the job together. The thought made David smile. And, he had to admit, it also made him feel a little uncomfortable.

Explanation

Under normal circumstances, things like lying, cheating, stealing, or killing are considered to be highly unethical. However, under certain circumstances, these behaviors might be morally justified. While all the ethical dilemmas we have discussed are difficult to navigate, Playing Dirty is perhaps the most difficult. This dilemma is similar to Skirting the Rules or Dissemblance in that you are using potentially unethical means for a positive end, but unlike the other dilemma types, this one always involves an unethical party (or parties). The trick with Playing Dirty is to make sure your ends really do justify the means, when you may have a personal or emotional interest in getting even.

Questions to Ask

1. Would your action really bring about justice or the greatest good?

Whenever you are being treated unfairly, your natural reaction is to strike back. In many ways, what makes people virtuous is their ability to rise above that impulse. When we act out of anger, our actions too frequently lead to further harm without solving any problem. Therefore, before playing dirty, you should consider whether your contemplated action will just create more harm, or whether it will actually create good. In David's case, manipulating the CEO into paying his employees does not create further harm; instead, it puts the money in the hands of those who rightfully deserve it.

2. Does your plan minimize the harm that must be done to the other party and how dirty you will play?

Unethical actions on the part of another party may provide justification for some response, but should not be viewed as carte blanche to retaliate in whatever way you desire. Rather, you should seek to create justice or achieve your ethical goal in as harmless a fashion as possible. Here, David's ethical goal was to ensure that his coworkers were fairly compensated. Was dissemblance necessary? It's hard to say.

3. Does harming the other party help anyone besides yourself?

Self-interest is not an inherently bad motivation, but interest for others is a stronger one. You will more likely be seen as being morally justified when you're doing things for someone else's benefit instead of just your own. As vividly showcased in the movie *Lincoln*, Abraham Lincoln ("Honest Abe") significantly misled his political opponents and paid bribes in order to pass the Thirteenth Amendment to the U.S. Constitution, thereby abolishing slavery. This act was clearly in the interest of others, not simply his own. Thus, he is still ranked as the greatest president in the history of the United States. In David's case, we might feel differently if he misled his CEO purely to recover his own compensation, rather than to help his coworkers.

4. Does this action harm your reputation or make it more difficult for you to do business in the future?

While acting unethically might bring about a greater good, it also might invoke other consequences and change the way others perceive you. For instance, playing dirty might damage your reputation with an opposing party of low character while simultaneously strengthening your reputation with a party of high character. In David's situation, he was willing to damage his relationship with his unethical boss to improve—and even save—his relationships with his colleagues. Since they likely viewed his prior inability to bring about justice as a major leadership deficiency, he hoped his plan would demonstrate his loyalty and win back their trust.

5. How will the other party react?

Inherent in this dilemma is the assumption that the opposing party has acted unethically. That does not mean, though, that the other party is necessarily unethical. Sometimes good people make mistakes. When they realize you were willing to go against your own principles to create social good, they might overlook your actions or acknowledge their own mistakes, or even commend your behavior. Alternatively, they might respond to your retaliation by escalating the situation even further and creating more harm. It is impossible to know how others will act, but being aware of the other person's personality and character can inform your decision. David believed his CEO would not react well—and would not be able to effectively escalate because everyone was leaving the company.

Pitfalls

Beware these pitfalls as you consider playing dirty.

Getting the Facts Wrong

Before you do something that is generally considered unethical, be as sure as you possibly can be that the other party truly is acting unethically. Because David's fiancé worked for the CEO, he was able to obtain very good evidence of the CEO's misdeeds. But he still doesn't have very good evidence of the CEO's intent. Before setting the tone for the surprise exodus, David might want to find out more about what the CEO knows and what he has tried to do to remedy the payroll problems.

Excusing Revenge

This is not the time to seek revenge; your action should right the wrong without escalating the situation. A lot of people have gotten themselves in trouble by seeking to punish the other party, as opposed to bringing about justice. The danger of seeking revenge is that others will be less likely to excuse your own bad actions. Society will often accept unethical actions for a noble purpose, but punishment, while sometimes necessary, is only considered legitimate when meted out by a third party. Any hint of vigilantism is distasteful and can hurt you in the end.

Bill's Experiences

Sometimes the boundary between clever, ethical business management and unethical business management wears thin. In my experience, this is especially true when those with whom you do business are seeking to take advantage or deceive. In those instances, playing dirty might help you protect yourself and your company. Here are two experiences from my career when I gave the other party a taste of their own medicine. You'll have to decide whether I made the right choice.

Patent for Plastics

Alcoa owned a patent for a quick new method of heat treating materials using microwave technology. Another company hoped to license our patent to process refractory materials—or so they led us to believe. Our negotiation centered on royalties around 0.2%, which we assumed was all this company would be able to pay, given the low profitability of the refractory business.

Then we learned the company actually planned to use our patent in the much more profitable plastics business. For a plastics manufacturer, we felt a royalty of 5% would be fair to both parties. But we didn't want to accuse them of lying.

So I wrote the license agreement as if I innocently believed they were engaged in processing refractory materials. I included in the license only provisions specific to the tasks they indicated they would do—no provisions for heat treating plastic. Imagine their surprise. Their negotiators then had to confess that they might be planning to use the new technology for plastics, after all. In the end, they agreed to pay us 0.2% of their revenues for refractory processing, and 5% of their revenues for any other materials processed. I felt great about this deal.

Last-Minute Orders

Our company produced huge electrical connectors (really big plugs) that allowed ships to plug into on-shore power when docked. We negotiated a contract to sell five of these plugs over the next year for $25,000 each. We delivered four of the plugs and anticipated an order for the fifth plug to come in over the next month or so. To our surprise, our customer called in a panic. Evidently a ship pulled out of the port in Norfolk without disconnecting the plug. This damaged the plug, such that they would need a replacement before the ship arrived in Charleston—in two days!

I explained that we didn't have a plug in inventory, but we could rearrange the factory schedule, work some overtime, and drive the connector to Charleston. But this would cost us an additional $7,000. The customer insisted that we had a contract price and I had to stick to it. He refused to pay our extra expenses and still insisted on the delivery. We worked through the night, made the connector, and shipped it to the Port of Charleston on time, all at the contract price of $25,000. With that fifth plug, our contractual obligation was complete.

Two days later I received a call from this customer. When the ship pulled out of the Port of Charleston, the plug had not been disconnected (again). It was damaged. He needed another one in two days. I offered to manufacture and deliver the plug—but it would cost $45,000 this time. With few alternatives, the customer agreed to pay.

Planning Ahead

Because playing dirty comes with significant risks, we invite you to consider the following recommendations well in advance.

1. Prioritize your values in advance. Playing dirty can be particularly difficult for people of character. Subjugating cherished virtues and acting in ways that under normal circumstances you would find despicable usually feels confusing and painful. As in many dilemmas, you cannot play dirty and still be true to all of your values—some kind of tradeoff must occur. Figure out now what's most important to you by completing the exercises explained in Chapter 17: Being Ethically Proactive.

2. Think about transaction costs. It is important to understand that while using questionable means to gain a positive outcome can be a worthy goal, as a general rule it can greatly hurt society. Instead of being able to trust one another, people can never be sure what another party will do. Economists see distrust as a transaction cost, dirt in the gears of commerce or other cooperative ventures that make doing business more expensive. Remember that your own transaction costs will increase if you lose people's trust by retaliating. Make sure, before you act, that you're willing to bear those costs.

3. Gather information through your social network. An important element of this dilemma is a clear antagonist who has already committed a wrong. But in many situations, it is difficult to know exactly what is going on or what the other person's motives are. Is the other party really doing unethical things, or does it just appear that way to you? If possible, use your social capital—the relationships you've built with others—to find out what is really going on before you act in ways that could bring harm to yourself and others.

What Happened

At the start of this chapter, David was preparing to leave his summer sales company. By engaging in a bit of deception, he thought he could get the CEO to pay his team members what the company had owed them for months.

Despite his distaste for hiding the truth, David felt he was obligated to make sure his sales reps were fairly compensated. He explained the situation to his team, and together, they came up with a plan.

David called the CEO and told him that the office was going to fall apart if the CEO did not fly out immediately, apologize for the accounting issue, and cut checks to everyone for all unpaid accounts. The following Monday, the CEO was in their morning meeting with a checkbook in hand. David sat with him and each rep and made sure he made things right. David also demanded—and received—a lump sum payment for himself.

David and the reps spent the next few days packing their bags and getting ready to leave. On the day they left, David called the CEO and told him he was quitting. And, by the way, the whole office was going with him.

Practice Dilemma

Ethan grinned as he looked over the bid from a new supplier. He could buy the custom molding from this company and save a lot of money. Even better, switching to this company would leave his current supplier with expensive unsold inventory. "Serves them right for breaking our contract so many times," Ethan thought.

Ethan had not yet graduated from college when his father asked him to handle the lease and possible sale of their lumber mill in Georgia. His father would be out of the country for a few years and had prepared for his absence by leasing out the property, plant, and equipment to a company called Westbrook Hardwoods. Westbrook would have the option to purchase the plant after three years. As part of the agreement, Ethan would have an exclusive right to sell Westbrook's products, at a specified commission, for the first fifteen days after each truckload of lumber was ready. If Ethan couldn't arrange a buyer within those fifteen days, Westbrook could find its own buyer and sell the load without a paying commission.

The president of Westbrook made no effort to conceal his harsh feelings about the deal, which he increasingly saw as constraining and unfair. Moreover, he felt it was wrong of Ethan's father to transfer sales responsibility to an unproven college student. He didn't hesitate to test Ethan's resolve.

Within Ethan's first month on the job, he made an unannounced visit to check on production. As he drove onto the mill property, he noticed a semi being loaded with finished units of alder. This was at least the third truck Westbrook had shipped to its own customer, outside of the brokerage agreement. This infraction could cost Westbrook the option to buy the mill—as both parties were well aware. Yet Westbrook continued to violate the agreement, even after Ethan had his attorney send a written warning. For a while, Ethan continued to sell Westbrook's lumber and tried not to let Westbrook's behavior derail his work. But then he saw a way to increase his power over the company—and maybe get even.

One of the better procurement deals Ethan had arranged paid $40,000 per container of custom-made corkboard molding—a product that was ideal for Westbrook because it profitably used scrap lumber. This customer routinely ordered one truckload a week, and Westbrook eventually began producing the corkboard in advance, whenever scrap lumber became available.

Now Ethan had found a lumber mill that would beat the price offered by Westbrook. If he quietly began filling purchase orders through this mill, instead Westbrook would soon be sitting on several loads of custom inventory they couldn't sell. They would have to beg for his help. "This could be very useful," he thought. "But would it be okay?"

CHAPTER 7

Challenge 7: Skirting the Rules

You could keep a rule for a worse outcome or bend it to achieve some good.

Nick's interview with Mr. Sandoval, a long-time customer, ended with a startling revelation: Mr. Sandoval has been using an invalid Social Security number (SSN). According to company policy, Nick should reject Mr. Sandoval's loan application and report the invalid number. But reporting would have disastrous consequences for Mr. Sandoval's landscaping business—and would harm Nick's company, as well. Nick wondered, "Can I approve the loan based on Mr. Sandoval's excellent credit history and let the invalid number slide?"

Nick works as a loan underwriter for Allegiance Financial, a nationwide lender that helps consumers and businesses purchase motorbikes, snowmobiles, lawn-care equipment, all-terrain vehicles, and personal watercraft through local dealerships. Allegiance earns revenue from the interest and fees paid by the borrowers, and from additional payments made by the equipment dealers and manufacturers.

Allegiance is known for its timely turnaround of loan applications. When individuals or businesses request financing, dealers submit an online application and Allegiance employees approve or deny the loan within minutes. If the loan is approved, Allegiance will underwrite, originate, fund, and service the loan. Dealers are paid immediately, manufacturers move product, and customers take home their equipment.

Nick's roles as an underwriter are to assess the customer's ability to repay, to foster relationships with a territory of dealerships, and to bring in business that will generate interest income. Almost all of his $500,000 in daily underwriting comes from local dealerships; consequently, one of his main goals is to support the dealers when they send client applications his way.

When a local dealer sent in Mr. Sandoval's loan application, it was flagged for containing a fraudulent SSN. Over 90% of flagged applications come from a typing error, so Nick called Mr. Sandoval to verify. When Nick asked for a copy of his Social Security card, Mr. Sandoval snapped, "Why are we discussing this? I've paid off seven loans with your bank already, and I currently have eleven loans open with you for my riding lawn mowers. You don't need more documentation!"

Indeed, Mr. Sandoval has been an excellent customer of Allegiance Finance. He has great credit and ample income, and he always makes his loan payments on time. In fact, his current loans of almost $90,000 bring in substantial interest income. Mr. Sandoval purchases the majority of his equipment from one of Allegiance's best dealerships. Nick knows this dealership sends borrowers his way because he can approve loans that other lenders won't touch. Not wanting to strain a customer relationship without doing more research, Nick politely asked Mr. Sandoval to hold on the line while he looked into a few policies.

Company policy states that when an invalid SSN is discovered, the employee should turn down the loan application and repossess any vehicles currently being financed with that SSN. If Nick follows the policy, Mr. Sandoval will lose his fleet of lawnmowers, his 20-year-old business, and his American dream. His employees and their families will be out of work in a tough economy. Allegiance also stands to lose at least $20,000 through legal fees and the transport and sale of Mr. Sandoval's depreciated equipment—not to mention lost future business from Mr. Sandoval and a favorite dealership.

Nick returned to the call and reiterated the need for more documentation. That's when Mr. Sandoval admitted the SSN wasn't valid. He told Nick he had tried to become a United States citizen, but wasn't able to. When he started using the invalid SSN, Mr. Sandoval was able to get credit and build his one-man lawn mowing service into a large landscaping company. Mr. Sandoval further pointed out that he had never received a letter from the Internal Revenue Service stating they didn't want all the taxes he paid using the invalid SSN.

Nick carefully thanked Mr. Sandoval for the additional information and promised he would be in touch. Within minutes Nick's phone rang. It was the dealership, requesting an answer on the loan application before this important sale was lost.

Explanation

Rules are part of almost every modern work experience. Usually, rules come out of experience and wisdom to prevent common mistakes. Other rules protect what's valued the most, like reputations, relationships, or financial well-being. Rules also create a standard of performance for evaluating everyone in an organization. But writing really good rules—rules that apply to every situation—is nearly impossible. Even thoughtful rules can have unforeseen consequences.

In this chapter, when we talk about rules, we are also talking about laws. Laws, like rules, are intended to prevent bad things but can have unintended consequences. That being said, laws differ from rules because they involve much weightier matters. We need laws for a harmonious and fair society. That's why penalties exist for breaking them. So here when we use the word "rules," it is used in a way that includes laws as well.

In either case, with rules or laws, we may find ourselves at an ethical crossroads. On one path, we get the better outcome while breaking rules or laws. On the other, we keep the rules or laws, but sacrifice very important things. We define the Skirting the Rules dilemma this way: you have to choose between a better outcome that breaks the rule or the worse outcome that keeps the rule.

Like Playing Dirty or Dissemblance, Skirting the Rules involves utilizing questionable means to obtain the right outcome. We are not endorsing rule- or law breaking merely for economic or personal benefit. Instead, we are describing those moments when rules stand in the way of a morally important end.

Keeping rules is an ethically important behavior. As a society, we value the rule of law, meaning no one should be above or better than the law; otherwise, laws have no value. Justice, a core ethical value, means rules and laws must have their effect, either through obedience or disobedience. Unequal application of rules or laws smacks of corruption and injustice.

Problematically, rules aren't always well defined. Rules often leave room for interpretation. This imbalance creates a strong temptation to interpret rules to fit your needs. Remember that just as the right to create rules belongs to certain people, so does the right to interpret them. If you could understand the rule better by asking for clarification, then you will get little mercy for deliberately interpreting the rule in a way that helps you get around the consequences.

If laws are unjust or rules are counterproductive, then it can be ethical to break them. But the way you break them matters. Two of the best examples we have of ethical rule breaking come from Mahatma Gandhi and Martin Luther King, Jr. They practiced civil disobedience, breaking unjust laws to get a just outcome. The way they broke laws gave them a great deal of moral authority. Specifically, they made sure to follow these four principles:

1. They were nonviolent, not deliberately harming others, even those asserting power immorally.

2. They disobeyed as a last resort, only when legal avenues were unavailable or exhausted.

3. Their disobedience was particular and proportional, responding only to the specific unjust law with disobedience to that law.

4. They were submissive to the penalties of breaking the law, recognizing the underlying importance of the rule of law.

These high-level moral principles may seem excessive if you're considering breaking a small company rule, like skipping supervisor approval to make a customer happy. But pay attention to the meaning of these standards of behavior. They stress the value of other people, the need to exhaust your options, minimizing rule breaking as much as possible, and respecting the authority of rule makers. Following these principles will give your rule breaking much stronger moral footing.

As with so many other dilemmas in this field guide, don't skirt the rules by offloading responsibility. Asking others to break rules for your benefit has the same moral effect as breaking the rules yourself. In fact, you have a responsibility to help your employees and agents keep the rules. This requires proactive effort on your part to make sure they understand the rules they need to keep.

Finally, it's worth noting there are a lot of rules and laws about disclosure. As a principle, confidentiality is ethically important and rules often institutionalize it. But disclosure might still be the right thing, even if a rule requires confidentiality instead. Use the tools covered in this chapter to decide if you should break a rule to disclose important information in order to obtain a morally important end.

Questions to Ask

1. Why does this rule matter?

Rules and laws have purposes. To ethically break a rule, you must consider why the rule matters. Ask yourself: Why would someone else think the rule was important? Why did those who wrote the rule think it was important? Be thorough. You may need to talk to the people involved to really understand all the reasons for the rule. You might even want to ask a lawyer why the rule matters.

In Nick's case, he needs to understand why the rules and laws for flagging fraudulent SSNs exist. He also needs to know the penalties for breaking the rules. Without knowing the purposes and penalties, Nick can't really make a confident decision.

2. Can someone give you proper permission to break the rule?

Within companies, rules can sometimes be changed or suspended based on circumstance. But you may not be the person with authority to make that decision. Don't assume you can take it upon yourself to decide if you can properly break a rule. Instead, consider asking for permission to break the rule.

Asking comes with an added advantage because it requires you to make a case for breaking the rule. Asking puts your ethical reasoning to the test. Asking may help you realize how poorly you've thought through the decision.

In our opening dilemma, Nick may have the chance to ask his manager for permission to extend the loan to a current customer in spite of the flagged SSN. But Nick could never obtain legitimate permission to break SSN reporting laws.

3. Would those with authority over the rule want you to break it?

Sometimes you can't ask for permission from those in authority. Time constraints, confidentiality requirements, or risk to others all could make asking unreasonable. If that's the case, put yourself in the shoes of those in charge. Would they want you to break the rule? Try to consider what those in authority would consider, like broader consequences, precedent, and fairness to everyone involved. This exercise will help you think through unintended consequences of the rule and important limits on what you can do. For example, most companies have rules for their employees that limit the value of gifts they can accept from vendors. But what if you're offered a gift from the company's first Asian vendor, where gift-giving has strong cultural importance? The rule makers in the company might want you to break the rule to preserve this relationship.

Looking specifically at the business decision, Nick might assume his company leaders wouldn't mind his breaking the rule. After all, approving the loan seems to help everyone involved. (Assuming that Nick and his company don't get caught, that is.) But how does Nick know what lawmakers would want him to do about the fraudulent SSN? It's hard to imagine that the people who made the reporting laws would want him to keep it a secret.

4. Does breaking this rule encourage inappropriate rule breaking by others?

Rule breaking always becomes an example for others to follow. This question invokes a line of reasoning from the All-Purpose Tools chapter. What if everyone after you were to break the rule in the same situation? How about in similar situations? Are there other rules that come into question if you break this one? If coworkers, for example, only see part of your circumstance, could they use your example to justify rule breaking in unethical ways? In the end, the choice you make here will become a standard for future decisions.

If Nick fails to report the fake SSN, it will probably mean continued business from Mr. Sandoval. But it might also mean his company gets a reputation for processing loans using fake SSNs, which could invite many more of these dilemmas to come across Nick's desk. There is also a possibility of government investigation and regulatory penalties should this reputation become widely known.

5. Whom is the rule intended to benefit? Does breaking the rule reduce that benefit?

Many rules and laws are designed to protect people, often individuals who are not in a position to protect themselves. For example, a rule about not accepting gifts from vendors protects the company and its owners when they can't be there to ensure your loyalty—and helps you avoid a Conflict of Interest dilemma.

As you consider breaking a rule, think about whom the rule is meant to protect. If you break the rule now, are you reducing what is rightfully theirs? If the answer is no, then the rule might be unintentionally overreaching. If the answer is yes, remember you can't simply exchange the costs to some with the benefits for others. The beneficiaries of a rule have a better moral claim, all else being equal. You'll need especially compelling moral reasons if you plan to break a rule at somebody else's expense.

Using a fake SSN doesn't cost Nick's company very much, at least in the short run. But fake SSNs cost taxpayers a lot through reduced tax revenue, identity theft, and increased security risks. Still, Mr. Sandoval doesn't seem to add to these problems. He's a dutiful taxpayer and his business contributes to the local economy. Here the law seems to be hurting everyone involved.

6. Does breaking the rule achieve fairness?

As we explained above, rules should operate on the basic principle of fairness. Everyone subject to the rule should be expected to follow it, and breaking a rule should have an equal consequence for all violators. Fairness preserves the rule of law that keeps us all together. Sometimes you may need to keep the rule at personal cost because of the importance of being fair.

But fairness that hurts everyone is not really fair. That's why organizations reconsider and rewrite rules to make sure the right outcomes occur. Breaking a bad rule might be the best choice for everyone involved. If that's the case, be active in changing the rule for the better.

In Mr. Sandoval's situation, fairness or unfairness could be interpreted in several ways. That's part of the reason immigration policy and reform are highly charged topics. Whatever Nick's political views, we can tell he is weighing benefits and fairness very seriously.

7. Can you accept the punishment and still achieve the better outcome?

Just because the rule is a bad fit for the situation doesn't mean you can escape the consequences of breaking it. Some of the great social reformers, like Gandhi or King, still submitted to punishment for violating unjust laws. This preserves the rule of law, which is essential to good laws having effect. If you rightfully break a rule, don't think hiding your act or shirking the punishment is always morally justified.

Without knowing the penalty for failing to report a fake SSN, it is perhaps too easy to say Nick should bear the cost of not complying. But if the penalty is severe enough, the consequence may give him (and us) pause.

Pitfalls

If you are going to skirt the rules, you must do so with great care. Watch out for the following hazards.

Signaling Disregard

Be thoughtful about the appearance of breaking rules, not just the direct effect. Following rules sends signals like loyalty, trustworthiness, confidence in leadership, and valuing the group or community. You might break a rule for the right reasons but send the wrong signals in the process. If your signals, in turn, encourage rule breaking for the wrong reasons, the ultimate cost of breaking the rule may outweigh the benefit you anticipate.

Leaning on Loopholes

We know poorly designed rules can be easy to get around. For example, if your company limits the amount that can be paid to contractors, you might be able to skirt this budgeting rule by breaking one contract into smaller contracts. But that doesn't mean you should. Use the questions provided earlier in this chapter to make sure you really understand the reasons for the rule you are skirting or breaking. Don't let the existence of the loophole be your only justification.

Skirting the Punishment

If it's right to break the rule, it's probably also right to accept the consequences. If you get away with breaking a rule, it's tempting to not go back and be accountable for doing so. You are now stepping into another ethical dilemma—the dilemma called Repair. Once you have made the choice to break a rule, don't assume you are out of the woods, ethically speaking.

Letting Rules Define Your Ethics

Sometimes we think behavior is ethical as long as it doesn't break any rules. But as we have discussed extensively in this chapter, rules are imperfect. They can be poorly drafted or have unintended consequences. In the law, we have, at best, an imperfect guide for ethics because the law comes from the bare consensus of our legal system. Laws embody the minimum that society can agree to as a standard of behavior. Good leaders do much better.

 ## Bill's Experiences

Rule keeping by leaders sends important ethical signals to an entire organization. But keeping rules can be just as hard, if not harder, for leaders than it is for everyone else. All of the experiences I share in this section involve opportunities

to skirt the rules. In each case, my ultimate decision was to keep the rule. That's not to say a leader should never skirt the rules. My personal observation, though, is that doing so doesn't often pay off.

The Tourist Visa

My boss once decided to hold his next staff meeting at my offices in Russia. One of the attendees, the general manager of a business unit in Europe, delayed getting her business visa. She called me and explained that because it was now too late to get a business visa, she planned to come to the meeting on a tourist visa. But she wasn't a tourist. She would be doing work, and I recommended she not come on a tourist visa.

On the day before the meeting, I got a call at 4 a.m. from the Russian airport authorities. They said the general manager had just arrived from Frankfurt on a tourist visa, and they wanted to know if she was a tourist or if she would be doing business. This was my chance to join in her rule breaking or to comply with Russian law.

Setting a high ethical standard in our Russian business unit had been an uphill battle. A small slip on my part would send all the wrong signals. I told them she was not a tourist. The authorities were prepared to take her to jail until the next plane departed to Germany. Luckily, I convinced them to place her in a hotel, which they did—with an armed guard. She was escorted out of the country the next morning.

Tax Advice

Rule-keeping counts in personal matters just as much as work situations. Prior to going on my assignment to Russia, I was offered accounting help to handle my tax obligations in multiple jurisdictions. I investigated the Russian tax obligation and understood I would owe the Russian government 13% of the wages I earned in Russia. My question to the tax advisor was whether I would owe the Russian government 13% of the investment income I earned in the United States. His answer was, "If you don't tell us about your investments, we don't know about them."

That didn't answer my question. Making his statement even worse, he knew his firm was also preparing my U.S. Individual Income Tax Return, so they would be fully aware of my investments. I told him I was interested in what my tax obligations were, not what he thought I could somehow get away with through pretense.

After reflecting on this, I thought the managing partner of the firm needed to know what advice his employee was giving clients. I sent an explanatory e-mail. The managing partner called me to say I had misunderstood the conversation. Of course I hadn't. I hope the employee got some needed ethics training.

Emissions Plan

Understanding the purpose of a rule helps you make better ethical choices. The environmental manager of a plant once explained to me how environmental permits for air emissions worked. I asked if we had difficulty with any of the permit limits. The manager told me we were allowed to emit 7 parts per million (ppm) but we often emitted 8–9 ppm. When I asked how to fix the problem, he told me one option was to install a fan that blew air into the stack and diluted the emissions below the 7 ppm limit.

Of course we didn't do that. It wouldn't reduce the actual pollution emitted by our plant. We reported our exceeding of the limit to the authorities and showed them our new plan for reducing the emissions legitimately.

Planning Ahead

Before deciding to skirt the rules, make sure you understand what you're getting into. Or better yet, play a role in creating good rules you won't want to skirt in the first place.

1. Know the rules. We've found this dilemma often occurs to people who didn't know the rules well enough beforehand. They might have been able to avoid the situation with proactive effort to learn the organizational or legal expectations.

Remember, ignorance isn't an excuse for this dilemma, but is a common cause.

2. Know the purposes. Preparation makes you less likely to think a rule is trivial. It also helps you make better informed ethical decisions. If you need help to understand the purpose of a rule, ask for insight from those who made or enforce the rules.

3. Seek professional help. Rules and laws can be extremely complex. Fortunately, there are almost always professionals, like accountants or attorneys, who can help you navigate the situation. They can tell you the fate of others who faced your dilemma. Professionals can also act as your advocate. When attorneys represent you, your conversations with them are private, allowing you to explore the whole situation frankly. (Just make sure the attorney actually represents you, and not the company you work for, because you don't have a right to privacy with a lawyer representing someone else.) If you are put off by the cost of professional help, weigh the expense against the cost of the career or legal trouble you might face without this help.

4. Care how you look. As noted above, appearances about rule-keeping are also important. Plan ahead so your technically compliant behavior also appears compliant. For example, an appropriately taken winter business trip to a warmer climate could look like a boondoggle. Make sure you do the extra things necessary—like keeping a full work schedule during the trip—so your obedience to the rules is apparent to others.

5. Make good rules. Don't sit by while others make bad rules or laws. You may avoid this dilemma altogether when you help plan good, thoughtful, and ethical rules that are fair to everyone. Even if you are not invited to be part of the deliberative rule-making process, you typically have a voice that will be considered. Share a well-crafted perspective; your influence can have a dramatic effect.

What Happened

In the opening dilemma, Nick had to decide whether to report a fraudulent Social Security number. Following the reporting rule would likely harm Mr. Sandoval, an excellent client.

Nick decided to notify Allegiance Financial about the fraudulent SSN and deny the loan. As an underwriter, his duty was to assess risk, and he felt that a borrower using a fraudulent SSN could be discovered and deported at any time, leaving Allegiance Financial with a loss.

Standard policy within Allegiance would have been to file a police report for the fraudulent SSN; afterward, the company's repossession team would go out and pick up all the lawnmowers currently being financed and then auction them off to recover as much value as possible. However, Nick chose not to pursue these further actions out of sympathy for Mr. Sandoval.

Practice Dilemma

Kim manages a global real estate portfolio worth more than $1 billion, with commercial properties in Washington D.C., Florida, North Carolina, California, Tokyo, and Bangkok. With millions of dollars coming and going each day, her company has created policies to safeguard its assets and employees. Like most of her coworkers, Kim has referred to a few paragraphs within the voluminous policy handbook, but has not actually read the whole thing. Who would have time? Still, she knows the policies that apply to her job and how to comply with those policies.

For example, she knows any capital expenditure over $15,000 is first approved by her managing director and then goes to the accounting department, so they can create a job code to track all related expenditures. This policy ensures her on-site staff are not over budget or spending frivolously. But it's complicated. Whenever she orients a new team member, Kim writes email after email to explain the bureaucratic mess.

On a warm July morning, Kim receives a phone call from one of her on-site managers. The air conditioning in an office building went out last night. Tenants have already begun arriving, and the building is not cooling down. Fortunately, a contractor can fix the rooftop HVAC unit by the end of the day, if he can get started soon. Unfortunately, because the total expenditure will be over $15,000, Kim can't authorize the repair without running it by her boss and setting up the work order through the accounting department. That could take several hours.

As Kim talks to the contractor, she learns that two separate parts will need to be replaced. One part costs $9,000, and the other $11,000, including labor. Individually, the parts do not add up to $15,000. Maybe she can treat the repair as two separate jobs and give the authorization to proceed now—especially with tenants already complaining about the rising temperature. Should Kim work around the rules to get the repair done quickly or wade through the proper process, with all the time it takes?

CHAPTER 8

Challenge 8: Dissemblance

Misrepresenting or concealing the truth could create a better outcome.

Shelley works as a customer service manager for RightBright, an industrial lighting manufacturer. Because of her time and position in the company, she is entitled to free tuition for classes and even degrees, as long as her direct supervisor approves the course of study as it relates to the job. Shelley decided to get her executive MBA at a local university and her supervisor quickly approved, noting that the company was interested in grooming Shelley for more leadership opportunities.

The HR director of Shelley's division found out she was interested in an executive MBA. He told her that, having sent other candidates to this particular MBA program over the years, he had a great relationship with the admissions director there. With his recommendation, Shelley could request a waiver and skip taking the rigorous GMAT admissions test. This not only saved time and money for Shelley, but also meant she could meet this year's application deadline instead of waiting until next year.

The only requirement was that she keep the GMAT waiver a secret. Some employees within the company, who were also alumni of the MBA program, had been required to take the test, and future employees would more than likely have to take the test as well. Shelley had proven her academic ability and qualified for the waiver; however, if word got out that she was granted a waiver with the HR director's recommendation, people would almost certainly complain.

Shelley applied and was accepted to the program. Then one day, a company vice president pulled her into his office to congratulate her on her admission. Also in the office was Shelley's colleague and friend, who was an alumnus of the program and had been pressuring her to apply for years.

"Congratulations, Shelley!" the VP boomed. "We're excited you got admitted to the MBA program. I know it's getting harder to be accepted there. You must have gotten a nice GMAT score. What did you get?"

The HR director was explicit. The waiver had to be kept a secret. But the vice president is an intimidating man, with a reputation for coming down on people for lying. And Shelley knew that her friend had been required to take the test. What should she say?

Explanation

Note that this dilemma isn't named "Dishonesty." Dishonesty brings to mind things like cheating, stealing, and other poor behaviors that don't fully fit this dilemma. Dissemblance, on the other hand, has a very particular meaning. It means hiding or concealing something, usually an intention or belief. You don't have to overtly lie to dissemble. Often people dissemble just by keeping their motives to themselves—usually to look better or to protect their interests. In fact, the Dissemblance dilemma occurs whenever misrepresenting or concealing the truth could create a better outcome.

When faced with the choice to dissemble for some greater good, it's tempting to rationalize that the end justifies the means. That statement itself hints, though, that there's something wrong with the means.

We prefer that others are truthful with us. More broadly, every society on earth to some extent values telling the truth and avoiding deception. It even appears to be a neurological preference. When presented with the opportunity in a lab experiment to lie for personal gain, people generally prefer to tell the truth and suffer the loss. But that doesn't hold true if the personal cost is high enough.

Because dissemblance is naturally disliked, even by those who engage in it, the real dilemma comes when telling the truth imposes a high cost. The higher the cost, the greater the risk of dissembling. Be sensitive to that risk.

Some other attributes of dissemblance deserve discussion.

First, dissemblance especially tempts us when the other party simply asks the wrong question. In the opening dilemma, Shelley has no way to answer that question without revealing that she didn't actually take the GMAT. Sometimes questions are worded in such a way that even a non-answer constitutes an answer. Taking our practice dilemma at the end of the chapter as another example, Jeff wouldn't even have a dilemma if Paul had simply asked a different question. Instead of, "Are you guys facing bankruptcy?" Paul could have asked, "Should the district be worried about you failing to keep the contract?" In fact, the second question is the better one for protecting the district. But that wasn't the question Jeff was given to answer.

Another troubling manifestation of this dilemma happens when silence or lack of denial will confirm the truth. For example, someone might ask, "I heard they've already made a pick for the new manager position. Is it you?" For questions like this, any answer other than "no" is a "yes." Even simply saying, "If I knew, I couldn't say," tells the questioner enough. These are especially hard questions to answer without dissembling.

Sometimes we are obliged to disclose the truth because of a position of trust that we hold. In those cases, keeping silence is a form of dissemblance. Remember that not speaking up tells others a number of things. It implies we don't have relevant knowledge or personal involvement. Failing to speak can be a failure to be truthful.

Finally, sometimes Dissemblance dilemmas appear because of a bad process, which can make it appear even more tempting. Within companies, the budgeting process provides one of the most common opportunities to dissemble. Departments are sometimes incentivized to inflate their budget requests—maybe to anchor high in the competition for resources, or maybe to cushion against unforeseen costs. But inflating the budget with pretend or wildly exaggerated numbers isn't honest. You may already be thinking of other processes in your workplace that encourage dissemblance. This chapter contains some tools that should help you manage those moments when you want to dissemble to achieve a better outcome.

Questions to Ask

Use these questions to help you decide the right time and the right way to tell the truth.

1. Do you have authority to reveal the truth?

Before you decide if you should tell the truth to the other party, be sure that you're entitled to tell it. Very often, we are entrusted with information that isn't ours to share with others. As you weigh the choice to be forthright, consider how you came to know what you know. Are there others to whom you owe an obligation of confidentiality? If you share what you know, contrary to your obligation, you trade one ethical misstep for another. Shelley made a promise to the HR Director that was important to his relationship with the MBA program. If she tells others that she skipped the GMAT, she could ruin a valuable resource.

Then again, just because information isn't yours to share doesn't mean it shouldn't be shared. If you do owe confidentiality to someone else, you might consider asking for permission to share what you know with others. Shelley, for example, could ask for permission to share her GMAT waiver with the VP. Explain the reasons behind your request. If you get permission, make sure to respect any new boundaries of confidentiality the confiding party puts in place. Allowing you to share something with one person, for example, doesn't automatically give you permission to share it with everyone.

There may be times when you need to share what you know—no matter what the confiding party wants—to keep others safe from harm. For example, lawyers have a responsibility to keep their clients' information confidential, unless what the lawyers know is furthering a crime or putting other people at risk of substantial harm. In those cases, lawyers have an obligation to disclose the information. Still, even in this case, lawyers can only disclose to the right people—typically law enforcement—and only with sufficient detail to stop the crime or prevent the harm. Similarly, it may be right for you to share someone's secret, but only to the extent needed to get the right outcome.

2. Why do you want to misrepresent the truth?

When trying to decide whether to misrepresent the truth, be sure to check your motives. Is the temptation to misrepresent motivated by a benefit to others or to yourself? Are you concerned about saving face? Are you trying to cover a mistake you made? It's very easy to assume our own reasons are just and noble, ignoring the various ways we happen to benefit personally.

This matters for more than just moral reasons. If later the truth comes out, your motives will be the first thing called into question. Shelley, for example, could face questions about her relationship with the HR Director. Some might question the reasons for the favoritism. Laid bare, your deception may look far worse to others than it did to you. Thoroughly examining your own motives has the practical value of protecting you against the accusations of others.

3. Would you tell the truth if the cost of truth telling were lower?

As noted elsewhere in this book, threshold issues in ethics are some of the trickiest. In this case, consider your decision whether to withhold or reveal the truth. How much needs to be at risk for you to dissemble? Would you tell the truth if there were no cost? (Almost certainly.) Would you tell the truth if there were a small cost to yourself or others? (Probably.) Taking another view, would you tell the truth if the cost to you was small but the cost to others was very high?

Changing the scenario helps you figure out what really matters to you. It helps you decide if the things you're valuing are worth the risk of withholding information from others. In our example, Shelley needs to consider what would happen if she told the truth to the VP and her friend.

4. Are you dissembling to protect others who need to be protected?

If your deception is discovered, people will be far more forgiving if they understand you did it in the interest of others who needed protection. But protecting others doesn't necessarily justify what you're doing. Would they want you to deceive someone else on their behalf? How do you know? It may be that you need to ask the people you're protecting if they are comfortable with your deception. Shelley, for example, could ask the HR Director if she has permission to share the GMAT waiver with anyone in senior leadership.

Dissembling to protect others feels noble, and that makes it dangerous. Remember that you're pitting one party's welfare against another's. Be sure that you're the right person to make this decision by considering your authority and any bias on your part. If you do make this choice, be sure you're choosing fairly the party who benefits.

5. Are you at fault for a misunderstanding—or do you have an obligation to clarify?

Many questions or assumptions that create a Dissemblance dilemma result from misunderstandings by other parties. For example, they may give you the benefit of the doubt when you don't really deserve it. Even worse, they might misunderstand or misread something in a way that benefits you. The default expectation in business is that each party must be thorough and diligent. If one party makes a mistake, the other party is rarely to blame.

But if you contributed to the misunderstanding, you probably have an obligation to clarify. Even an accidental miscommunication on your part is tantamount to deception if you let it go unchecked. Once again, remember that silence is just another form of communication.

You may also have an obligation to clarify even if you didn't create the misunderstanding. This is especially true when you're in a position of trust with the other party. If professional expectations require you to put the other party's interests ahead of your own, then you need to correct their false understanding. Professional rules of conduct for your job may also require complete disclosure. Some roles come with fiduciary duties that impose a higher standard of behavior.

6. Is there a way to get what you need without dissembling?

Don't get caught in the false dichotomy of either (a) deceiving to get what you need or (b) telling the truth and bearing the hard outcome. Think creatively about how you could both be honest and get what you need. You might prevail by being forthright and then asking for the other party's patience and understanding. You might also find that your honesty is valuable enough to them that it brings long-term benefits. Don't let immediately apparent pressures blur your vision of a more prosperous future.

Pitfalls

Avoid these common dangers when faced with a Dissemblance dilemma.

Ruining Your Reputation

Few ethical errors will stay with you more tenaciously than being caught in a lie. A reputation for deception stains everything, and people will hesitate to trust you under a wide range of circumstances. In a very real way, one deception could cost you financial opportunities and personal relationships and could label you for a long time.

Making Assumptions

Don't assume that your silence isn't dissemblance. If someone else reasonably expects you to correct a misunderstanding, then your silence could be equivalent to telling a lie. This is especially true if the other party misunderstands something that you have an obligation to clarify.

Also don't assume you know what others will do with the information. Sometimes we're afraid to be truthful because we think someone will use the information in a way that hurts us or others. We fear the worst and so our fears drive us to dissemble. It's our experience that people are usually more kind and understanding than not. Also, they may be asking for the information for reasons you don't know or understand. Put yourself in the other party's shoes and consider what you would do after learning the truth. Be willing to trust their better natures.

Letting Negotiations Pressure You

Be especially careful in negotiations. These are often high-pressure situations where you have to make quick decisions. It's easy to tell small (or big) lies when working out an agreement. This is especially true when the other party doesn't have a chance to confirm what you've told them. Your best bet is to take time and be thoughtful before you let the pressure of negotiation lead to mistakes you'll regret.

Thinking You Can Lie Just Once

Lies breed lies. You might think that your dissemblance will be a one-time event, but that almost never happens. People usually need more information than one answer can give them. You'll quickly find that one lie necessitates many more. You may be less comfortable with dissembling if you consider that you're likely committing to an entire series of deceptions.

Avoiding Coming Clean

If you've already deceived someone, don't discount the value of coming clean. Knowing how costly a lie can be to your reputation, consider telling the truth before someone catches you in a lie. Everyone lies at some point, and everyone knows that. We are far more forgiving of a person confessing their dishonesty than of a person who is caught and only then comes to regret the lie. Consider coming clean now, both to do the right thing and to salvage your reputation.

 ## Bill's Experiences

False understandings happen all the time. When two people are talking or negotiating with one another, rarely are both parties equally educated, experienced, knowledgeable, or aware. Many times one party knows more than the other on a certain subject. Sometimes one party relies on the other to be truthful. In these situations, you could create an advantage by not clarifying a misunderstanding, by not telling the complete truth, or by lying. How will you act?

"How Much Do You Make?"

My father taught me that half a truth is a whole lie. I recall being challenged one day. As a new general manager, I decided to travel to all 17 warehouses and meet the employees. I visited the largest warehouse first and met with about 75 union workers toward the end of their shift. I talked about our goals, then asked for questions.

The first question was, "How much money do you make?"

I don't think the man expected me to answer. He was clearly trying to show off in front of his coworkers. I could have easily danced around the question—explained that I am paid under a fair compensation system based on education, experience, accountability, problem-solving, and so on. Instead, I decided to answer. I told them my base annual compensation to the dollar. That number was surely higher than the compensation of anyone else in the room. I added, "And a year from now, I want you to tell my boss that I'm worth more."

I earned a lot of trust with my answer. Later in that assignment I would get straight answers from these workers when I asked them questions. And sometimes I'd get valuable, unsolicited advice. This experience reinforced my belief that honesty is the best policy.

The Wrong Question

Later, I found myself in a situation that I still don't feel good about. I was asked to testify in court in a personal injury case. An individual was killed when a large mining machine was activated while he was in the line of fire. Proper procedure was to lock out the machine before getting into any vulnerable position. The deceased had locked the machine.

In a trial, I was asked, "Was there a master cutoff switch on the control panel?" The easy answer to that question was yes. But it was the wrong question. This machine had two master cutoff switches. That's just bad design. There should be only one master cut-off switch, so nobody can activate the machine when it's locked. But this machine had another master cutoff switch that was not locked.

I was uncomfortable answering "yes," so I asked for time to speak with my attorney. I explained my dilemma. My attorney explained that my job was to answer the question asked—no more, no less. He explained that the plaintiff was represented by counsel who was being paid handsomely and who had the responsibility to ask the right questions. It was not my job to clarify.

I returned to the stand and answered "yes." The existence of the second switch was not revealed. That didn't feel good. I didn't lie. I didn't even misrepresent the truth. But the entire story was not told. Afterward, I investigated to assure that the faulty design was corrected—and it was.

Budget Bluffing

A common annual exercise in most corporations is to assemble and present for approval each corporate function's budget for the next year. In my company, the annual budget process was usually initiated with a general directive such as, "Cut 5% from last year." Then the bluffing would begin.

The first step of crafty budget managers was to select a favorable baseline. The baseline might be last year's budget, this year's actual expenses to date (annualized), the average expenditures for the last five years, or something else. Managers could usually devise a baseline that was very high. Then a 5% reduction would be easier to achieve. The next step was to obfuscate or bury revenues and expenses in an effort to arrive at the most favorable and easiest-to-achieve budget. In a corporation where trust between department heads and their bosses was so important, this budgeting process built a foundation of misinformation and mistrust.

After a short while, I decided not to play the budget game. In presenting to my boss, a man I trusted immensely, I put all my cards on the table—all of them. I showed all the baselines (last year's budget, current actual expenses, and historic budget performance) and suggested the "right" baseline. I then followed the directive for reducing my budget, often by 5%, without requesting any exceptions or exclusions. Finally, I told my boss where I still had some "fat" in the budget, by account and amount, but asked him not to take the fat unless he really needed it.

That openness and honesty was refreshing for my boss, and he awarded me for it. I know he appreciated my coming clean with all the numbers, rather than turning the budget process into an inquisition in which he attempted to find what was being hidden. My boss and I would review and approve my budget rather quickly, without arguments, name calling or worse. In the end he would thank me for the information, approve my budget, and ask me to tell my peers that the budget meeting was "rough."

"Third-party" Opinion

Sometimes you may need to insist that others not dissemble on your behalf. Don't hesitate to take a stand.

Under United States patent laws, willful and intentional patent infringement can carry triple damages. To avoid the triple damages and to demonstrate that conduct is not deliberate, it is prudent to seek and document an opinion from an independent third party. Then, if a court later rules that you've infringed on someone's patent, your careful advice-seeking can be used as evidence that the infringement was not intentional—that is, not worthy of treble damages. These opinions often cost from $10,000 to $25,000. They are expensive because you are soliciting independent advice.

The usual practice when we were introducing a new product or process was to conduct a patent infringement search. In one instance we discovered a patented process that was fairly close to our own new process. I felt that our process was sufficiently different to not be considered infringement. But, to be prudent, I sent all the relevant material to a reputable law firm and asked them for their independent opinion.

I soon got a call from a law partner asking me, "What do you want our opinion to say?"

I was paying for an independent opinion, but this person was prepared to tell me whatever I wanted to hear. I asked him to package all the material and send it back to me. I sought my opinion elsewhere.

Planning Ahead

Consider these strategies to avoid a Dissemblance dilemma in the future.

1. Anticipate the questions. Sometimes we lie simply because we've been caught off guard. It's better to think through what someone might ask you and carefully prepare thoughtful answers that avoid dissembling. Don't use this as an opportunity to be ticky-tacky with the meaning of words. Use it as a chance to get the truth across in the best way possible.

2. Clarify expectations. Often dissemblance occurs when we've misunderstood what others were expecting from us. To avoid this, set expectations right, both yours and the other party's. Try to anticipate where there might be misunderstandings. Be clear about your interests and intentions. Don't give others a reason to make bad assumptions.

3. Invite honesty. Finally, take care to avoid putting other people into this dilemma. When you're going to ask questions to try to get at the truth, make truth telling as easy as possible. Parents know this is especially important with children, but it works for everyone. Show patience, express trust, and remember the importance of the relationship. You'll find others will be more honest with you as a result.

What Happened

In the opening story, Shelley had to handle the vice president's query about her score on an admissions test she didn't actually take. An honest answer in this situation would betray the HR director's request that she keep the test waiver a secret.

Shelley decided in the moment that protecting the confidentiality of the GMAT waiver was more important than telling the full truth about it. She gave a nonspecific answer to the VP about having gotten a good enough score. Later, Shelley went back to the VP in private and explained the situation. Luckily for her, he was very understanding and apologized for putting her in that position. Shelley never did explain the truth to her coworker who was also in the room, deciding that doing so would cause unnecessary problems for the HR director.

Practice Dilemma

Jeff works as a sales rep for Great Rides, a large fleet maintenance company. Great Rides offers a full range of services to keep commercial vehicles running at their best. Lately times had been tough for Jeff's company, mostly because of some lost clients. There wasn't enough work to keep everyone employed. At first the company simply didn't hire replacements as workers left. But eventually Great Rides had to let several mechanics go. The layoffs left employees and others with the impression that the company was on the verge of bankruptcy. The truth was that the company really might go bankrupt—but only if it couldn't renew its largest contract, a yearlong engagement with Carterville School District.

That renewal hinged on Jeff's upcoming negotiation with Zach, the district's head of procurement. Thankfully, the terms of the contract weren't a problem for either side. All the details, including payments and service schedule, were arranged in advance. Jeff was basically expecting to show up and collect signatures.

That's why Jeff was startled when the district manager asked if Great Rides was facing bankruptcy. Zach said he had "heard some things." He said the district was nervous about recommitting the care of its vans and buses to a company that might not be around for much longer.

Jeff's mind started racing. Should he answer the question truthfully, at the risk of losing this critical account, or misrepresent Great Rides's financial situation in order to keep the company in business?

CHAPTER 9

Challenge 9: Loyalty

You're not sure how much you should give up to honor a relationship.

Ellie was thrilled when her manager granted permission for her to enroll in a two-year executive MBA program and attend classes every other weekend. Her company, a large wireless services firm, would even support her with partial tuition reimbursement. Then, almost halfway through her program, a large restructuring took place. Ellie began reporting to Barbara, who was unwilling to let her continue with school.

Things are so tense with Barbara that Ellie would be more than happy to quit her job—if she could get a generous severance package. But suing the company to obtain that severance might cause problems for her former manager, a boss she really liked. What should Ellie do?

Ellie manages accounts for wireless retail and B2B dealers. Over nine years, she rose in the company and earned the respect of regional management. When her sales and distribution channel was restructured, Ellie's position was eliminated. However, upper management recommended Ellie for a new sales manager role, directing retail distribution throughout North and South Carolina.

The new director, Barbara, interviewed several candidates before giving Ellie the job. Ellie accepted with enthusiasm. But when Ellie returned from a weeklong vacation, Barbara abruptly informed her that she'd given the positon to someone else. "You were one of our leading candidates, but I didn't formally offer you the job," Barbara bluffed.

Barbara found a position for Ellie that was similar to her old account manager job. Disappointed and frustrated, Ellie decided to stand up for herself. She appealed through every possible means: her previous manager, her director, the regional vice president, the human resources division, and the company's ethics hotline. While many were sympathetic to her situation, no one was willing to confront the director or attempt to grant her a sales manager role.

Ellie's good friend and previous manager, Paul, who had signed the written approval for her MBA, was especially empathetic. But Paul was low on political capital and was under extreme pressure from above to not make waves. He told Ellie that his director was now angry with him for signing the MBA authorization in the first place. Paul felt his own job was not secure.

At this point, Ellie requested a severance package in exchange for voluntarily leaving the company. During the restructuring, severance packages had been provided to hundreds of employees. But Ellie's request for severance was denied. With five children to feed, Ellie started working in the account manager position while aggressively looking for new employment.

Over the next few months, the situation with Barbara went from bad to worse. Barbara was angry that Ellie had publicized their "misunderstanding" about the sales manager role, and she begrudged the flexibility Ellie required to go to class on Fridays. Eventually, Barbara said Ellie's job was not compatible with being a student. She threatened to terminate Ellie unless she gave up school right away.

Ellie was shocked. She gave Barbara and Barbara's up-line ample evidence the company was supporting and even sponsoring her participation in the two-year program. But, as before, all levels of management ignored her appeal.

At this point, Ellie decided to explore her last option: litigation. She explained her situation to several experienced employment law attorneys; all confirmed she had legal ground to sue the company. Her case was very well documented and they felt certain she would receive a yearlong severance with 100% commission and benefits. This would give Ellie plenty of time to finish school and find a better job.

Then Ellie spoke with Paul about her plans. To Ellie's surprise, Paul asked her not to sue the company. He feared he would be held responsible if she filed suit and, given his own rocky employment status, would almost certainly be fired, too. Based on her own recent experiences with the company, Ellie felt pretty sure Paul's assessment was accurate.

Explanation

Our research into ethical dilemmas has made one thing abundantly clear: relationships matter. We all build important connections with our family, friends, coworkers, bosses, neighbors, and so on. These connections influence our choices in many important ways. In Ellie's case, a relationship is at the heart of her dilemma, specifically the dilemma of Loyalty.

The Loyalty dilemma happens when you are not sure how much to sacrifice in order to honor a relationship.

For this dilemma, we are not talking about relationships necessarily formed out of legal obligations, like a contract or some sort of fiduciary duty. Those relationships come up in different dilemmas, like Made a Promise or Conflicts of Interest. Instead, the Loyalty dilemma springs from the unwritten obligations we have for others, usually because of a special connection we have with them. But being unwritten doesn't make the obligations any less compelling.

Loyalty most often emerges in two kinds of relationships: one where you have benefited from someone's generosity or one where you share an identity with someone. Ellie's dilemma involves the first kind of relationship. She is not sure if she should litigate at the expense of a boss who has been so helpful to her. Our practice dilemma at the end of this chapter involves the other kind of relationship. The actor is part of a professional group that shares the same interests. Sometimes both types of relationships manifest in a single situation.

Exactly what we owe to individuals in these relationships is hard to define. Because our duties are at times unclear, the boundaries of loyalty tend to be vague. It can be hard to know exactly what or how much to give in order to be loyal to our relationships.

Think of loyalty as a form of capital, specifically social capital (as we discussed in the Standing up to Power dilemma). Loyalty is how we build valuable resources through our relationships. We appreciate how others have helped us in the past, so we help them when the time comes. Reciprocal relationships fill gaps where things like contracts don't quite fit.

In terms of what we must sacrifice, loyalty usually involves a personal cost of freedom, value, or opportunity. Sometimes we must choose between conflicting loyalties (and those sacrifices are some of the stickiest versions of this dilemma). Often loyalty works in kind: we give what we receive in a relationship. For example, Ellie's boss is asking for special consideration to protect his job and reputation within the company, something he gave Ellie over the years.

Despite their nebulous boundaries, loyalties are rarely complete or all-encompassing, even in our closest relationships. We have all experienced the moment of being asked too much by a friend or family member. The problem is that we all disagree about the right amount of sacrifice.

Generally, the right answer to a Loyalty dilemma is one that helps you remain loyal. The conflict will be around the boundaries of what loyalty demands of you. Remember that loyalty and trust belong together. Make sure your choice reflects the trustworthy person you want to be.

Questions to Ask

When the demands of an important relationship test your loyalty, use these questions to figure out how much you should sacrifice.

1. Has the individual shown loyalty to you?

As noted in our explanation, loyalty is reciprocal. If the person (or organization) is asking something of you when he or she hasn't done much to earn your loyalty, you are more likely to be facing the Showing Mercy dilemma.

This perspective may seem callous, but it is an important distinction. We wouldn't say Ellie is being disloyal to her old boss if he had no special relationship with her or if he had not treated her well. His past loyalty to Ellie is what creates the current dilemma. The same might be said for a situation you're facing. Be sure to fully consider and appreciate the loyalty you have been shown.

2. Did you ask for this person's loyalty?

There's a saying, "You shouldn't let the Mafia do you any favors." The idea is that once the favor happens, the Mafia will demand your loyalty in return for their generosity. Sometimes people will give us things we do not ask for or need. They likely hope the action will build a relationship. When you accept this kindness, you suddenly feel an obligation to reciprocate. And usually you do have an obligation of some kind. But remember, the strongest loyalty is based on mutual benefit, not unasked favors.

Ellie's relationship with her old boss probably involved things she asked for and things he simply offered without her asking. Both kinds of exchanges deepen her obligation to him, making her proposed lawsuit harder to justify.

3. Does your choice make you trustworthy?

This question deserves special attention because loyalty is built on trust. You need to decide if your choice reflects the fact that you are a trustworthy person. Does your choice show others you deserve their trust? Can people have confidence relying on you in the future?

If Ellie decides to sue, her old boss might see her choice as disregard for ways he helped her career to grow. Others who see Ellie's suing the company to his detriment might be less willing to be her friends. Ellie will need to weigh the benefits of legal action against the cost to her trustworthiness.

4. Is this person taking advantage of you?

Your loyalty cannot be limitless. Perhaps the other party is asking for more than he or she is entitled to ask. Loyalty is rooted in trustworthiness and reciprocity. Is the individual being trustworthy in their request to you? Is the person asking more from you than they would offer or have offered in return?

This question is a tough call for Ellie. She has seen her career opportunities grow because of her old boss. But now she's facing losing both her job and her MBA degree. Instead of a chance for direct reciprocity, there seems to be a direct tradeoff: will it be Ellie's financial wellbeing or her old boss's? Ellie has to figure out if her old boss is asking more than he should when requesting she forego her lawsuit.

5. Would they want your loyalty if they knew all of the costs?

Sometimes people ask more of us than they realize. Without knowing all the facts, they may make a request that turns out to be a huge burden. We may feel bad pointing this out or asking for a reprieve because we don't want to look disloyal. In these situations, we are unintentionally taken advantage of by the other party.

Ellie should make sure her old boss knows what he is asking of her. They should explore options that will benefit both of them. In fact, this moment might be an opportunity for them to deepen their relationship by showing mutual self-sacrifice. But if Ellie never has this conversation with her old boss, she'll never know if he understood what he asked of her.

6. Does showing loyalty in this situation unfairly sacrifice other loyalties?

Like commitments, loyalties can come in conflict. When this happens, we should always weigh our loyalties carefully.

If you have a conflict of loyalties, take time to think about each one. Consider how your current well-being relates to what others have done for you. Consider the needs of those counting on you. Without fully appreciating the reasons why others trust you, you might unfairly cast aside one loyalty for another. For example, helping a friend or coworker at the expense of your spouse—someone who has given more and deserves more in your relationship—would clearly be unfair. Ellie needs to be sure she doesn't make an unbalanced decision in favor of her boss.

7. Does showing loyalty sacrifice your ethics?

Loyalty is an ethically dangerous principle because it invites you to give your decision-making power to someone else. For example, someone to whom you owe loyalty might ask you to lie or cheat for them. When your ethics are at stake, remember, loyalty is not boundless. Your character is always more important.

If you are going to show loyalty to someone, make sure you still own your decision. This will help assure your choice is an ethical one. Loyalty may mean sacrificing many things; do not let it lead you to sacrifice your ethics.

Pitfalls

Before you make a decision based on loyalty, study up on these common mistakes.

Offloading Accountability

Loyalty is not a substitute for personal responsibility. Make sure each act is your own, not just something required of you by someone else. Don't be loyal in an unthinking way. Accountability, a core ethical value, means you are always responsible for your choices, even if you are doing what someone else has asked of you.

Trusting Blindly

Loyalty, properly considered, brings us closer to each other. It deepens our relationships and builds value for everyone involved. But not everyone who asks for your loyalty deserves it.

Beware those who disvalue loyalty, themselves. It's easy to throw relationships out the window if you don't feel beholden to anyone. The advice of disloyal people is probably driven by their own self-interest. Don't feel you owe loyalty to them.

At the same time, beware those who overvalue loyalty. These people make the same mistake as the disloyal—selfishness—just in the other direction. They demand more than they give and expect more than they share. They are usually not interested in your wellbeing or in your character. Those who overvalue loyalty are more likely to ask you to act unethically.

Taking Advantage

Be careful about what you let others believe about your relationship with them. As we noted, sometimes others can make sacrifices for you that you didn't ask them to make. If you sit by and let them help you, thinking that you don't owe them a thing because you didn't ask for their help, you take advantage of them. You are acting in a way that is untrustworthy.

Bill's Experiences

Loyalty is essential in organizations. Trusting, reciprocal relationships help us do business every day. But it's easy to misdirect loyalty in a way that lets people off the hook. It's also easy to forget how much others have done for you.

Values vs. People

In my decisions as a leader, I find that loyalty to a value often takes precedence over loyalty to a person.

Our company had a rule that any employee who intentionally visited pornographic websites through company equipment or Internet would be terminated. Such behavior was considered inappropriate and would not be tolerated. When I was the chief information officer, our information technologies security manager sent me a monthly report with the names of people who had accessed these websites. I reported the offenders to their managers, and termination would result rather quickly.

One report listed as an offender the vice president of sales for a major division. I gave the report to the division president, who questioned whether there was any room for an exception. He felt loyal to this vice president. I explained that we also owed loyalty to appropriate conduct—a value that should outweigh our loyalty to any one person.

After our brief discussion, he released the offender from the company.

Losing Loyalty

On the other hand, it's a tragedy how easily loyalty can be tossed aside.

I once shared a secretary with my boss. The secretary was leaving on maternity leave and expressed concern for her job. Aware of the difficult economic environment, she worried she would be an easy target for a layoff while she was gone. My boss assured her that her job was safe. He promised her job would be waiting when she returned from maternity leave and told her she had nothing to worry about.

Three weeks later, in a meeting to decide on department layoffs, my boss offered up our secretary—who was still on maternity leave—as his first candidate. I reminded him of his assurances to her and he dismissed those assurances as ancient history. I urged him to honor his oral commitment but was overruled. (He was the boss.)

How do you think this affected my relationship with my boss? Do you think I relied on anything he said after that experience?

He didn't just lose the secretary's loyalty. He also lost mine.

Planning Ahead

Loyalty dilemmas can sometimes be prevented if you emphasize loyalty to a shared value or goal, rather than loyalty to a particular person. Here are a few tips.

1. Choose loyalty to values. "Bill's Experiences" articulate this well. Loyalty to values will be a constant source of ethical courage and will help you make a strong case when you're pressured to be loyal to a person over a principle. Also, don't let loyalty to an organization feel like loyalty to a value. Organizations, in the end, are just groups of people.

2. Be trustworthy. As we say throughout the book, when others know what you stand for, they won't be surprised when you are loyal to your values. Remember, loyalty is based on trustworthiness. Loyalty to good values makes a person supremely trustworthy.

3. Lead through shared commitment. Encouraging loyalty to shared values is a better way to lead than encouraging people to be loyal to you. Because loyalty between people is reciprocal, some of those you lead will see loyalty as being merely transactional. You'll encounter people with a "What have you done for me lately?" view of your relationship. Bring in and cultivate the people who are loyal instead to the values you share. Together, you'll sacrifice to protect important principles, something far more motivating. As a promoter of those values, you'll benefit, too.

4. Correct over-reliance. If anyone is counting on you more than they should, be wise enough to correct that problem early. Don't wait for the moment of crisis. You might be tempted to let the misconception continue because it brings benefits today, but the cost of having to abandon someone will be expensive to you. If you make expectations clear right now, you will still be able to call yourself trustworthy.

5. Inspire loyalty. Be worthy of loyalty from others. Be trustworthy. Be generous. Value the people in your life and consider their welfare along with your own. Constant concern for the welfare of others brings incredibly protective power when you face an ethical dilemma.

What Happened

Let's return to the dilemma that began this chapter. Ellie's boss, Barbara, was forcing her to choose between staying in school and keeping her job. Ellie had a strong case for suing her company, but suing might bring retaliation against Paul, her former manager and loyal friend.

Despite her fear of being unemployed without a severance package, Ellie did not feel comfortable bringing a lawsuit that would endanger Paul. She told Barbara she was going to stay in school. Barbara began the termination process.

Hours before her final day at work, Ellie received an unexpected call. It was a job offer from a company she knew she could trust. She stayed with that company and finished her MBA.

Practice Dilemma

"Well-Known Plastic Surgeon Accused of Botching Nosejob" is the leading line on the local evening news. Being a plastic surgeon himself, Keyshawn's interest is piqued. "Plastic surgeon Ben Pennington is under investigation by the State Medical Board after two women complained about their nose surgeries. Both claim Pennington is responsible for their permanent disfigurement," says the investigative reporter.

The next morning, Keyshawn receives a call from Dr. Lucinda Costa, president of the State Society of Plastic Surgeons. Dr. Costa asks him to sign a letter she is sending to the news station and to the local newspaper, condemning the news story as inappropriate, unprofessional, and libelous.

Dr. Pennington is an experienced senior plastic surgeon who has practiced in the area for more than 30 years. When Keyshawn first started his own practice, Dr. Pennington was someone he looked to for advice. Although Keyshawn has never operated with him, he knows Dr. Pennington is well respected by his peers and has several outstanding achievement awards to his credit.

The previous day's news story started by posting an unflattering picture of Dr. Pennington as the reporter interviewed the patient who alleged permanent disfigurement in complaints filed with the State Medical Board. Apparently a complication with her surgery had resulted in severe tissue degradation, destroying most of her nose. The patient said she was devastated and ashamed of her appearance. She also criticized Dr. Pennington for handling her post-operative care very poorly, repeatedly telling her that everything was "spectacular," she was "healing well," and she looked "fabulous."

Keyshawn recognizes the news report only told the patient's side of the story. Dr. Pennington did not grant an interview, and the reporter made this sound as if he were hiding. The reporter would have known that federal law prohibits physicians from discussing patient information with third parties. She could easily have found another physician to speak about surgical complications, their relative infrequency, and their effective treatment. The bias in the reporting was blatant, and the overall message was negative toward plastic surgery. Keyshawn and his colleagues often joke about the negative messaging their field receives from the press— even though most actors and TV reporters have gone to a plastic surgeon for one procedure or another.

Dr. Costa wants to rally a unified front from local plastic surgeons. Her letter states that plastic surgeons make every effort to provide outstanding care for every patient, but even with outstanding care, there are still risks to every procedure. Those risks are explained to patients and they sign consent forms acknowledging that they understand the risks. Surely, Dr. Pennington did the same. He is an exceptionally gifted surgeon with hundreds of satisfied patients. Some patients, however, can be unrealistic and a few are impossible to satisfy.

Somehow, Keyshawn feels uncomfortable with the wording of the letter. It implies support for Dr. Pennington to the same degree as for plastic surgery in general. What if Dr. Pennington did do wrong by this patient, and possibly by others? Keyshawn doesn't want to add his endorsement without knowing the full story.

He hints as much to Dr. Costa. She counters that he is the only plastic surgeon in the area who has not yet signed. If he doesn't add his name, she implies, he is basically turning his back on their professional community.

Does Keyshawn sign the letter out of loyalty to his colleagues? Or does he refuse to sign, even if that signals he doesn't trust their collective judgment or ability?

CHAPTER 10

Challenge 10: Sacrificing Personal Values

Living true to your own beliefs might impose a burden on others.

"For a media startup, this company is doing surprisingly well," Arthur said to Joe. They were waiting in the client's lobby, preparing to close an employee benefits deal.

"Not that surprising, considering the services they provide," Joe laughed.

Arthur returned a confused look. "What do you mean?"

Joe chuckled. "You don't know?"

"No, I don't," Arthur said uncertainly.

"They produce adult entertainment for hotels. Pay-for-view stuff."

"Oh." Arthur didn't know what to say. He avoided adult entertainment himself, and he had some strong feelings about the industry, especially the way it tended to objectify women.

"It's all pretty mild," Joe assured him, "Just soft porn. Does your company have a problem with that?"

Cautiously, Arthur replied, "I don't know if my company has a problem with it, but I do."

Arthur was two years into his first job with a large insurance and financial services firm. As an account executive, he marketed and sold his company's products to intermediaries, including retirement plan advisors and employee benefits consultants, like Joe. After a sale, Arthur would stay with the account to provide management and administrative services for the client.

So far, Arthur had mostly been assigned "C" relationships, clients the senior account executives viewed as not worth their time. Joe was one of those "C" relationships, an intermediary with whom they had limited business. Arthur's job was to change that.

But his skittishness in the lobby had clearly irritated Joe. "You can walk out now if you don't want my business," he told Arthur.

"We want to do business with you, Joe," Arthur insisted. "I just might want to talk with my supervisor about this particular client."

That's when the HR director appeared and invited them into the conference room.

Walking the halls, Arthur felt sick to his stomach. He excused himself to the restroom to collect his thoughts. Immediately he noticed that the pictures on the bathroom walls were of nude women. He supposed these still frames could be considered art by some. Could the actual pay-for-view media be much worse?

Once the meeting began, everything moved quickly. They reviewed the agreements Arthur had drawn up, and the client signed where requested. Joe looked relieved. "See, that wasn't so bad," he joked as they left the building.

Arthur smiled and thanked him for the sale.

But on the drive back to his office, Arthur's thoughts raced. Could he really take commissions from a company whose products were in opposition to his values? Even in the pornography industry, workers deserve employee benefits, he told himself. He didn't want to burden anyone with his personal hang-up. And he didn't want to lose out on future deals with Joe.

Explanation

While most values tend to be universal—such as love, justice, or freedom—many of us hold values that are unique to our personal or cultural beliefs. Some of these values might originate in religious traditions; for example, work being suspended on certain days of the week (Fridays for Muslims, Saturdays for Jews, and Sundays for most Christians). Other personal values might stem from ideological convictions or commitments to health. Some business people, like Arthur, feel uncomfortable supporting industries they view as harmful, perhaps including gambling, pornography, weapons production, or the sale of tobacco. Other business people try to avoid being involved in any human use of animals (e.g., for cosmetic or medical testing) or environmental abuse.

This chapter deals with the issue of having particular values that are not broadly shared by others in your organization or community. How do you stay true to your values while also participating in the larger group?

Conflicts between individual and organizational values are often driven by the clash of cultures. For example, a vodka toast in Russia is an important relationship-building tradition for business leaders, while in Sudan, alcohol is forbidden. Whenever you leave your like-minded community, you will almost certainly be confronted with the challenge of trying to live your values in circumstances that make it difficult to do so.

As a general rule, organizations will not require you to engage in practices directly opposed to your values. In other words, it's unlikely that your organization requires you to gamble, drink alcohol, use tobacco, or view pornography. (One exception to this rule would be when an employer requires you to work on a day that you reserve for religious worship.) However, in an interconnected world, it is nearly impossible not to be involved in at least a tangential way with products or activities that conflict with your values. For example, you may be asked to audit a company that produces pornography, to invest in a company that produces weapons, to give a loan to a company that creates meat products, or to be the caterer for lunch at a tobacco company. Such circumstances might involve you in something you deem reprehensible without requiring you to directly participate. Thus, you will need to decide how to allocate your effort and resources, given these potential value conflicts.

There may be values you will not need to compromise at all. On the other hand, sometimes you will have to balance your values, as we learned in Conflicts of Interest. This is especially the case when living your own values imposes a burden on others.

This dilemma might be amplified if you feel pressure from others to act in a way that contradicts your values. However, be aware that sometimes this perceived pressure can be more imagined than real. Consider the experience of Tagg Romney while interning with a top consulting firm. On his very first day in the office, for his very first assignment, he was staffed on a project dealing with a state lottery operator. Gambling was an activity that conflicted with Tagg's personal beliefs; he could not in good conscience accept the assignment, but he also knew that turning down an assignment was simply not done. When he went to speak to the partner who oversaw assignments, he felt for sure he was going to lose his job. Instead, to Tagg's surprise, the partner said there was no problem. He simply reassigned Tagg to another project.

Questions to Ask

1. Does involvement directly promote the behavior that conflicts with your beliefs?

As stated earlier, in an interconnected world it is virtually impossible to be entirely uninvolved in activities or products that we do not support personally. For example, most workers have retirement accounts that are in broadly diversified mutual funds, meaning that they are invested in companies in virtually every industry. It is probable that your organization has received business or donations over the years from companies involved in practices that don't match your values.

Recognize that not all involvement is the same. Directly promoting an activity you don't agree with would probably feel more uncomfortable to you than being indirectly involved. There is a difference between being a tobacco marketer and accepting a donation from a local tobacco company for your airport expansion project. The closer your work is to the actual promotion of the activity, the greater the likely violation of your values. In the example dilemma, Arthur is not directly involved in the production of pornography, which might make him less concerned about going forward with the deal.

2. Are you acting on your own behalf or as an agent for others?

In some organizational situations, we act for ourselves. But often we are acting as agents on behalf of others. When we are acting as agents for others, we might not necessarily want to impose our values, particularly if doing so causes the others some harm. However, that does not mean that we should completely abandon our values. Instead, such a situation calls for a more delicate balancing act. While we give up some level of autonomy when working on behalf of others, we should never completely abandon our own judgment. (This is an ongoing dilemma for politicians.) In Arthur's situation, he is acting as an agent for his company and as an advisor to Joe—not solely on his own behalf.

3. What burden is placed on others by living your personal values?

Some values can be lived with minimal impact on others because they deal solely with personal decisions and outcomes. However, other values necessarily impact the people around us. For example, if you choose not to work on a religious holiday, you may be requiring that someone else has to work that day. If you are hosting a department party at your home and you don't drink alcohol, your decision to not provide alcohol could place a burden on others in that they don't have the freedom to engage in a commonly accepted social practice. If Arthur refuses the account, other employees would be happy to manage it. But he may do damage to Joe's opinion of his company.

4. What costs are you willing to bear for your beliefs?

Placing a burden on others or not following through in the way your company or clients hope may come at a cost to your career. You have to look deeply inside and decide for yourself how much you are willing to sacrifice for your values. Before taking an all-or-nothing approach, be sure to think through all of the consequences to you and to others who will be affected.

There is an upside to consider as well. Because of their cost, Sacrificing Personal Values dilemmas provide an opportunity to demonstrate your commitment to what you believe. Hakeem Olajuwon, a Muslim and one of the all-time greats in the NBA, famously respected the fasting requirements of Ramadan. That meant he played a month's worth of games each season while only eating and drinking before sunrise and after sundown. During Ramadan, he would lose up to ten pounds because of the rigorous physical demands of professional basketball. Instead of a burden, he saw Ramadan as an opportunity to educate others about his religious faith.[1]

For Arthur, asking to be removed from the account would show the depth of his personal conviction. Refusing to accept his commission would send an even stronger message.

5. Do you believe the product or service hurts society?

If you believe that by supporting some practice you will be harming society, that provides a greater justification to avoid it than personal conviction does alone. For example, tobacco use brings negative social consequences by reducing air quality and increasing healthcare costs. Gambling could lead to negative social consequences as its participants form addictions, lose their money, and burden their families and communities. Arthur believes pornography is harmful to participants and damages family relationships. While using that justification to guide his personal choice, he should keep in mind, when speaking to others, that they may not share his viewpoint.

6. Were you sufficiently aware of this conflict to have avoided it?

As a general moral principle, once you have agreed to do something, it is not right to back out. If you take a job or accept a role knowing that it might require you to forfeit a personal value, you have little excuse when such an expectation becomes a reality. However, when the role expectation is new, you might have greater moral justification for refusing to engage in the questionable activity. (We discuss this at length in the Made a Promise dilemma.) In Arthur's case, he did not know that part of his job would involve working with a pornography producer, so it would have been difficult to avoid this conflict in advance.

Pitfalls

When you consider sacrificing personal values, be cautious about the following common mistakes.

Forgetting Your Family

Because the consequences of your decisions can affect the entire family, it is critical that you and your loved ones have a mutual understanding about the sacrifices you are willing to make to uphold your values. Without that unity, your unilateral decision to either maintain or abandon your values could cause discord at home.

Seeing only Yourself

Be careful not to be the person who only thinks about his or her own values; reciprocity matters. By actively recognizing and personally sacrificing to allow others to live their values, you are more likely to get support for your own. For example, being willing to work unpopular shifts might encourage others to work the times you need off.

Further, be careful to not assume your worldview or standards are better than others'. People quickly catch on to any sense of superiority. Work hard to notice the commitments you and your coworkers share—for example, the desire to help others, do your best, or be kind. Use those commitments to build common ground.

Bill's Experiences

Staying true to your personal values is noble. It reveals your character and establishes your reputation. By keeping your commitments, even at a cost, you will inspire others and will feel good about yourself. Occasionally, though, it's even more noble to sacrifice a personal value. You make that sacrifice to achieve something you value even more.

Beyond Bribes

When I went to Russia on assignment from Alcoa, I was adamant that my personal values did not condone bribes. I would not participate in any sort of bribing scheme, whether or not corruption was accepted as a norm of doing business there.

On one occasion, my car was stopped by the police—a standard practice in Russia. Typically, the police will detain you until you agree to pay them a few hundred rubles, and then you are allowed to go on your way. My colleagues frequently justified these payments by saying that the cost was minimal and they couldn't afford to waste any time. Their time was worth more to them than the petty bribe. However, I chose not to pay. I instructed my driver to have all the necessary papers in order—insurance certificates, owner's card, driver's license—because we were not paying any bribes. While we were stopped regularly, in over three years we never did pay any bribes.

I took the same stance whenever I was detained in airports, something which happened regularly as well. It would be suggested that I could go to the banking machine and withdraw a few thousand rubles to give to the guards, and then I could be on my way. I declined, saying that I would prefer to wait and work it out. Although it would have been easier to make the payments, I wanted to make a point to our employees: my reputation and dedication to playing fair were more important to me than sacrificing my values and saving time. During my years of travel to and from Russia, I ended up being detained in every Russian airport. Once I was detained in the Rostov airport for nine hours. But I never did pay a single ruble in bribes. My conviction communicated a powerful message to our workers.

Sacrificing for Safety

Many of our employees faced a similar dilemma over whether they would sacrifice their personal values. Because our company operated globally, many of our workers came from cultures with strong traditions of wearing particular clothing or religious adornments, such as necklaces, rings, or bracelets. Our company insisted on safety, and the clothing of our workers was a vital part of that safety, so sometimes these two expectations would conflict.

Many workers decided to accept our safety standards for dress. I imagine this was a difficult decision for some. Other workers did not feel they could make that sacrifice. We showed respect for their values by offering them alternative assignments. I admired their conviction, but I would not *compromise our commitment to safety, even if they said they would accept the additional risk.*

Donation Dilemmas

Often with a Sacrificing Values dilemma, you can find a way to meet your job requirements and still feel you are being true to yourself.

I was the head of our procurement organization when a popular charity selected our CEO as the honoree for their fundraising gala. The charity instructed me to write a letter to all of our suppliers, urging them to donate to the charity in honor of our CEO. In return, they would get a table for the event and could advertise in the gala's program.

I saw this as somewhat inappropriate. In our arrangements with our suppliers, we were committed to quality, delivery, and price. I worked very closely with them to reduce the cost of goods and services. Now I was supposed to go to these same suppliers and ask them to spend more money?

My CEO felt differently, however. Even after I asked him how he would feel if one of our customers asked the same of us, he still wanted me to invite our suppliers to contribute. So I wrote to our largest 50 suppliers. In a very carefully worded letter, I advised them of our CEO's being honored and told them if they were inclined to participate please do so directly with the charity. I also told them we would not know whether they had chosen to be involved. I assume some suppliers donated to the charity, but I'm not sure. The wording of my letter and the separation I made clear between us and the charity made me feel a little bit better about what I needed to do. I still do not like this practice.

On another occasion a well-known environmental charity contacted me with the good news that Alcoa was selected to receive their annual award. After much discussion, I was able to discern that, as the winner, we were expected to buy ten tables to the award dinner—at $10,000 each—for both this year and next year; to contribute $50,000 to the organization; and to purchase a gift, such as one of the charity's environmentally focused books (worth $25 to $50) for each of the 400 dinner attendees.

I declined the award.

Planning Ahead

When you worry your personal values and your job tasks may conflict, keep these ideas in mind.

1. Investigate ahead of time. Organizations can have strong cultures. You need to be as informed as possible about the culture and related expectations before you accept a job. While some organizations are accommodating of diverse values, others are not. You can increase your likelihood of being able to uphold your values by selecting organizations that won't require you to compromise your convictions.

2. Explain what and why. It's important to share your values with others so that they don't make false assumptions about why you do or don't do things. Consider a young father who leaves the office early to coach his child's soccer team. If he doesn't explain what he is doing and why he wants to do it, coworkers might wrongly assume that he is lazy or uncommitted to the organization.

Being open about your values has two components: (1) clearly communicating your values to others, and (2) providing the reasons behind your values. If values are not communicated clearly in the first place, you may end up with assignments you could have otherwise avoided. While your personal preferences may not always be accommodated, an awareness of your values can encourage coworkers or clients to help you be true to your values. Providing some reasons for your values—in a gentle and nonjudgmental way— can make others more likely to understand your point of view and honor your convictions. Vocalizing your values can also have the added benefit of empowering others to share and uphold their own values.

3. Be gracious about what matters to others. Go out of your way to understand the values of those around you. While personal convictions and religious beliefs are sensitive topics in the workplace, it's impossible to honor others' beliefs without first being aware of them. Proactively respecting the values of others can help you gain goodwill and may increase their willingness to respect your values. When learning about someone else's values, be careful to respond in a way that is open and understanding, even if their values seem foreign or strange. Never discount or disparage their beliefs.

4. Look to your boss for help. While from your vantage point, you may not see many options to your dilemma, individuals higher in the organization often have greater information and vision. This allows them to see ways in which your values can be honored. A new employee, like Arthur, might worry that if he does not feel comfortable doing business with a client there could be negative consequences. However, his manager might be fully aware that the account can be easily transferred to another employee with minimal repercussions. Managers are often aware of multiple acceptable ways of accomplishing a task. Having important information about employee preferences provides them with the ability to choose preferable options.

5. Seek others' guidance. If your values come to you from a religious tradition, you may be able to look to that religion for guidance. For example, the Vatican recently published guidelines for Catholics regarding their participation in business. You may also glean helpful ideas by watching other business people who share your faith tradition and whose integrity you admire.

What Happened

In the opening story, Arthur had just signed a deal with a company he did not want to work with, based on his personal beliefs. But he didn't want to offend anyone or lose valuable business for his firm.

Back at the office, Arthur immediately found his manager. He explained what had just happened and asked if there was any sort of policy for the situation. To the manager's knowledge, there were no industry restrictions related to clients. Arthur let her know that supporting a pornography company presented a difficulty for him, personally, and asked for help in exploring some alternatives. Arthur also told the manager that he did not know how he felt about being paid on the account once it funded.

To Arthur's relief, the manager did not dismiss his concerns. "I understand how this could be uncomfortable, especially if you have to go back there to manage the account," she said. "Let me give this some thought and get back with you."

Later that day, the manager returned to propose a solution. "We are going to move ahead and submit the new business application and agreement to compliance," she said. "So you don't feel compromised, I will assign the client to another account manager today." She explained further that she would be crediting Arthur for the new business sale, seeing as he had done the work and should be compensated for it.

Fresh out of school, with a new baby and wife at home, Arthur certainly appreciated the bonus. He hesitantly agreed to be paid. Years later, when Arthur shared this story with us, he was still questioning his decision to accept payment. Did he do the right thing?

Practice Dilemma

Selma grew up in a religious family, for whom Sundays were a day of rest, reflection, service, and worship. Her parents never worked on Sundays, themselves, and Selma hoped to follow their example.

A few months before her eighteenth birthday, Selma decided it was time to enter a field that was aligned with her long-term professional interests. She applied for a job as a technical support professional at Pathways Corporation.

In the interview, she made it clear that she would not be available to work Sunday shifts due to her personal beliefs. The recruiter said this arrangement wouldn't be a problem.

Selma completed a two-week training program and worked for several months on the call floor with the night shift team. She worked hard and quickly became a top performer. Her manager upheld the recruiter's promise and gave her every Sunday off.

Then, during the summer, Pathways moved her to the day shift. To her surprise, she started receiving assignments to work on Sundays. She spoke with her new manager about the situation and mentioned her initial agreement with the recruiter. But the manager did not believe Selma and questioned whether the company would ever make such a commitment. Unfortunately, Selma had not asked for the promise in writing.

Selma repeatedly attempted to help her manager understand her resolve to avoid Sunday work, but her manager refused to alter her work schedules. In order to uphold her personal beliefs, Selma would take sick days or vacation time whenever she was assigned to Sunday shifts.

After this had gone on for about two months, Selma's manager confronted her with an ultimatum. She told Selma that if she failed to appear for work on her next assigned Sunday shift, she would be fired. Selma was just starting college, and she needed the job. She knew that being fired would make her forever ineligible to work for Pathways Corporation and could impact her ability to get other jobs in the future.

She had to make a difficult decision. Would she hold to her personal commitment and sacrifice her job, or work on Sundays in order to pay for her education?

CHAPTER 11

Challenge 11: Unfair Advantage

You have the opportunity to wield an unfair upper hand.

Stephen is the managing partner at a private equity firm. Private equity involves large transactions, generally millions of dollars at a time. With such high stakes, negotiations are typically extensive.

Stephen's firm recently ended a negotiation with Peter, the CEO of Volo Financial. The deal involved a routine transaction fee, which would cost Volo Financial $1.5 million. Volo said the fee was too high for them, so Stephen's firm ultimately agreed to eat the fee to make the deal happen. With the major points hammered out, Stephen and Peter left their junior partners to finalize the details of the contract. A few days later, both companies signed.

Everything was going smoothly until Stephen received a phone call from Peter, who was angry. "Stephen," he explained, "I'm just now finding out that the agreement we signed included the transaction fee we had agreed to toss out. What's going on here? This mistake is going to get me fired by the board."

Stephen hadn't looked at the agreement for months, so he asked for some time to figure out what happened.

He called the junior partner, Liza, who had drafted the final version of the agreement. To Stephen's surprise, Liza seemed proud of the outcome. "I thought they might not read the agreement closely enough. I put the transaction fee back in, thinking nobody would notice. Sounds like they didn't," she said with a grin.

Stephen knew the contract had an integration clause, a provision which says the final, written version of an agreement trumps any prior discussions. This clause gave the fee full legal force. Peter wouldn't be able to argue they had agreed to different terms. A judge would just tell him to read his contracts more closely before signing.

Stephen had to decide what to do next. The payment in question would certainly be a nice, added profit. But it wasn't part of the intended agreement, and Peter's job might be on the line. Then again, Peter should have read the final agreement. At this point, he was basically asking Stephen's firm to hand over $1.5 million. Should Stephen work out a solution with Peter, or go with the agreement as signed?

Explanation

Good fortune is never unwelcome. We are happy to enjoy all the success we can find, which means we hesitate to question our good luck. Sometimes though, these moments come in a way that is problematic, because someone else is left in the lurch. Like two sides of a coin, our good fortune often comes together with some-one else's bad fortune.

Happenstance doesn't negate our right to the position we enjoy, but something else might. If our current benefit requires an unjust cost to someone else, then good luck can mean bad ethics. In the dilemma above, for example, Stephen comes out ahead in a way that may not be fair.

Unfair Advantage happens when you enjoy a benefit or position that comes at another's expense—without a good reason. In other words, you have the opportunity to wield an unfair upper hand.

You will notice right away that this dilemma feels a lot like Conflicts of Interest because you weigh a personal benefit to you against a cost to be borne by someone else. But in this kind of dilemma, you do not have a traditional obligation to the other party. Your duty to others doesn't come from the same type of relationship. This makes the question of fairness much trickier.

Because judging fairness is hard, we should discuss some of the contours.

Mistakes. Perhaps the most common source of an unfair advantage is someone else's mistake. No one is perfect, but a momentary oversight, like the one made by Peter, can have dramatic consequences. Sure, someone's loss may be your gain. But the other person's mistake, potentially one you'd easily make, too, may not justify you in claiming the benefit. You might be holding the other person to a standard you would not expect of yourself.

Power. Some advantages come from size and power. The world sees a difference, though, between an outperformer and a bully. For example, we don't begrudge a company using its success to enter new markets, but we do forbid abuse of a monopoly position. Consider this: You have a problem if others cannot say no to you. In fact, your power and position may mean you have an obligation to help others, not take advantage of them.

Information. Imbalanced information can be an unfair advantage. Knowledge is power, and you might have power you do not deserve. For example, you might have been tipped off by a friend about the details of a competing bid, allowing you to make adjustments your competitor cannot. Imbalanced information is especially tricky in negotiations, when it is hard to know what you ought to disclose.

Costs. Finally, your unfair advantage may be over a third party. This situation occurs if you can offload a cost onto another party, without justification. For example, you might place blame for your own mistake on coworkers who are not present to defend themselves. The pressure of the moment can make these situations especially tempting.

Questions to Ask

These questions will help you manage dilemmas of Unfair Advantage when they come your way.

1. What makes the advantage unfair?

Fairness can be hard to define, especially because people often disagree strongly about what is fair. Our definition of fairness asks if the advantage comes at someone's expense without good reason. A good reason could be hard work, creative strategy, substantial investment, or even simple luck. Bad reasons for an advantage obviously include things like deceit, coercion, promise-breaking, and illegal activities.

If you are unsure whether your advantage comes from a good reason, consider if others would call the reason good. For example, you might have inside information in a sales competition because your high school friend is on the competition committee. Would you consider your advantage to be fair if the roles were reversed? Would you trust someone who claimed the same advantage you are claiming? If you answer no to either question, your advantage is most likely unfair.

In the opening example, Liza would argue that the other company's lack of attention is their own fault. Stephen might feel otherwise.

2. Who else stands to benefit from or be hurt by the unfair advantage? What obligation do you owe them?

Because we rarely act solely in our own interest, consider how the advantage you enjoy might benefit others besides yourself. For example, you might win a bid because you unfairly found out what the competitor was bidding and so you changed your bid. In this case, your employer could stand to gain from the advantage, too. Consider all those who might come out better because of your position.

You also need to consider the other parties who could be hurt by your advantage. Innocent people, like families or communities, could be hurt if you exercise your power. Remember there are people on both sides of the situation, not just on your side. If your advantage hurts others, you may need to balance justice by helping them in some way.

Stephen's business could be at risk if he decides to enforce the contract, because he could get a reputation of being untrustworthy. If the company suffers because of the bad reputation he would earn, then more people than Stephen would pay the price.

3. Did you contribute to the unfair advantage?

Some advantages come purely from luck; others from hard work and ingenuity. But some advantages come from putting your thumb on the scale. If your unethical behavior leads to an unfair advantage, you do not deserve to keep it.

Keep in mind that good behavior, not just dishonest behavior, can lead to an unfair advantage. What reasonable expectations do others have of you? Have you made promises or conveyed information in a way that earned their trust? If you have invited others to rely on you, and their reliance gives you unfair influence, fairness may require sacrificing your position.

Liza clearly contributed to the unfair advantage in this case by slipping in the contract term last minute, hoping no one would notice. She has a much harder case to make that enforcing it now would be fair.

4. Did the other party play a role in the advantage you have?

Everyone trips up from time to time. What matters is how you handle the errors of others. Of course, you can't bear the cost of every mistake someone else makes. You may need to let especially irresponsible behavior bring consequences to the person who persisted in that behavior. But innocent mistakes, the kind we might make ourselves, probably don't justify taking advantage of others.

Stephen's dilemma is tricky for this reason. In such a big business deal, both sides have the obligation to be thorough in their agreements. Stephen has to decide if he's going to capitalize on their mistake.

5. Can you make the advantage fair?

This last question is the most valuable. You don't need to give up an advantage, just because it is unfair. Instead, keep the advantage by making it fair.

Disclosure usually comes first. You need to reveal your advantage and where it came from. Second, invite the other party to help solve the dilemma with you. This collaboration gives everyone a chance to voice concerns and represent their interests. People commonly make concessions in these moments, either out of gratitude or because they recognize your integrity and choose to reciprocate.

A disclosure conversation might diminish your advantage in the moment, but will most likely boost your reputation and future opportunities. A trustworthy reputation only comes from trustworthy decisions. As we've noted before, trust makes business faster and cheaper in dozens of ways. Being trustworthy is a hard-won advantage that no one can call unfair. Stephen would need to consider all of this before he decides whether or not to enforce the contract.

Pitfalls

Think carefully about your situation to avoid the pitfalls of unfair advantage.

Counting on Your Current Position

If you exercise unfair advantage, you are setting yourself up to be treated the same way when power shifts. You can't always count on being in your current position, but you can count on interacting with the other parties throughout your career. If their experience with you invokes feelings of distrust or anger, you will face potentially great expense or, even worse, retaliation.

Remember that power does shift. Don't be overconfident. In fact, a regular habit of taking unfair advantage of others could speed your downfall because you are inviting people to look for opportunities to unseat you. If, on the other hand, you show a preference for fairness, people will be more likely to support you and come to your rescue when needed. Think of fairness as an investment or insurance policy. Fairness begets fairness.

Justifying Your Abuse

Avoid the temptation to justify your abuse. There are many ways to rationalize an unfair decision. You might, for example, imagine some overblown offense against you. You might pretend you are acting in the best interest of others. You might claim that you have earned your position and have every right to claim it. If you find yourself trying to justify an unfair advantage with these arguments, remember you cannot manufacture fairness intellectually. Fairness has everything to do with the situation and not with your interpretation of the situation.

Blaming the Other Party

Be sure you do not blame the other party for not catching you in your bad behavior. The idea that anyone should suffer because he or she failed to police you is unsustainable. People reasonably assume good faith from others around them. People's trust in you should never be considered a weakness. That's a crook's defense.

Bill's Experiences

Whenever I'm in a position of power, I think hard about where that power comes from and how it should be used. In my observation, wielding power unwisely or unfairly will ultimately come back to hurt you. On the other hand, a pattern of fairness, over the course of your career, builds a reserve of trust.

Negotiating Fairness

Being fair doesn't mean giving up all advantages. Often, you can keep your advantage, and keep things fair, with some quick thinking.

I was sitting in the St. Louis Airport waiting to board a plane for Pittsburgh. Four individuals came into the waiting area and took the seats directly behind me. They then proceeded to discuss their upcoming negotiation with my company. This wasn't just any negotiation, either; it was one of the biggest annual contracts my company negotiated. They were loud enough for me to immediately understand what they were discussing. What was I to do?

These negotiators had no expectation of privacy because they were in a public place. Furthermore, it was not illegal to listen. Recording a conversation without the speaker's knowledge is unlawful in some jurisdictions, but listening is always allowed. Were these individuals acting inappropriately? Yes. But their conduct was not my concern. My own conduct was what mattered to me.

It is commonly taught that gathering intelligence is a crucial part of preparing for a negotiation. The information these individuals were discussing would have cost Alcoa tens of thousands of dollars to ascertain through independent research, and yet here, right behind me, they were offering that information for free! The thought crossed my mind that maybe I even had a duty to my shareholders to eavesdrop.

The spectrum of decisions I considered, in a flash, ranged from "listen and take notes" to "walk away." I had my work spread out in front of me and I didn't want to gather all my things and move. But I was uncomfortable listening—it seemed wrong and unfair.

So instead, I got up from my seat, turned around, and introduced myself. I shook hands with all four individuals, giving my name and my employer's name. One of them commented that they were headed to my company the next day. When I sat back down, they continued to discuss the negotiation.

Had I then fulfilled my ethical obligation, allowing me to listen and take notes? I thought that I had, and so I did. Afterward I called my friend, who would be leading the negotiation, and told him what happened in the airport.

The first thing he did—before I could share any information—was to ask if I had told them who I was and where I worked. The fact that he asked that question showed a lot about his personal ethics and the ethical culture of our company.

When I speak to students and executives about ethical conduct, I often ask them to consider the following scenarios.

- During a negotiation your opponent takes copious notes. At the end of the negotiation, she throws the notes into the wastebasket. Can you retrieve those notes and read them?

- Your opponent leaves his folder or briefcase in your office by mistake. Are you free to look inside and see what you can learn?

- Your competitor copies you on an email containing confidential information that was clearly not intended for you. What do you do?

In each case, consider the insights from this chapter. If you're enjoying a benefit at another's expense, and without good reason, you may need to reconsider your approach.

Softening the Blow

When you must exercise an advantage and things feel unbalanced to you, see what you can do to make things better for anyone who stands to be hurt or inconvenienced. The way that decisions are carried out can often soften their ramifications.

I was acting as the head of procurement when a new CEO was named in the company. During a review of my function, the new CEO was surprised to learn that we paid our suppliers promptly in thirty days. I explained that we received good prices, quality product, and on-time delivery because we were excellent customers and followed the provisions of the negotiated contract with our suppliers. The CEO said that we needed to delay our payments to suppliers to sixty days because he wanted to live off the suppliers' money a bit longer.

This presented a dilemma. Most of our suppliers were much smaller than we were, and they needed the contracts with our company. Many were living day-to-day, and so having to go an extra month without being paid would be an extreme hardship. In addition, our current contracts stated that we would pay within thirty days.

To avoid unfairness, I met with each of the suppliers and explained that the company would be moving to sixty-day payment terms when the next contract was negotiated. Until then, we promised to honor the current contracts. I proposed that we extend the term of the new contract, which would help suppliers qualify for loans, if needed, to help them get by. I even offered to accompany the suppliers to their banks. Most suppliers appreciated these accommodations. I felt better about making them than hitting suppliers with an abrupt switch to sixty days, or worse, dragging payables to sixty days without giving them any warning.

Planning Ahead

In business, it's a great thing to have an advantage—at least, if it's an advantage you have earned or truly deserve. Take these steps to ensure you accrue your advantages in ways that are fair.

1. Work hard. Do your research and planning. The more you earn your position, the more likely it is to be fair. Being the best at what you do provides an advantage that others will have a hard time denying you.

2. Think long term. An advantage today could be a disadvantage tomorrow. Short-term gains from an unfair advantage are tempting, but could carry a much larger cost later on. Consider how the current moment could find its way back to you in the years to come.

3. Practice fairness. Look for opportunities to be forthright and even-handed, even in small ways. Habitual fairness will help you see the bigger, tougher moments more clearly. You'll have more confidence in a level playing field. You'll also make an investment in earning others' trust, which will pay off in the long run.

What Happened

At the beginning of this chapter, Stephen discovered that a junior partner, Liza, had quietly altered a contract in their company's favor. Now that the contract was signed, the other party was legally bound to pay a large transaction fee.

When Stephen found out what Liza had done, he viewed the situation as a teaching moment. He explained to this junior associate that their business was built upon trust. After emphasizing to Liza that being clever is not nearly as important as being honest, he immediately called Peter, the other company's CEO, to let him know that a mistake had been made and that they would not be expecting the $1.5 million. He had Liza rewrite the contract, which was then signed by both parties. The transaction went through without further issue.

Liza internalized the lesson she had learned from Stephen. Years later, she became a senior leader in the firm.

Practice Dilemma

Derrick, the manager of new commerce at HealthTech, has a meeting with a vendor at 1:00 p.m., but neither he nor Amanda, the chief operating officer, can remember who is scheduled to come in. Amanda frequently invites Derrick to sit in on her meetings with vendors to discover what they offer or to explore a more concrete partnership. For the past few months Derrick has been battling with Amanda over a new organizational structure, so he has been looking for every opportunity to rebuild their relationship. Showing support for Amanda and her efforts with this vendor would be a great opportunity to do just that.

No one else can make the meeting, so it's just Derrick, Amanda, and the vendor—who turns out to be Phil, a sales rep from a small tech firm. Phil goes directly into his canned slide presentation. Five slides in, Derrick still can't figure out what Phil's company does. Then Phil mentions a familiar company name, KBO Conglomerate. Immediately Derrick feels on edge.

KBO Conglomerate is the parent company of twenty-six health-care-related organizations. One of those organizations is Convention Healthcare, a large direct competitor with HealthTech. What's more, there's a bit of history between their companies.

Last year, Derrick was in charge of selecting and implementing a cost transparency solution. In the process, another KBO company named KeyHealth won the bidding process and started contract negotiations. After months of delay by KeyHealth, Derrick learned that KBO's CEO had only been using the bid as leverage in an unrelated business deal. Derrick rescinded their offer, signaling his distaste for KBO's negotiation tactics and removing the CEO's bargaining chip.

As it turns out, Phil's company is another of the twenty-six owned by KBO. Derrick determines immediately that he will never do a deal with any KBO business. Essentially, the sales call was a huge waste of time for Phil and his company.

Derrick waits for Amanda to react, perhaps even to send Phil away, but she doesn't. As Phil continues his presentation, Derrick realizes that Phil has something very valuable to offer. The idea he's pitching is eerily similar to an idea that Derrick has been working on with HealthTech's chief financial officer. This fortuitous meeting presents the perfect opportunity for Derrick to ask key questions that can help his own company—and help him impress the CFO. Showing enthusiasm for Phil's product will also help Derrick repair his relationship with Amanda. The only problem is that Phil would never answer his questions if he knew that Derrick had no intention of becoming a customer. Does Derrick take advantage of the chance to improve his own career prospects and string Phil along?

CHAPTER 12

Challenge 12: Repair

You are responsible for a mistake.

Claire is the CEO of Know Your Company (www.knowyourcompany.com), which delivers weekly insights to small-company executives about the internal aspects of their business.[1] These regular reports cover simple things, like employees' favorite movies, and critical information, like problems in employee satisfaction. Two years in, Know Your Company has grown rapidly based on its uniquely valuable service.

Because reporting the right information matters so much to its business model, Know Your Company often rolls out new features. Software-based products always carry the risk of buggy code getting out the door, but thus far Claire's company has avoided any major glitches. Now Claire has found out about a big bug, one with potentially disastrous consequences for her clients.

About six months ago, a misplaced bit of code within a new feature accidentally gave privileged information to new hires. Specifically, when they were added to Know Your Company, these employees could view private responses that only their CEOs were supposed to be able to access. It was a horrible mistake, affecting hundreds of employees in about 80 companies. Claire felt sick just thinking about it.

Making matters worse, it was a client who had noticed the error. Luckily, the client was kind enough to report it so it could be fixed. Claire assumed other clients had seen the problem but hadn't reported it. And there was no way to tell how many new employees had read information they shouldn't have seen.

This left Claire with a terrible decision: should she tell the affected clients? On the one hand, if customers hadn't noticed, why say anything? The damage was already done, and the problem was now fixed. On the other hand, as a CEO herself, Claire knew she would want to know if her employees had had access to those supposedly private responses.

Explanation

We're often terrible at admitting our mistakes. They make us feel exposed. Even if we work in a place where mistakes are tolerated, we worry that a mistake will hurt our reputation. We have to choose if we want the attention that comes with disclosing a mistake and trying to repair the damage we have caused.

We call this dilemma Repair: You've made a mistake that perhaps should be reported, but you can get away with not disclosing it or not fixing it.

It's tempting to fix things in secret, but this is a risky strategy. You risk getting caught, which reinforces the idea that you're untrustworthy. You also risk making a fix the other party doesn't actually want. Besides, doing things in secret removes your chance to apologize.

Hiding your mistake gets even more tempting if the costs to you in exposing it are high, but the costs to others, if you do not, are low. For example, what you did wrong might be covered by an insurance policy. Or it might create only a few hours of extra work for your coworkers. It might be something your client can clean up without knowing you made the mess.

The Repair dilemma gets more complicated if your mistake was itself an ethical failing. Put on the spot, you might have told a client something untrue. Now you need to decide if you explain the misstatement or stay silent and hope that the client never needs to know the truth. In these cases, correcting your unethical mistake might reveal something about your choices you don't want others to know. Worse, it might tell a story, true or not, about your character. Ironically, revealing your unethical mistake, though the right thing to do, could actually make you seem less trustworthy.

While it is clear that owning up and trying to repair the damage is the most responsible way to follow up when you make a mistake, there are some situations that require a more nuanced approach.

Questions to Ask

Thinking through these questions will help you determine how to proceed when you find yourself in a Repair dilemma.

1. Is the blame shared?

If you were not the only person involved in the mistake, your repair strategy will need to consider more issues.

First, are the others who contributed aware of the problem? If not, what's the best way to inform them and should you be the one to do it? The harm done could be embarrassing to one or more people. Also, if a superior in the organization was involved, it may be their place to tell the others.

Next, should you decide on the repair strategy yourself, or should you decide in collaboration with the others? It may not be your right to decide how to best fix the problem; the others may have better ideas than yours. On the other hand, coming to the group with a thoughtful solution may be the difference between their doing the right thing or covering up the mistake. Particularly if the mistake is the work of a group, it may be appropriate to address the problem or its solution as a group.

Be aware that shared blame creates the opportunity for everyone to escape accountability. Don't give in to that temptation; work to get the right outcome for everyone. Be sure that you understand the ways you contributed to what happened. Be sensitive to the way others in the group may avoid blame.

2. Is it really your fault?

This question is not intended to make you feel better, nor should you use it to find convenient excuses. Asking if you're truly to blame helps you better orient yourself to the problem and assume responsibility for what you've done.

You may have been underprepared for the moment, leading to your mistake. If that's true, knowing this will influence how you and others address the problem in the future. Make it your responsibility to help your organization be better prepared to avoid the same mistake and others like it.

3. Did you act unethically?

Determining whether your mistake was unethical is important to your repair strategy. That's because people will be more lenient toward a well-intentioned mistake than they will be toward a morally suspect action. If your mistake involved an unethical choice, you will need to approach the repair even more humbly.

Do not attempt to cover, rationalize, or distract from the immorality of your choice. Repairing the problem while justifying your poor ethics will still leave a bad impression with people, invalidating your efforts to fix your mistake. Own your behavior and be willing to apologize sincerely. You may get scolded for what you did. Take your lumps so you can move on.

4. Who should bear the cost?

Doing the right thing means that those who ought to bear the costs are the ones who actually do. As noted before, the temptation to hide your mistake is partly rooted in the fact that repair might be expensive to you. Hiding your mistake possibly spreads the cost out on others. Be willing to pay the cost if the responsibility lies on you.

The question about who should bear the cost is complicated if several people contributed to the mistake. Teams of people can make mistakes together, creating the problem of joint culpability. Put simply, when it's everyone's fault, it somehow becomes nobody's fault.

Of course, this isn't really true. That's why in the law there's a concept called joint and several liability. This means when a group of people caused a problem, each one is responsible for the full cost. The injured party never gets more than they're due, but if one of the wrongdoers can't afford his share, the others are liable to cover the difference. So in a legal sense, just because you were one of multiple people who are at fault doesn't mean that you only bear a fraction of the cost.

5. Was the error foreseeable? By whom?

In the law, foreseeability is an important measure of fault. For example, if I go skydiving, it's foreseeable that I might get hurt or killed. Unless the others around me do something that's out of the ordinary protocol for skydiving, then I'm the one assuming the risks involved and can't really blame anyone else if I get injured.

Your mistake may have been a known risk the other party reasonably assumed. But be very careful not to take that concept too far. Don't pretend that they should've known that everyone makes mistakes, so they're to blame for trusting you.

If you caused a problem because you took on a task that was beyond your expertise, then the issue is whether you warned the other party that you did not have the know-how for this task. Pretending to abilities you didn't have make you the one who should've seen the potential for mistake, and thus bear the burden for repair. However, if you were honest about your abilities at the beginning, the problem could be reasonably foreseeable by the other party, so you may not bear the full burden of repair. That's why we recommend always being frank in your abilities, with others and with yourself.

6. Does the other party want you to fix the mistake?

You might reasonably assume that the injured party would want you to fix the problem, but that could be false for many reasons.

They may not trust you. If you made the mistake to begin with, they might prefer for someone else to step in to fix what was broken. As far as they know, you are a risk. Be respectful of their preference. Though very humbling, handing off the repair to someone else shows sincerity.

Further, the damage you caused might create an opportunity for the other party. Not unlike how people will use insurance money to replace a totaled car instead of repairing it, this might be a chance for them to be better off than they were before.

The other party may want an apology more than anything else. As we note later, an apology is a form of emotional repair. They might be happy to clean up your mess as long as they feel that you've learned your lesson and that you respect them.

You won't know any of this if you hide your mistake. Communicate openly to learn the other party's interests; then you can jointly develop the best repair strategy.

Pitfalls

Be careful to avoid these mistakes as you navigate the Repair dilemma.

Fixing Things by Yourself

You'll be tempted to fix your mistake on your own. Your instinct tells you that you've already imposed a burden on others, and involving them in the repair will only become more of a burden. But fixing things by yourself is usually a mistake.

First, there's a high likelihood that people will be particular about the way the problem is repaired. They may be concerned about things like privacy, input from others, or timing. Really any number of concerns could justify their input, and not all of those concerns will be unpleasant for you.

Second, when people have been hurt, they can find a great deal of emotional satisfaction in participating with the solution. Fixing a mistake is an inherently social thing. Be sure that people have a chance to engage in the repair so they can enjoy the fulfillment and confidence from being a part of a better outcome.

Of course, the injured people may want nothing to do with you. Be sure to respect that. Still, ignoring their interests in the repair may make matters worse, so try to give them a chance to participate.

Not Apologizing

Another common mistake is to avoid apologizing, a tactic almost universally recommended by lawyers. The idea is that an apology is an admission of fault, exposing you to legal liability. In reality, this can be bad advice even from a legal perspective. For example, doctors who apologize for malpractice are much less likely to be sued than doctors who don't apologize.[2]

Apologies matter because they are a sort of emotional repair. You might restore someone financially for a loss you caused, but the feeling of being hurt usually doesn't go away with a payment. Apologies also inspire confidence that you'll make sincere efforts to avoid this mistake in the future.

This is why you should also avoid making a false apology. Be sure your apology is sincere and meek. Saying, "I'm sorry this happened," is not the same as saying, "I'm sorry I made this happen." Sincere apologies reflect ownership of your choices and their outcomes. Insincere apologies make things worse because they heap disrespect on top of the carelessness of your mistake.

Delaying

Finally, avoid delay. Although it's important to be thoughtful and deliberate in solving the problem, waiting too long can just make the problem worse. While you wait to fix your mistake, the injured party may consider options that may be very costly to you, including a lawsuit. In general, it's best to be quick to claim ownership for your error.

And remember, it is far, far worse to wait until you get caught. The problem may worsen if you're the only one who knows about it. You will lose a great deal of influence and trust if it appears you were hiding the mistake. You lose your chance to influence the outcome. Besides, hiding your mistake will almost certainly be evidence against you if a lawsuit is brought.

 # Bill's Experiences

Sometimes we find ourselves in the middle of a mess that needs to be repaired. Acting is always the right choice for those with a sense of justice, fairness, and concern for the injured parties.

I began this book with perhaps the biggest Repair dilemma of my career—the discovery of contaminated drinking water near our plant in Texas. In that situation, we disclosed the problem and offered a solution right away, even though there was no way to know whether our plant was at fault. Interestingly, I had an easier time handling that multi-million-dollar choice than a 50-cent choice I faced as a young paperboy.

Christmas Lights

I delivered newspapers in my neighborhood for years. One day when I was collecting the weekly payment from my cus-

tomers, a friend came along with me. We talked and maybe tossed a baseball while we walked from house to house, then he waited on the sidewalk when I went up to the door.

At the end of the route my friend pulled four colored Christmas lights from his pocket and enjoyed smashing them on the ground—just for fun. I asked where he got those lights, and he identified a home where the neighbor invited me inside while she found her coins. He said he unscrewed the lights from their Christmas display. I was hurt. How could he do that to my good customer?

I agonized over how I should repair the situation. I was reluctant to make a formal apology because I hadn't done anything wrong. Or, I thought, maybe it was my fault for bringing my friend with me that day?

I decided I would not collect money from this customer the next week, and that amount would reimburse her for the missing lights. So I skipped her house when making my next collection rounds. Two weeks later, she reminded me that I hadn't collected from her last time. I assured her I had been paid. That was a lie, on top of not telling her what happened to her lights. I felt that I had technically made the repair, but still felt uncomfortable. When repair opportunities came my way in the future, I decided, I would be as honest as possible, as quickly as possible. This has been an excellent guide.

The Pepsi Repair

When something needs fixing, ethical people often take steps to correct the situation—even when they might not be to blame. In fact, I see repair beyond one's obligation as more than ethical; I see it as virtuous. Sometimes it takes a virtuous leader to make things right.

Allow me to share one very small act as an illustration. I once purchased a beverage during halftime at a football game. Immediately behind me, I heard two young boys in an argument. There had evidently been a collision and one boy had dropped his Pepsi on the ground. They were arguing over who was at fault.

It was not my mistake. But I was in a position to give the boy who dropped the Pepsi my beverage. The argument stopped. The repair was made. I bought another Pepsi.

Sometimes we are fortunately in a position to see that individuals are treated with dignity and respect. We don't need to be told to do so, and we don't need to have a specific obligation. It's just what ethical people do.

Planning Ahead

In a simple world, the best preparation for the Repair dilemma is to never make mistakes. Knowing that won't be the case for any of us, here are some tips to help you be ready in the future.

1. Learn from your mistakes. You won't stop making mistakes, but you will make fewer mistakes if you understand why you made them. This process requires time and attention. Write down your thoughts and, where appropriate, discuss them with a friend or mentor. Doing this has the added benefit of making you more open to feedback from others.

2. Develop strong friendships. We've said it before, and now we'll say it again: Remember the power of social capital. You'll need to draw on others' patience and kindness to forgive your mistakes. A psychological phenomenon called the fundamental attribution error predicts that we are less understanding of people we don't know well.[3] Make sure your associates know you and like you. This will make your mistakes more tolerable to them.

3. Be open to criticism. We all tend to be uncomfortable with critical feedback. Whenever we hear it, our brains invoke defense mechanisms to help us preserve our self-image as capable, successful people. But practicing an openness to criticism does two important things relative to repair. The first is that others' insights help us make better decisions. The second is that humbly accepting criticism builds relationships with those giving feedback. Those relationships are a great resource when you need to repair a mistake.

4. Encourage a culture that allows for mistakes. Your mistakes will be more tolerable to others if you, yourself, are more forgiving of others' mistakes. Research into firms that launch satellites into space shows that those that saw failure early on experienced more success down the road, because they learned more from the failed launches than the successful ones.[4] View your work as an iterative process. Iteration requires mistakes and learning from mistakes. As much as possible in your organization, create a culture that enables this iterative process, incorporating mistakes into improvement.

5. Review your work to minimize mistakes. On a personal level, an iterative approach to your work will also increase your performance. As you plan your tasks, be sure to include time to review, assess, and improve what you produce. If you don't build this into your timing, you'll develop a habit of finishing work just as it's needed. Without time to review what you've produced, you expose yourself to more errors. Be sure that, whenever possible, everything you create goes through more than one version. Remember that the first version of your work is never the finished version.

What Happened

In the Repair dilemma at the beginning of this chapter, Claire was advised about an embarrassing software glitch in her company's product. Once the problem was fixed, she wondered what, if anything, she should tell her clients.

Claire called her co-owner, a more experienced executive, for advice. His response surprised her. He said, "I like moments like these. This is an opportunity to show what kind of company we are. We get to show our customers what we stand for."

That was what Claire needed to hear. She sent a short, personal email to each CEO. She explained the problem and expressed regret. She also offered a small account credit, acknowledging that the credit would not, of course, make up for the mistake. After repeating her assurance that the problem was now fixed, Claire included her personal cell phone number and invited the CEOs to call her anytime with questions or concerns.

Then she braced herself for their reaction.

In Claire's own words, this is what happened next:

> I received a flood of replies from customers. Not a single one was negative. A few folks were concerned (as they ought to have been!), but no one was angry. No one left. In fact, the response from customers was overwhelmingly positive. People said, "Thank you for letting me know," and, "No biggie, these things happen." One of our Dutch customers emailed, "We have a saying in Dutch: *Waar gewerkt wordt, worden fouten gemaakt.* That translates to 'Mistakes are made if you're doing work.'" Another person replied, "We all screw up from time to time. Go have a cocktail. ;)" I even had one customer who said he was so impressed with the email I'd sent that he'd forwarded it to his entire company as an example of how to handle a mistake.

In Claire's assessment, the mistake became a defining experience for her company. It solidified who they, as a company, were and what they stood for. It also demonstrated that customers' best interests would be put first. Claire believes she gained her customers' trust and confidence as a result.

Practice Dilemma

Annie manages supplier relationships for a large defense contractor. One of her suppliers is providing the software for a multi-year research and development contract worth more than $100 million. A few months before the project's final deadline, Annie's engineering team discovers that the software provided by the supplier does not reflect recent changes to the government's requirements. These changes must be incorporated, and quickly. The success of the entire project—and the final performance-based payment—depends on meeting all of the government's requirements.

Linda, the director overseeing the project, calls and berates the supplier about the noncompliant software. Pointing out the fixed-price contract, she insists that they update the software at their own expense. The supplier apologizes and agrees to make the changes at no extra cost. Problem solved.

However, after hearing about Linda's phone call, Annie feels uneasy. She returns to her desk to do a little research. Rereading the contract, she discovers that her own company is at fault. The software changes requested by the government had not been express mailed to the supplier as the agreement requires. To be clear, the project glitch is not particularly Annie's mistake. She doesn't manage day-to-day communication between the engineers and the suppliers. But a gaffe this big reflects poorly on her and her team.

On one hand, Annie knows that the supplier has executed perfectly to the contract. They are not legally obligated to make the software changes, so they should be paid for the extra work they are doing. On the other hand, the supplier has agreed to do the work at no extra cost. Is it her fault that they aren't enforcing the contract?

Complicating things even more, if she draws attention to the discrepancy, the supplier will need to prepare and submit an updated proposal. Annie will then have to negotiate with them and issue a contract change to the government. Both of these tasks take considerable time. Given the late stage of the project, initiating a contract change now could put the whole project schedule in jeopardy.

What should Annie do next?

CHAPTER 13

Challenge 13: Showing Mercy

You could grant forgiveness or forbearance, but don't know if you should.

"I just got a text message from Alan, and I don't think I was supposed to receive it."

Over the phone, Julie's client sounded confused and slightly frustrated. The office manager, Alan, had mistakenly texted her client with another client's information—a major privacy breach.

Julie apologized profusely and thanked the client for letting her know. After hanging up, she stared at her phone, trying to decide how to handle Alan's mistake. It was his third major blunder this week.

When Julie left a large law practice to start her own firm, Alan had been one of her first hires. With his personable demeanor, he recruited his friends, family, and acquaintances to use Julie as their lawyer, making him responsible for a large chunk of her early clientele. Although Alan never caught on to new tasks quickly, he eventually completed them adequately, and all of the clients seemed to like him.

In the last several months, however, Alan had started to struggle. Initially, performance discussions with Alan helped improve his deficiencies, but these discussions had become more and more frequent, to little effect. Once or twice she had mentioned to Alan that continued mistakes would put his job at risk, but she doubted he believed he might actually be fired. Obviously, Julie's recent plea that Alan check and recheck client information before sending texts or emails hadn't helped.

To meet the strict deadlines and attention to detail required in legal work, Julie's other employees—who were junior to Alan in experience and pay—had started to cover many of Alan's responsibilities. Since they were very busy with their own jobs, this created added tension. More than once, Julie had considered hiring an extra part-time employee to manage some of Alan's tasks. But this would be a financial hardship for the firm. Even with her growing client base, Julie was barely able to cover all of her expenses and begin to pay off her hefty loans.

Clients were beginning to be affected by Alan's mistakes, too. In just the last three months, Julie had waived about $2000 in fees to preserve client relationships and her firm's reputation after Alan dropped the ball on one task or another. There simply wasn't financial room for this poor performance.

Whenever she thought about firing Alan, though, Julie felt guilty. She knew his wife was in remission after a long battle with cancer; she had not yet been able to return to work; and many medical bills remained. Alan, himself, would soon be out of the office for two weeks for a medical procedure.

To make matters worse, Julie had recently received a phone call from a loan officer. Apparently Alan and his wife were applying for a home loan, and the officer asked her to confirm Alan's salary, his tenure in the job, and his prospects for continued employment. Caught off guard, Julie told the loan officer that Alan would continue to be an employee. Now she might have to go back on her word.

Explanation

Everyone makes mistakes. Everyone has bad luck occasionally. Everyone needs help from time to time. It's natural for a coworker, friend, or even a boss to come seeking rescue. You're probably willing to help, but the trouble is that doing so can be expensive.

The Showing Mercy dilemma happens when someone needs your help, forgiveness, or forbearance, and you don't know how to respond.

Healthy working environments usually tolerate some mistakes and failures, as long as everyone learns from them. But some failures cost too much. These costs can be more than financial. Failures often hurt reputations and relationships. If not directly expensive, they might impose excessive risk. Part of the difficulty in this dilemma lies in knowing when the cost of showing mercy is too high.

Adding to the difficulty of this dilemma, people sometimes take advantage of the mercy that others show. Once you start allowing for errors, it's hard to know where to stop. The line has to be somewhere, otherwise you're encouraging bad behavior instead of preventing it.

Don't assume that this dilemma will only appear when someone asks for mercy. It might come because you see the need to extend mercy, unsolicited. Some people are too proud or shy to ask for help, but that doesn't absolve you. The right thing may be to rescue the person who didn't ask to be rescued.

Most important, mercy always comes at a cost. You might bear that cost through extra work or lost compensation. The company might bear it through lost profits or reputation. The cost may fall on the community by damage done to its environment or economy. But someone, somewhere along the line, pays the price for the mistake or failure. That doesn't mean you shouldn't forgive or forbear. But it does mean you need to think carefully about when and how you will grant mercy.

Questions to Ask

Consider the following questions when faced with a situation in which you could show mercy.

1. Is mercy yours to give?

It is easy to assume that you're the right person to extend mercy if someone is asking you for it. Don't automatically accept this assumption. For example, a company wouldn't let just any employee forgive customer debts. Giving mercy in that way comes at the expense of the many people who rely on the company's profitability, so the person making the decision to give mercy needs to have visibility and responsibility for the effects of those decisions.

Ask yourself if extending mercy in this case falls under your assigned responsibilities. If not, are there other reasons you'd be the right person to make this decision? For example, you may be able to personally bear the cost of the mercy.

If you're not the right person, the next best choice may be to find the right people and help them decide whether to be merciful. You may decide the ethical thing is to advocate for mercy, even if it's not yours to give. Whatever you do, don't refuse to get involved just because the choice of whether to be merciful belongs to someone else.

2. Does showing mercy in this case hurt others or put them at risk?

Workplace failures almost always have real-world consequences. It's too easy to see only the costs to the company. In reality, a mistake at work can hurt families, customers, and others. You need to consider anyone who may be hurt or at risk if you grant mercy.

In the opening dilemma, Julie bears much of the cost for Alan's poor performance, but that cost is also borne by Julie's family because of the reduced income she is taking home. Further, clients are at risk of having confidential information disclosed by one of Alan's mistakes. This could lead to Julie's disbarment. The cost to her and her clients may be too great.

3. Who bears the immediate cost of showing mercy?

As you consider the costs mercy imposes and who will bear them, it's hard to know how far-reaching a mistake or failure can be. Fortunately, you can reasonably give preference to those who will bear the immediate costs of showing mercy. Don't let distant speculation keep you from seeing the problems right in front of you. Ultimately, you have to make a choice, and recognizing the immediate consequences makes the decision easier.

4. Is this a precedent you want to set?

Extending mercy in one case may require you to extend it in all similar cases. Ethical behavior is consistent, irrespective of individual preference. Because mercy always comes with a cost to someone else, extending mercy may be seen as unfair. But the process for deciding when to be merciful should be fair and reliable.

If you show mercy (or withhold it) in this situation, are you prepared to do the same for all similar situations in the future? If not, why is this situation different? To really understand the difference, consider how someone else might view your choice if you were merciful to one person's failure but not to another's identical failure. If this isn't a choice you could make the same way every time, it may not be the right choice now.

5. Does granting mercy violate organizational policy?

Knowing that failure is an inescapable component of innovation and growth, company managers often tolerate some mistakes. They may even specify under which circumstances extending mercy is acceptable. Unless you have power to change those rules, be sure to include your organization's policies in your decision. Policies may help you make a much better choice than you could make on your own.

Pitfalls

When deciding whether to show mercy, be careful to avoid these traps.

Endorsing Poor Behavior

By forgiving mistakes, you may inadvertently send the message that you endorse bad behavior. If you choose mercy, be sure to make future expectations and penalties clear to everyone involved. Moreover, remember that intentionally poor behavior differs from honest mistakes. When you forgive intentionally bad behavior, you have to be especially clear about the standards for future choices. Intentional behavior against corporate values is the most serious because it carries a cultural message to the whole organization. You might need to have an especially low tolerance for choices that violate your company's values and culture.

Punishing Improperly

Remember that punishing in the wrong way sends the wrong message. If too severe, your punishment will damage trust with others in the company. Alternatively, you might be inclined to forgive completely, which could harm your credibility. In the end, a light punishment might work better than no punishment at all. It could send a message to everyone in the organization that you don't endorse the mistake, but you value the person who made it.

Avoiding Transparency

It is tempting to keep the mistake and the outcome hidden from view. Not being transparent about the decision and your reasoning behind it will cause others to assume the worst. You will lose their trust. By contrast, transparency in your decision adds precedential value, guiding others who will make the same choice later. By following the advice in this chapter, you'll have great insights to share with others about how and why you made the decision you did. (Of course, be careful in your disclosure to maintain others' privacy and confidentiality.)

Forgetting Conflicts of Interest

The choice to show mercy can be influenced by a conflict of interest. You may owe an unrelated obligation to the person seeking mercy. This can make it hard to refuse their request, even if the costs will be enormous. If you find yourself swayed by conflicting obligations, also read our advice in the Conflicts of Interest dilemma.

Ignoring Cost

Whatever you do, don't forget who bears the cost. Extending mercy that isn't yours to give is unethical and puts the burden unfairly on someone else.

Bill's Experiences

Having spoken to federal judges about their roles, I've learned a lot about mercy. To a person, they claim that the most difficult part of their job is sentencing. Even with the many sentencing guidelines, these judges are expected to use their discretion to dispense justice in the punishment. That involves considering the myriad factors involved and arriving at the right, just conclusion. In my mind, discretion exercised wisely, consistently, and fairly distinguishes good bosses from great bosses.

The Right Information

First and foremost, remember that you need the right information when making choices about mercy. A former employee, Mike, comes to mind. Mike was irritating his colleagues by arriving to work 20 to 30 minutes late each day. All it took was a conversation with him to find out that he was caring for an ailing parent late at night. Mike was also staying later at work to make up for the missed time. No one else was staying late, so no one knew this. My choice to give Mike flex time was an easy way to show mercy. He was a great employee who needed some basic help.

Mistakes through Ignorance

Employee mistakes can be costly, so when it comes to employee mistakes it's important to determine if the mistake was through ignorance or if it was made knowingly. I have little tolerance for intentional wrongdoing. However, many mistakes are made through ignorance.

For a time, I had to deal extensively with antitrust law compliance. Some of the antitrust laws are quite complex and require a strong understanding of regulations, case law, and the rationale behind the laws. This kind of understanding doesn't come immediately.

We had a high-level employee with little to no experience in antitrust law. As a recently promoted business unit president, he took over a business unit with frequent customer and competitor contact. That carried inherent risk in being able to discern what information can and cannot be discussed. Price, markets, market share, and other topics were off limits in most of these situations, according to antitrust laws.

Our company hadn't sensitized this president to the importance of these issues and he crossed the line. The investigation into his mistake cost the company a great deal of time and effort, and his mistake eventually carried a significant fine.

But this employee was exemplary in many, many respects. Should he be fired? If the behavior were intentionally wrong I would say yes, but there was a large degree of ignorance here. I was sure that this business unit president would learn from this mistake.

After long discussions with a number of the corporate leaders, we decided that there needed to be consequences, but termination was not necessary. Given this person's seniority, his expectations of a pension, and all his good work in the past, we wanted to extend mercy. In the end, he lost his bonus and stock options for a year. This was a significant slap on the hand, which allowed us to show commitment to following the law and allowed him to bear some of the cost of his mistake. I felt the punishment fit the crime.

A Second Chance

Twice in my career I was brought allegations that a specific employee was either "an alcoholic" or "on drugs." These allegations can sometimes be baseless. Other times they stem from observations of irresponsible or erratic behavior, such as coming late to work, missing deadlines, missing team meetings, producing illogical reports, or having episodes of anger. Each instance is unique.

People struggling with substance abuse are troubled and need help. But don't try to help them alone. Professionals should be involved in the determination, the diagnosis, and the treatment.

I learned early on to send these employees for evaluation. Then, after evaluation, I needed to stay involved in the matter—not as the medical professional, but as the business leader interested in the performance of the company and the growth and development of the employee.

In one instance, I noticed an employee who was habitually late to work, had excessive absences, and was missing goals and deadlines. I approached his direct manager, who reported to me, and asked if there was anything wrong with Ron. The manager told me he didn't know for sure, but he suspected Ron was drinking excessively. Other employees in the department had complained of Ron's excessive drinking, and the manager offered me many more examples of missed goals, missed meetings, and missed deadlines. We had ample basis to terminate Ron for lack of performance.

We discussed the situation and decided that we had some obligation to give Ron a chance to turn his life around. We confronted Ron, first with the evidence of his poor performance, then with an offer to be evaluated by a professional psychologist. We made the arrangement very clear: if the resulting recommendation was that Ron required treatment, he would attend that treatment. The alternative was termination.

Ron agreed to be evaluated. The evaluation concluded that he was abusing alcohol. The recommended treatment was that Ron go to a reputable treatment center for six weeks. Ron agreed to go. The other employees were told that Ron needed extended medical care for six weeks, and his duties were redistributed.

The morning after Ron was admitted to the treatment facility, I arrived at work early, as usual, and sitting in my office was Ron's wife. She was in tears. I expected her to be angry, but her tears were tears of joy. She explained that their family had been trying to get Ron to change for years, but their efforts had been unsuccessful. It was only when he faced the loss of his job that he realized he had to change. She was very grateful that the company offered to help.

Ron returned to work in six weeks. I still hear from him periodically. He tells me he has not had a drink of alcohol in over fifteen years now. He is happier and healthier, and he is successful in his work.

Planning Ahead

Consider these strategies to make a Showing Mercy dilemma easier in the future.

1. Leave room for justice and mercy. Policies can be overly rigid—and so can leaders. Be clear in how you apply the rules, but be willing to evaluate the circumstances surrounding each infraction. It's a fine balance to strike. Make sure that everyone in your organization anticipates that you will make wise decisions, whether they lead to punishment or forgiveness. You can communicate this in small mercies or punishments involving less critical matters.

2. Empathize often. Even if the right choice is to punish, remember that a real person will receive the punishment. Don't be unreasonably cold or cruel. Express your concern in sincere ways. Be sure to avoid insincerity or empty platitudes, which can be especially damaging. If those around you know that you regularly consider their well-being, they will trust your choices.

3. Encourage open communication. People make fewer mistakes when they can share their concerns, doubts, or troubles. Help your employees understand that communication brings all the best resources to bear in fixing or preventing a failure. Set the example by inviting their insights when you are facing a challenge and could use their help. Without this, they may be tempted to hide a problem and then make it worse.

What Happened

In the opening dilemma, Julie had to decide how much mercy to extend to Alan, a long-time employee who was making costly mistakes. Julie felt two competing concerns: responsibility for Alan's well-being and responsibility for her business performance. She created a document with specific examples, showing the gaps between Alan's current performance and her performance expectations. Then she set up a meeting with Alan for the following day.

Julie began the meeting by expressing gratitude for Alan's contributions to her law practice, especially in the early years. She thanked him for his efforts every day. Then she very clearly set her expectations: certain chronic mistakes could not occur again if he wanted to maintain employment in her firm.

Julie asked Alan how he felt about his performance. He indicated that he felt overwhelmed with his job responsibilities, especially with how fast the business was growing. She thanked him for sharing his assessment. Julie shared with Alan that his job would continue to become busier. She told him she had tried to make the numbers work so she could hire a part-time assistant for him, but that option was not financially feasible. As it was, he was already managing fewer responsibilities than other employees in the firm.

Julie had Alan sign a performance discussion documentation page, indicating he understood her expectations moving forward. She reiterated her care for him and her desire that he be happy as well as successful.

While Alan was away from the office for his medical treatment, he called to tell Julie he had decided to retire. He expressed gratitude for his employment and said he harbored no hard feelings. Over the next few weeks of transition, Alan was much happier at work. Julie and her staff celebrated his contributions by giving him a retirement party.

Practice Dilemma

Once again the general ledger is messed up. It is late on a Friday night and management has just sent Omar their third request for the numbers. A quick glance at the data is all Omar needs to confirm that his coworker, who is walking out the door to handle some personal issues, has again uploaded half of the data in reverse. She promises she will jump back online by 10 p.m. to make everything right, but both she and Omar know that will be too late. As Omar pulls up a blank email, he wonders what he should tell management this time.

Omar is one of a small, six-person finance department in a medium-sized outerwear company. He is one of the founding members of the team, and as company demands have grown, his boss has added additional people to share the load. To meet their stressful deadlines, each person relies heavily upon the others.

Bridget, the coworker walking out the door, is responsible for uploading the general ledger from the company's accounting software into the larger accounting software package of their parent company. Omar must wait until this upload is complete before he can start analyzing the results and ensuring that all the necessary entries have been booked. The turnaround window has already been reduced from five days down to three, and there is continued pressure to close it even faster. With all the accounts that need to be checked, there is hardly any time for fixing errors.

But month close after month close, despite her promises to do better, Bridget causes delays. She misses lines that need to be uploaded, uploads entries in reverse, or has to leave early to take care of personal matters at home. Often she does not respond to urgent emails.

Except for these frustrations, Omar likes Bridget. They have worked together for two years. He knows she is the only legitimate source of income for her family, which includes four young children. If she were to lose this job, they would likely lose their home and move out of state to whatever family can take them in.

One evening at a dinner with old friends, Omar learned that his best friend from high school is Bridget's next-door neighbor. The friend asked Omar about Bridget's personality and performance at work. Before Omar could figure out how to respond, the friend proceeded to tell him that he suspected Bridget's spouse was involved in drug dealing. He shared neighborhood rumors about domestic violence in the home and recounted several visits there by police. This revelation helped Omar understand why Bridget's personal life always seemed to be interfering with her ability to complete her work. He sympathized with her situation.

Still, Omar is tired of staying many hours after closing time to clean up Bridget's mistakes while management waits for the month-end report. He knows this pattern of lateness reflects poorly on his team, and he worries that one of these days he will overlook a big mistake.

CHAPTER 14

Becoming an Ethical Guide

Congratulations. You made it!

We hope that reading these chapters has increased your aware-ness of, and confidence in dealing with, ethical challenges in the workplace. Each of us is on an individual journey to develop the knowledge and skills necessary to be a strong ethical leader. It is fun for us as educators to see our students mature and grow on their own journeys. It makes us reflect upon our own.

In this chapter, as a transition to the next section of our book, we (Aaron and Brad) share a few ethical dilemmas that were formative for us. These experiences shaped our feelings about the importance of ethics in the workplace. As you read these stories, we hope you'll think about your own ethics stories—the experiences that increased your commitment to becoming an ethical guide.

Brad's Stories

The first ethical dilemma I remember in business involved driving a full-size tractor five miles through the city. I was a teenager at the time. This tractor was owned by my employer, a large hospital in town. My father, a vice president at the hospital, had instructed me to use the hospital's landscaping tractor to dislodge a large trailer that was stuck in the mud. We were using the trailer as part of a fundraiser for my local Boy Scout troop. In addition to being scared about driving that tractor on the streets of town, I wondered if it was really appropriate to use company property for this purpose. I suspect I didn't know the term "conflict of interest" at the time, but I think I understood the concept. While nothing came of this incident at the time, years later my father told me that he had actually gotten in some hot water over borrowing the tractor without getting permission from the hospital CEO.

Perhaps I was sensitized to conflicts of interest because my job at the hospital was obtained through the influence of my father. I remember hearing the grumblings of some of the maintenance workers about their inability to get jobs for their teenaged children at the hospital. My father was a wonderful man, and a man of strong integrity, who worked diligently to make sure his boys learned how to work. It worked. Both of my brothers and I are hard workers. However, like most of us, he may have had a bit of a blind spot when it came to understanding the full implications of one of the ethical dilemmas we've discussed.

The second major event in my life to make an impression on my growing understanding of business ethics occurred while I was doing a college internship at IBM. I had received permission to take off a Wednesday and work a Saturday so that my wife and I could go on a one-day cruise to Grand Bahamas Island on a weekday (when it was inexpensive). When I received my next paycheck, I was surprised that it was slightly higher than normal. Apparently I had received a differential for working on a Saturday. I eventually realized that this wasn't appropriate, because I had worked the Saturday for my benefit and not for IBM's. However, before I came to that conclusion, I was kind of excited about the extra bit of money I had received. I mentioned my good fortune to one of the experienced IBM workers in my department. I will never forget his reaction. He didn't say anything, but his face communicated his displeasure. In fact, to this day I don't know how he communicated so much with a look. He made me feel as if I had just reached around into his pocket, pulled out his wallet, and stolen money from him. At that point in my life, I was still immature enough to think of a big company as having a lot of money and to enjoy getting some of it. This good man made a strong impression on me.

The third event involved my first full-time job at a large bank. The bank recruited me as I was finishing my undergraduate degree. During that process they described several benefits I would receive by working for them. Shortly after moving my family to another state for the job, signing a lease on an apartment, turning away other job options, and starting my job, I found out that the company had made a mistake in its recruiting presentations. I would not be receiving the promised benefits. While out of necessity I stayed with the company for over two years, I was never particularly excited about working there.

I started my PhD studies after working at that bank. I suspect the recruiting experience was part of the reason I was so interested in my business ethics classes at the University of Washington. Because of my doctoral training, I could have very easily ended up primarily teaching business strategy or business–government relations. However, I began noticing challenging ethical situations all around me and was intrigued by their difficulty. I also found that my students routinely faced these challenges and were looking for help in confronting them. I have faced several subsequent significant ethical challenges in my career and wondered how I could have handled them better. This challenge continues to motivate me. To this day, when my students tell me about their ethical dilemmas, I know I will have to think hard about how I would manage them effectively.

I am also inspired in my journey by the notion of virtue in business. Business ethics is not just about challenging difficult situations, but also about the creation of virtue through commerce. While many people are understandably cynical about business (just read the headlines about unethical business practices in any paper on any given day), I'm constantly amazed at the wonderful things business people do for me. Every day I enjoy a wonderfully climate-controlled house, office, and car. I eat nutritious and delicious food. I enjoy wonderful entertainment, drive on well-maintained roads, and am well cared for by the health care industry. I am writing this on my wonderfully dependable Mac computer and have the world at my fingertips through the Internet.

I am reminded of how my father fought to ensure that parking continued to be free at his hospital when on several occasions the board of directors proposed making parking a revenue source. My father contended that because the community had helped to pay for the hospital, they should receive some benefit therefrom. He also sacrificed his time to teach my brothers and me the value of good honest labor. When I was a young teenager he bought three acres of land to help his church and to teach his city boys how to work. For two summers, my brother Brian and I cultivated and harvested an acre of pickling cucumbers under his watchful eye and helpful encouragement.

I am also reminded of the many businesspeople who inspire me daily with their acts. You've read about my friend Bill O'Rourke. I'm also inspired by the leadership of Pat Hassey, who upon retirement from his position as Chairman and CEO of Allegheny Technologies, was given union shirts by the leaders of the unions because of the positive way he had interacted with them. I'm inspired by the leaders of Merck, who chose to develop a drug for river blindness in 1978—even though the villagers who needed the drug would not be able to pay—because they felt it was the right thing to do.

Aaron's Stories

Like Brad, I want to explain my passion for business ethics. I'll share a bit about my professional life and then tell a favorite story. These personal experiences shaped me dramatically as a professor.

After graduating from law school, I worked as an attorney and also in a startup company that sold legal software. For confidentiality reasons, I can't go into much detail about the ethical dilemmas I faced and the ethical misbehavior I saw. But I can say that my observations quickly validated this insight from a favorite law professor, Jim Gordon: "It's not that lawyers are inherently more dishonest than other people—it's that they're given so many more opportunities to be dishonest."

One example comes to mind. I represented a client in a settlement negotiation over a bad business deal. I'd spent weeks working out an agreement, relying in part on a specific piece of information I had shared with the other party's lawyer. As we were nearing a final agreement, my client told me casually that they'd misestimated on that point, and the new estimate was much less favorable to our side. To make things worse for me, my client didn't understand why I needed to tell the other side the truth. This made for a difficult conversation as I tried to get my client to come around. This sort of dilemma happens constantly for lawyers.

I also encountered shady business dealings. One business had a clear organizational policy of enrolling clients at any cost. Someone had actually forged my client's signature on a contract—a contract with terms that differed from what had been agreed to over the phone. This was clearly the result of a culture of bad ethics in the company. Luckily for my client, some great consumer protection laws added teeth to our case.

For me, working in the law made it abundantly clear how much good business relies on good people. Many times I saw shortsighted ethics come back with a bite. Thanks to wise mentors, I learned to think carefully about how ethical choices will matter down the road.

One specific experience really drives the point home. Back when I was a poor, married grad student, I owned a 1982 convertible Fiat Spider, a holdover from my days of being single. It was silver and a lot of fun to drive. It also broke down a lot. After yet another mechanical failure, my wife and I decided it was time to sell the car.

My classified ad ran for about a week before a buyer finally came to look at the Fiat. We met in my apartment building parking lot, where he took some time inspecting the body, tires, interior, and so on. When he asked to take it for a test drive, I realized that I had left the keys up in my apartment. I ran upstairs to grab them. It took me a few minutes to find the keys and get back down to the car.

Imagine my horror when, as he drove off in the car, I watched gasoline pouring out of the bottom. I chased him down before anything set fire. We pushed the car into a parking place, and that's when this buyer started haggling down my asking price. In fact, he was so quick to start talking about a lower price, I was suspicious that he had sabotaged my beloved little Fiat. Instead of agreeing to a sale, I sent him on his way, telling him I wanted to investigate the problem before I sold the car.

When a few hours later I climbed under the car to look around, I saw the problem right away: a newly shredded gas line. The white fibers around the cut stood out from the rest of the gas line, which was dirty from years of driving around. Luckily, a new gas line was just $15 and easy enough to repair on my own. I ended up keeping the car for a few more years.

Let's fast forward four years. Now my wife and I were in the market for a van. We visited a local used car dealership that was known for carrying the brand we hoped to buy. After we spent a few minutes with one sales person, another one butted his way into the sale, taking over our potential purchase. That was off-putting enough, but something else was wrong.

I couldn't put my finger on it at first, although alarm bells were going off in my head. Then I realized that this sales guy was the person who had come to buy my Fiat and sabotaged the fuel line!

Needless to say, we left quickly and luckily found a great deal on a van with another dealership.

I share these two stories because they teach me that good ethics always matter, and often in the ways we least expect. If you haven't already come to the same conclusion through your experiences, I'm confident you will. I hope our book can play some part to help you consistently do the right thing.

Our Challenge to You

Hopefully these chapters have helped you in your quest to be a strong and courageous ethical businessperson. Making sound decisions is an ongoing challenge for us, as it will be for you. We hope you'll return to the *Field Guide* often for insight.

The following chapters provide you with more help, derived from theoretical insights from great thinkers throughout history, as well as from findings from current social science research. We challenge you to do the work required to develop ethical decision-making skills. Then you can find your own way in the wilderness and guide others as well.

Essential Knowledge and Preparation

The Business Ethics
FIELD GUIDE

CHAPTER 15

Perils

During your ventures in the business world, you have likely already encountered dangers. Just as a hike into a national forest can bring you exhilarating sights, sounds, and a sense of sheer wonderment, so, too, that hike can expose you to possible dehydration, harmful insects, dangerous animals, and other risks. The better you understand the risk factors for unethical decision making, the more likely you are to avoid harm and help others stay safe as well.

Let's begin with an illustration. Fire comes from the combination of heat, fuel, and oxygen. Put these three together and you can usually count on combustion. A similar pattern emerges for unethical behavior. Scholars have identified three factors that are nearly always present when an ordinary, otherwise decent person commits fraud or acts in unethical ways.[1] The evidence is clear: no matter how strong your resolve, you're more likely to deviate from your values when you experience the combination of:

1. Perceived Pressure

2. Perceived opportunity

3. Rationalization

In textbooks, these three elements sometimes appear in the shape of a pyramid, the "fraud triangle."[2] This fraud triangle illustrates how making a poor choice, or falling prey to an organizational pitfall, can be due to a combination of seemingly innocent and unseen factors.

In discussing these and other factors, we will use several social science concepts related to cognition and social functioning. We group the factors into *internal dangers*—harmful ways of thinking that we easily fall into, because we're human—and *external dangers*—forces outside of the mind and body that can exert undue influence on our decisions, particularly if we are not aware of them.

Internal Dangers

Our brains play tricks on us. For a variety of reasons, the mind engages in thinking errors, such as rationalization—often to convince itself that we have made a solid choice. This allows us to make unethical decisions and still feel that we are ethical people.

Rationalization

Here's how rationalization works. As individuals, we are predisposed to thinking of ourselves in positive ways. Whenever we engage in unethical conduct, we face two options: (1) accept that the action is unethical, or (2) decide that the action actually is ethical. If we accept the action as unethical, we experience a painful mismatch between our actions and our desired identity, which threatens our positive self-concept. Therefore, we are highly motivated to convince ourselves that the action actually is ethical in order to preserve that self-concept.

The process of rationalization has been described as self-deception,[3] cognitive errors,[4] moral disengagement,[5] and moral fading.[6] Often the process involves neutralization techniques.[7] Whatever the rationalization process, it usually happens at the edges of consciousness—such that it often goes undetected.

Neutralization Techniques

Psychologists have identified a number of strategies we use to construe our unethical behavior as somehow ethical. These neutralization techniques are dangerous because they allow us to make decisions that upon deeper introspection, or when confronted by others, we find to be unacceptable. As you read about these techniques, consider moments in your life when you have felt yourself beginning to rationalize ethically questionable behavior.

1. Denial of responsibility. Also referred to as the agentic shift, denial of responsibility means we place the responsibility for our actions on someone or something else. Our brain insists we are not accountable for our behavior.

2. Denial of injury. To help us feel better about something we did or plan to do, we tell ourselves that no one was (or will be) hurt by our actions—or, at least they won't be hurt very much.

3. Denial of the victim. Sometimes called victim blaming, denial of the victim occurs when we want to excuse poor behavior. Using ideas like "She should have known better" or "He had it coming," we convince ourselves that the wounded party is actually the party at fault—and thus not really our victim at all.

4. Condemnation of the condemners. To combat the criticism we fear because of our actions, we focus on finding fault in the entities or people who might criticize us.

5. Appeal to higher loyalties. As noted in this book, ethical dilemmas often require you to choose one value over another.

This makes appealing to your higher loyalties a particularly effective neutralization technique. You'll know you're in this trap when you feel fine about doing harm on the way to achieving or honoring something important to you.

6. **Moral ledger.** Like "cheat day" on a diet, the moral ledger technique gives you permission to act less ethically in some domains because of the good you have done in others. It's as if unethical acts can be paid for, on balance, by the ethical choices you've made.

7. **Defense of necessity.** Sometimes there is a compelling reason something *has* to be done. More often, our brain exaggerates the necessity to help us feel better about what we are about to do.

8. **Claim of normalcy.** This is the "everyone's doing it" excuse. By noting cultural, national, company-specific, or industry norms, you convince yourself that your course of action is acceptable. (Hint: Look again. More often than not, everyone isn't doing it.)

9. **Denial of negative intent.** You admit that your actions hurt people, but you tell yourself it's okay because you didn't mean to hurt them.

10. **Claims of relative acceptability.** To justify whatever you've done, your brain feeds you examples of people who have done much worse. Your actions seem not so bad by comparison.

11. **Postponement.** Action is needed but you stall, reasoning that if you don't make any decision, you are not responsible for the consequences. (Remember, as discussed in the Intervention dilemma, that choosing not to act is also an act.)

12. **Use of euphemisms.** Subtle changes in the words you choose can disguise your action's full impact—even from yourself. For example, the word "restructuring" may feel better than the word "firing"; a "breach of safety protocol" may carry less moral weight than a "debilitating accident."

Perhaps the most dangerous aspect of neutralization techniques is that they generally rely on some element of truth. Without that bit of truth, they would seem obviously erroneous and could not salve our self-concept so effectively.

Luckily, awareness goes a long way in neutralizing the neutralization techniques. When you are familiar with common mistakes, you can recognize when your thought processes are headed in erroneous ways and, through self-honesty and introspection, get your thinking back on track.

Locus of Control

What people believe about destiny affects how they act. People who believe that their destiny is controlled by their own actions are said to have an internal locus of control. By contrast, those who believe that their fate is determined by factors they can't influence have an external locus of control. According to research, those with an external locus are more likely to act unethically, probably because they don't see themselves as responsible for the outcomes of their actions.

Script Processing

Our brains have amazing capabilities, one of which is to create scripts, or memorized patterns of behavior, for tasks we perform often. Scripts are highly functional because they act as mental shortcuts, allowing us to expend less cognitive effort. For example, most people have a "brush your teeth" script, a "drive to work" script, or a "grocery shopping check-out line" script. Chances are, you can let your mind wander while walking home and still end up at your door.

However, scripts can blind us to information in our environment that tells us we need to act differently this time. Our automatic response is not always the correct response.

One example of the potential blinding effect of following scripts comes from Denny Gioia.[8] He worked for Ford when the Pinto was released with major manufacturing defects. As the recall coordinator, he had developed a script for processing large amounts of test data. This allowed him to finish the task without being overwhelmed. Unfortunately, following this script when reviewing the Pinto model caused him to overlook critical issues in the car's performance. This model had a flaw that made it blow up, and over time the explosions injured many people. If Denny had not been blinded to the patterns in the data because he was following a script, he might have recalled the car and prevented harm to customers and the company. We can minimize the chance of mindlessly making a decision with potentially harmful consequences by observing and, when needed, circumventing our scripts.

External Dangers

In addition to internal influences, social scientists have identified influences outside of ourselves that can influence us to act in unethical ways. As illustrated in the Fraud Triangle, unethical behavior comes about when people perceive opportunity in their environment for getting gain or avoiding loss, and feel pressure to act in unethical ways. Think about how the following external forces have influenced your decisions.

Obedience to Authority

In order for society to function well, we need authority structures as well as obedience to those structures. Thus, as a general rule, obedience to authority is a positive virtue. However, there are times when having obedience as the highest priority, or even blindly carrying out an authority figure's orders, can lead to unethical behavior. We have learned through history and through famous social science experiments, such as the Milgram electric shock trials[9], that most people will be obedient to an authority figure—even when he or she asks them to do something unethical, like administering electric shocks to an innocent victim.

Role Taking

To help us know how to act within our social contexts, we all take on various roles. You might be a student, an employee, a parent, a team member, and so on. Roles generally come with a set of expectations. Meeting such expectations is normally considered a virtue. But, as with obedience, role taking can go too far. Experiments such as the Stanford prison experiments[10] demonstrate that individuals can easily disregard regular behavioral expectations in order to fulfill their role expectations. For example, when typical graduate students were given the role of prison guard, many of them became surprisingly abusive. In business, when given a particular role such as Chief Financial Officer, it's easy to become so engrossed in your immediate role requirements that you forget about ethical obligations and implications beyond your role.

Diffusion of Responsibility

In some situations, the person who is responsible for acting is clear. However, in other situations, the responsibility to act is shared. We find that in situations where (1) an action is clearly necessary and (2) only one person can act, that person is likely to act. However, when there are multiple people who are all capable of taking the action and there is no clear responsibility, we often find that no one acts. Each hopes that somebody else will take care of the problem.

One classic example of this diffusion of responsibility, also referred to as the "bystander effect," is Kitty Genovese, who was pursued and then stabbed to death in New York City while dozens of onlookers were at least somewhat aware of what was happening but mostly did nothing. They anticipated that others would act.[11] The same phenomenon can occur when employees see corporate misdeeds in the workplace. A review of the Enron and other corporate fraud scandals reveals that many people, not just the whistleblowers, knew what was happening and yet said and did nothing.

Group Norms

Any time one joins a profession, institution, or team of any sort, one is socialized into the existing norms of that organization's culture. Those norms, when positive, can motivate teammates to encourage one another, to practice diligently, or help one another in a pinch. However, group norms can also be destructive. For example, in the 1980s it became normal for baseball players to use performance-enhancing drugs. An even stronger example can be found in professional cycling during the 1990s, where doping became standard practice on some cycling teams. In business, consider the case of price fixing in the electrical equipment market during the 1960s and '70s, where an entire industry succumbed to an unethical norm without recognizing it as problematic.[12]

Psychological Distance

Research suggests that we treat people who are like us with greater respect, dignity, and justice. Psychological distance is created when we perceive others as being different from us—perhaps of a different race, gender, nationality, creed, political persuasion, age, socioeconomic background, alma matter, and so on. Psychological distance can also be created by geographic distance.

Societal Culture

Similar to groups and organizations, societies have also developed norms over thousands of years. Anthropologists refer to these norms, values, beliefs, and rituals as elements of culture. Such elements of our society's culture profoundly affect the way we act and think. Indeed, anthropologists argue that the most powerful aspects of culture are the ones we don't even think about. For example, no one in the United States has to think about whether to put on a shirt when they're going to work because being clothed is such a strong cultural norm. Some norms have strong moral implications, such as the lack of respect for women found in certain cultures.

As documented by Transparency International, many national cultures are corrupt, where entrusted power is abused for private gain in the form of bribes, fraudulent reporting, and various other corrupt activities. We cannot always rely on the norms of societal culture to help us act ethically.

Conclusion

In this chapter we have introduced you to an array of influences— both internal and external—that inhibit individuals' abilities to make sound ethical choices. By increasing your awareness of such common dangers, you can better prepare yourself to avoid them when confronting ethical dilemmas in the workplace. Additionally, you can become a more skillful manager by recognizing these tendencies in yourself and those around you and putting safeguards in place to help everyone avoid unethical conduct. (We return to this idea in the final section of this book, "Leading Others in the Wilderness.")

We caution the reader that awareness of ethical pitfalls does not guarantee immunity from them. Constant vigilance and disciplined morality are also necessary in order to ensure ethical behavior. In the following chapter, we offer a battery of questions and perspectives that can help you maintain awareness and make choices that accord with your own values, as well as those of your organization.

CHAPTER 16

All-Purpose Tools

The business world is full of difficult situations. Frequently these involve your interaction with and treatment of other people, such as coworkers, customers, or clients. Whenever your actions or decisions impact others, you enter the ethics realm. That's when the tools in this chapter will come in handy.

Some of the decisions you make that affect others have a small impact. For example, what color you decide to paint your office is generally not a decision high in moral controversy. There may be implications for the natural environment, depending on the type of dye needed for such a color, or there may be cultural or other implications connected to the color you decide on. However, as a general rule, such a decision would be low in what has been described as "moral intensity."[1] On the other hand, decisions high in moral intensity could include deciding where to build a new dam that will flood thousands of acres, or choosing to market a new medical product that has health benefits for many, but may pose serious risks for a few.

Part of your challenge, as outlined in the previous chapter, is being sensitive to the ethical content of decisions you make. The less the moral intensity in a decision, the greater the probability you'll miss the ethical dimension altogether. However, when you do see the ethical dilemma you're faced with, the question becomes: "How do I think through this decision so I make the best decision possible?"

As you've seen in this book, ethical dilemmas are usually complex and difficult. Fortunately, you are not the first person to be confronted with such challenges. People have been dealing with moral challenges for centuries. Many very smart individuals have provided us with their ideas on how to think through ethical issues. This chapter consolidates their wisdom.

We begin by introducing a formal decision-making process—a step-by-step framework for structuring your deliberation and actions when faced with an issue of moral relevance. We then provide an overview of various perspectives, or "tools," that can be used to address ethical issues. Like the all-purpose pocket knife you'd take backpacking, these tools will be useful to you in a wide variety of situations.

The Ethics Toolkit, at the end of the chapter, provides a chart outlining the tools, including decision criteria, weaknesses, and questions raised by each approach. Table 1 provides questions, based on the tools, that you could ask yourself when confronted by any ethical challenge.

As you will see, each of the tools, while helpful, also has limitations. For this reason, thinking through ethical dilemmas using multiple tools will provide greater insights and will help you to make better decisions.

Decision Process

Ethical dilemmas often trigger emotions and fears that shut down our best thinking. (Review the "Dangers" chapter for a few of the ways this happens.) A structured decision process can keep your thinking clear so you will arrive at a solution you won't regret. We encourage our students to use the following steps.

1. Identify the important facts. What do you know about the situation, and what other information could you quickly obtain that would be helpful in making your decision?

2. Identify the ethical issue(s). What about this circumstance gives the decision moral weight or moral intensity? Write down the values you would like your decision to honor, and note how those values may compete. Also attempt to place your ethical issue in one of the thirteen common dilemmas discussed in this book.

3. Identify the stakeholders. Stakeholders include the decision makers, the actors, and those who will be influenced by the action. Although you usually can't please or benefit everyone, it's important to think through which stakeholders are most important to you and why, and what kinds of benefit or harm are likely to accrue to them.

4. Identify potential solutions. List all of the alternatives that come to mind, then use your creativity to think of more. Could a combination of solutions achieve a better result than one solution alone? Remember that "choose to do nothing for now" is sometimes an alternative as well (which can be a good thing or a bad thing, depending on the circumstances).

5. Assess the solutions using ethical perspectives. Run your solutions through the time-honored principles explained in the following section. As noted, one principle alone can lead you to shaky conclusions, but in combination, these perspectives supply important rationales as well as talking points. Also, utilize the questions provided for each of the thirteen common ethical dilemmas discussed in this book.

6. Assess any new potential solutions. Usually, working your way through the ethical perspectives will bring new possibilities to mind. Add them to your list and weigh them against the alternatives previously listed. Which solution(s) bring you a sense of wholeness or peace?

7. Act in accordance with your ethical analysis. Here's where you *do* the thing you decided was best. This can be uncomfortable, but it may be easier than you anticipate, especially when you've done so much preparation work.

8. Assess your actions and the outcomes. Incorporate this new knowledge into your decision-making process. How did it go? How do you feel? If you can, discuss the situation and its results with someone close to you. Write down what you learned and how this experience might help you process your next ethical dilemma.

This decision-making model has proved useful to students and professionals for the past several decades. Our model is a modification of the one developed by Treviño and Nelson in their book *Managing Business Ethics.*[2] We hope you'll give this process a try with the practice dilemmas throughout our book.

Questions I Should Ask Myself with Every Ethical Challenge

- What are the core principles at stake?
- Am I protecting others' rights? Does my decision preserve others' dignity and ability to choose?
- Would I be willing to be the other party to the transaction?
- Will this decision be fair to all involved?
- Who will be affected by my decision? Who will benefit? Who will be harmed?
- Who am I? What kind of person would this action make me?
- How would I feel if my reasoning and decision appeared on the news?

- Am I fulfilling my societal duties? What are my obligations or promises (explicit or implicit) to others?
- Am I taking care of the people who are most important to me, or those who are most vulnerable?

Ethical Perspectives

The questions in Table 1 are based on formal ways of looking at ethics—frameworks that have been used in various ways for decades or centuries. While these philosophies often point to disparate courses of action, and thus are not sufficient for definitively "solving" a dilemma, they can help you think through your choices in important ways. They can also help you explain your decisions to others.

We outline several moral philosophies, or ethical perspectives, here. (Note: These are the perspectives we mentioned in Step 5 of the decision process.)[3]

Deontology

Deontology refers to the idea that ethics should be based on unwavering adherence to a set of rules. Four of these rules include universal principles, rights, reversibility, and justice.

Universal principles. Also referred to as universalizability, this rule suggests the ethical thing to do is follow the moral principle that should apply in any situation. For example, a universal principle might be "don't lie," "don't steal," or "don't sleep with anyone other than your spouse." When you use universalizability to make an ethical decision, you identify the universal principle governing the behavior and then make decisions based on that principle.

An alternative way of thinking about universalizability would be to ask yourself the question: "Would I want to live in a world where in similar circumstances everyone acted in the way I'm contemplating acting?" If your answer is yes, you could say you're willing for that principle to be "universal."

While an attractive way to think about ethics, universalizability has multiple challenges. First, in our experience, most people can find very few principles they consider to be universal. Most of us would agree with the following universal principle: "never torture children for fun." However, when it comes to principles like "do not kill" or "do not lie," people make exceptions. For example, you may believe it is okay to kill someone who is threatening your life, or to tell a "white lie" to friends or spouse when they ask how they look. Most believers in honesty think it would be best to lie to Nazi soldiers if you were harboring Jewish neighbors.

So, the challenge for you, if you want to live by universalizability, is to bound principles in such a way that they become "universal" for you. For example, "never lie, unless someone's life is threatened, or the lie is only intended to spare someone else's feelings." This exercise is difficult, but it is particularly helpful when thinking through corporate decisions. One way we can think about universal principles is to think of them as personal commitments or corporate policy.

Rights. Virtually anytime you experience an ethical challenge, someone's rights are involved. Your duty, according to a rights perspective, is to act in a way that preserves everyone's rights, or if this is not possible, to do that which preserves or protects the most important rights.

People and organizations have many rights. Most rights can be categorized as legal (arising from government); contractual (arising from agreements entered into); or what have been referred to as natural rights (arising from one's existence as a person). For example, the Bill of Rights in the United States Constitution provides certain legal rights, such as the right to speech, the right to assemble, and protection from unreasonable search and seizure. Contractual rights arise when individuals or organizations voluntarily enter into agreements with one another. Note that contractual rights don't need to be formally written into a contract in order to be binding. Natural rights are identified in the Declaration of Independence: "We hold these truths to be self-evident, that all men are created equal, that they are endowed by their Creator with certain unalienable rights, that among these are Life, Liberty, and the Pursuit of Happiness." The UN Declaration also identifies natural rights including equality, freedom of movement, freedom from arbitrary arrest, and so on.

When you use a rights perspective to determine the correct action to take, you must consider the other parties to your actions as ends unto themselves. This means other individuals have rights that should be taken into account and are not merely means to your desires or ends.

The challenge in this type of reasoning is to first identify what rights others have and then balance those rights to preserve the most important ones. This balance is made all the more difficult because people disagree over which rights are most important. After 9/11, for instance, the United States attempted to balance the rights of national security and individual privacy through the Patriot Act. Some argue it is wrong to give up some level of individual privacy for supposed gains in national security, while others don't believe the law went far enough in providing security.

Reversibility. Also referred to as the "golden rule," reversibility asks you to "do unto others as you would have them do unto you." This principle has been identified in all major world religions. Reversibility invites us to put ourselves in the shoes of the other parties and then to behave in the way we would want to be treated.

One of our favorite ethical principles, reversibility unfortunately has limitations. The first limitation is that people often don't accurately perceive the experiences of others and thus misjudge how others would like to be treated. The second, and generally more significant, limitation is the difficulty created when dealing with multiple parties. Generally doing unto one also means doing unto another. The difficult ethical challenges usually require you to behave toward at least one stakeholder in ways that you would not want to be treated. Thus, you will be required to do your best to treat all parties as well as possible, even if you can't treat all ideally.

Justice. With most of the justice dilemmas in your career, you will be dealing with fairness as it relates to the consequences of your decisions. When you think about who will gain, and how much, versus who will lose, you must decide on whether the result is fair to all parties. Your challenge is to come up with a solution that is fair, as much as possible, to everyone.

Of course, the primary limitation of the justice perspective is deciding on the meaning of fair and how fairness can be justly achieved. We offer a few suggestions here.

You can think about justice in at least three different dimensions: the fairness of an opportunity, the fairness of a process, and the fairness of some set of outcomes. Additionally, there are two main ways to conceptualize how fairness is achieved: fairness through equality, and fairness through merit.

While there are certainly disagreements about whether equality or merit is the correct principle to use when thinking about fairness, in general, many people feel that opportunities and processes should achieve fairness through equality; that is, everyone should get an opportunity, and processes should treat everyone the same. Conversely, many people feel that fairness in outcomes should be achieved primarily on merit. This type of rationale shows up in the adage, "May the best man win."

Let's use voting as an illustration. Very few today argue that voting should be based on merit (for example, only landowners or those with an IQ over 120 should get to vote). It is also not particularly controversial that all citizens should get an equal vote—one person, one vote. In this sense at least, voting could be considered fair, based on equality in process.

Sometimes justice involves the distribution of rights or goods. The job of the purveyor of justice is to see those rights or goods distributed fairly. The emblem of a scale, often used in the legal profession, symbolizes the balance that must be achieved.

Distribution becomes more difficult when it involves several parties. One mental device that can help you in this task was proposed by the philosopher John Rawls. Rawls suggested we use the "veil of ignorance" when deciding on how to be fair.[4] Because we all tend to be biased, Rawls proposed that when making a decision, we pretend we don't know which party to the decision we will be. This primes us to make the most fair decision—one we'd be willing to live with no matter which stakeholder we ended up being. Some of our students have referred to this technique as "the multi-party golden rule."

Consequentialism

The consequentialist approach assumes that the rightness of an action can be judged by its outcomes. This school of thought includes the theories of egoism and utilitarianism.

Egoism. To be clear up front, we have multiple objections to egoism. Proponents of egoism argue that you should always make the decision that is best for yourself or your organization. The assumption of self-interest—the idea that people are selfish and will always choose what benefits them most—undergirds many economic theories, corporate policies, and government regulations. However, if unchecked, this assumption rarely results in ethical decisions. In processing your own dilemmas, think about the egoism framework in reverse. You might ask yourself, "Am I giving too much weight to what's best for me?"

Utilitarianism. Utilitarianism asserts that people should attempt to maximize social welfare. In other words, when you make an ethical decision, think about all the potential good and harm your action could produce and then act in a way to produce the greatest benefit to all. You've probably heard "the ends don't justify the means." Utilitarianism asserts the ends (or outcomes) are the only things that justify the means (or actions).

There are two variants to this theory: act utilitarianism and rule utilitarianism. Act utilitarianism asks you to make a decision based on the outcomes that will occur from your single act. Rule utilitarianism asks you to think about the outcomes that would occur if you were to use your act as a rule for all similar situations.

One way of illustrating these principles is to think about the legal principle of attorney-client privilege. Because providing good legal counsel to people who are not trained in the law is an important aspect of supplying justice, our legal system demands attorneys keep information given by their clients private. However, it is easy to imagine how breaking attorney-client privilege could easily lead to social good. What if a defense attorney leaked information that put a serial murderer behind bars? That act, considered alone, might seem to lead to greater social welfare; after all, we have taken the murderer out of society and prevented future deaths. However, if it were a rule that an attorney could break attorney-client privilege any time he or she thought it would be better for society, most people would not be willing to divulge all information to their attorneys. Even innocent people with incriminating information would likely keep their silence. In this scenario, people would not receive the kind of legal counsel necessary to provide a just system. According to rule utilitarianism, breaking attorney-client privilege fails to maximize social welfare.

While interesting, utilitarianism has some significant limitations. Both act and rule utilitarianism require us to put a value on all things, calculating the benefits minus the harms. There are many things that are difficult to place a value on, for example, your children's lives, lack of an ailment, the ability to go from zero to sixty miles per hour in six seconds, and clean air. It's also impossible to predict all of the outcomes of our actions. Nevertheless, thinking about the possible outcomes of your ethical decisions can provide insights into your decision that other tools cannot.

Virtue Ethics

This framework, also referred to as "character ethics," asks you to think about the type of person you want to be, and then to contemplate how your decision might affect who you are. In other words, when you think about a decision, ask yourself: "Will this act help me become the type of person I want to be?" Or "Is this action in harmony with my best self?" The virtue ethics perspective also invites you to think about your community's values and whether you are living up to those values.

Several helpful questions grow out of the virtue ethics framework. We call these the mirror test, the pillow test, and the disclosure test.

Mirror test. The mirror test appeals to your identity as a good person and your need for a positive self-concept. Ask: "Based on my proposed action, when I look at myself in the mirror, will I like the person looking back at me?"

Pillow test. This is a test you can think about in the abstract or actually try. Ask: "Based on my proposed action, will I be able to sleep well at night?"

Sunshine or disclosure test. Transparency is a great motivator for ethical behavior. It's also highly likely that somehow, sometime, people will find out about your (un)ethical actions. So it pays to ask yourself: "Would I be willing to have my proposed actions accurately reported to the public?" This rule is sometimes referred to as the 5 o'clock news test, or the *New York Times* test. It is a favorite among organizations.

We really like the virtue test of ethics. However, it has limitations. Some people lack a developed sense of ethics or of self, and thus can smile in the mirror and sleep very well at night having done terrible things. The disclosure test isn't foolproof, either—particularly when public values support unethical behavior. (Just think about the public opinion of slavery in the southern United States in the early 1800s.) Still, there's a lot of merit in thinking about the person you want to be and striving to make your actions consistent with that ideal.

Social Contracts (Duties)

Social contract theory endorses actions that create a harmonious or better society. People who subscribe to this school of thought think about the duties they have to others and make decisions based on those duties.

Social contracts are similar to the rights perspective discussed above. In parallel with rights, we have legal duties (duties based on governmental requirements), contractual duties (duties based on voluntary agreements we've entered into), and moral duties (duties based on being human). Your task in doing a duties analysis is to understand what kind of duties you have to others and then act in a way that best fulfills those duties. When it is impossible to fulfill all of your duties, you must decide which duties are most important.

As with rights, the challenge is to balance competing duties while fulfilling the most important ones. For example, on a daily basis we have to decide on how to prioritize our duties to our company, family, and society.

Ethics of Care

Ethics of care acknowledge that our duties to every person are not necessarily equal. We have special obligations to those who are closest to us, such as our families, our coworkers, and our clients. We also have special obligations to individuals or organizations who might be vulnerable for one reason or another. The ethics of care perspective asks us to think about the important role relationships play in our world and suggests that ethics is about maintaining those relationships.

Of course, this perspective also has limitations. We have often heard about managers who are willing to do all sorts of question-able things, reasoning that they have to take care of their family financially. Fortunately, we find when we ask these individuals whether their primary obligation to their spouse or children is to maintain a certain lifestyle based on finances; or to be a husband, wife, or parent of integrity; they generally favor the second.

A second limitation for ethics of care has to do with the danger of psychological distance. It's easy to consider our duties toward people who are similar to us as more important than our duties toward people we view as different from us. Be sure that in embracing the ethics of care, you don't inadvertently discriminate.

Conclusion

On a backcountry adventure, an all-purpose pocket knife doesn't just make tasks easier—in some situations, it could be the difference between a comfortable excursion and a struggle to survive. Experienced hikers keep their all-purpose tools close by.

Similarly, we hope you'll bookmark this chapter and refer to it often. When you're confronted with an ethical dilemma, let the eight-step decision process guide you. Use the ethical perspectives and their associated questions to explore your options and test your ideas.

Finally, take time to practice with the process and tools, ideally well in advance of a major dilemma. Practice is an important part of being prepared. In the next chapter, we share ideas for keeping your ethical reasoning skills sharp and ready.

Marriott School Ethics Toolkit

Developed by Brad Agle, Jeff Thompson, and Dave Hart

Theoretical Roots	An action is ethical when...	Questions I should ask myself
Deontology	I would be willing for it to become universal law (Universal Principles)	What are the core principles at stake?
	It treats other people as ends in themselves, and not just as a means (Rights)	Am I protecting others' rights? Does my decision preserve others' dignity and ability to choose?
	It is reversible (as per the Golden Rule) (Reversibility)	Would I be willing to be the other party to the transaction?
	Benefits and costs are equitably distributed (Justice)	Will this decision be fair to all involved?
Utilitarianism	It provides the greatest benefit to the most people	Who will be affected by my decision? Who will benefit, and who will be harmed?
Virtue Ethics	It helps me become a better person (Mirror Test, Pillow Test)	Who am I? What kind of person would this action make me?
	I would be willing to have it broadcast to the public (Sunshine or Disclosure Rule)	How would I feel if my reasoning and decision appeared on the news?
Social Contracts	I am fulfilling my obligation to contribute to a harmonious society (Duties)	Am I fulfilling my societal duties? What are my obligations or promises (explicit or implicit) to others?
Ethics of Care	It benefits those with whom I have a special trust and obligation or the most vulnerable	Am I taking care of the people who are most important to me, or those who are most vulnerable?

Limitations	Discussion starters (in "business speak")
Difficult to manage competing principles Difficult to bound the conditions	"Would we be content if others (competitors, employees, partners) did what we plan to do?"
Difficult to balance conflicting rights Lack of agreement about rights	"Will our decision make some people feel that they are just being used?"
Multiple parties to satisfy Difficult to anticipate how others really feel	"Are we treating our stakeholders as we would like to be treated?"
Difficult to measure costs and benefits Lack of agreement on fair shares	"Will any of our stakeholders feel this decision is unfair to them?"
Difficult to measure costs and benefits Majority may disregard rights of the minority	"Let's talk about whom our decision will impact the most. Who are the key stakeholders here?" "What decision would add the most value to us and our stakeholders?"
Relies on individual feelings All have implicit self-serving biases	"Let's consider what kind of organizational identity we want to convey to the public."
Public isn't always right Historical/cultural biases	"How will this decision affect our image or reputation if it becomes public?"
Difficult to balance conflicting duties Lack of agreement on duties	"What do we owe our stakeholders?" "How might this decision affect our environment (the market, the national economy, our industry) at large?"
Danger of favoritism and nepotism Difficult to balance competing relationship demands	"How does this decision affect the people or groups who trust us the most (e.g., employees, customers, etc.)?"

CHAPTER 17

Being Ethically Proactive

If you were venturing out into the wilderness, you would prepare by studying maps, packing the necessary items, and developing contingency plans. Similarly, it is easier to face ethical challenges in the workplace when you've put in some work ahead of time.

In this chapter, we will discuss how you can proactively prepare to avoid, and when necessary, handle, ethical challenges. Specifically, we will discuss four areas of preparation for your journey: (1) identify your values and commit to living them, (2) develop the right social structure, (3) earn a reputation as an honest and ethical person, and (4) create habits of ethical reflection and skill building.

Clarify What Matters Most to You

You're a good person. You want to do what's right. Unfortunately, ethical dilemmas usually force you to choose between two right things, or two things you highly value. As you saw in the "Tools" chapter, moral philosophies can provide answers to right-versus-wrong dilemmas, but they only provide some insight into right-versus-right dilemmas. Ethics scholar Joseph Badaracco refers to the decisions we make in right-versus-right dilemmas as "defining moments" because these decisions reveal and test our values while shaping our future behavior. For example, many businesspeople value important clients as well as familial relationships. However, someone's true priority is revealed when he or she must make a decision between a client's demand for a meeting and a daughter's championship tennis match.

Time spent evaluating your priorities—ideally, in advance of the defining moment—can help you align your choices with the things that really matter most to you. To borrow a metaphor from Stephen R. Covey, you don't want to climb a ladder only to find that it is leaning against the wrong wall. By identifying your values and committing to live them, you can avoid improperly prioritizing short-term actions that conflict with your long-term goals.

Identify Your Values

While clarifying one's values is not an easy task, the rewards can be life-changing. Here are some suggestions for discovering what matters most to you.

- Complete a values clarification questionnaire, such as those available at ethics.byu.edu.[1] These exercises will help you to identify and prioritize your values, set related goals, and create a life mission statement.

- Make a list of people you admire. Write down which of their characteristics you aspire to develop. Then write down ways you could demonstrate those characteristics in your current circumstances.

- Examine your perspectives on a set of ethical dilemmas, including the ones you encounter in this book. As you think through what you would do in these situations, answer the question, "What values are honored by my choice?"

- Read thoughtful books. Learn all you can from the perspectives of experienced authors. We recommend *How Will You Measure Your Life* by Clayton Christensen and *The Last Lecture* by Randy Pausch.[2]

If possible, complete these exercises with the assistance of people who care about you. They may have insights about your values based on their experiences with you. In addition, if you are married or have a life companion, it is important to realize your decisions no longer impact your life alone, but both of your lives together. Include your partner when identifying life values and goals.

Commit to Living Your Values

It is not enough to merely identify your values—you must commit to living them. One way to remember your values is to write down and display them in a prominent place. Make sure to periodically update your values and goals to keep them current and meaningful. Expect some setbacks and use them as opportunities to learn about yourself. Share with people close to you your personal commitment to practice moral discipline; that is, to "choose the right because it is right, even when it is hard."[3] Ask for their feedback and support.

Build a Social Structure that Facilitates Ethical Behavior

Don't underestimate the value of social support in ethical decision making. To return to our wilderness metaphor, hike with people you trust and whose risk tolerance is similar to yours, stay far away from natural hazards, and pack appropriately. The same advice applies in the organizational world.

Research has demonstrated that our surroundings and social networks significantly impact our personal behavior. In his book *The Social Animal*,[4] David Brooks confirms that the decisions we make are as much a subconscious product of our environment as they are a conscious result of our cognitive thinking. Disciplined individuals make good choices not because they possess strong willpower in decision-making moments, but because they are disciplined in creating an environment that reinforces their values and objectives, thereby minimizing the number of difficult decisions they have to make. Here are a few suggestions for making your decisions easier.

Join an Organization that Shares Your Values

Through organizational socialization, the companies we work for exude an important influence on how we view what is appropriate in an organizational setting. Thus, it is critical to join an organization that promotes your most deeply held values.

Keep in mind that organizational ethical cultures vary significantly. For many years, Brad required his executive MBA students to perform an analysis of the ethical cultures of their companies. On one occasion, Brad called a CEO to congratulate him for cultivating the remarkable ethical culture documented by one of the students. In response, the CEO quickly brushed off the congratulations and began to ask for advice on some current ethical dilemmas he was facing. By contrast, another Fortune 100 CEO, as reported by a student in the same class, openly reveled in having a reputation for being unscrupulous.

One way you can determine the values of an organization is by looking at their expressed values, such as those found in mission statements or codes of conduct. However, we know from examples such as Enron and WorldCom that expressed values are not always lived values. In order to determine an organization's real values, we suggest discussing the ethics of the organization with the interviewer, your peers, and former employees. Because platitudes are easy in ethics, interview those individuals utilizing short ethical dilemmas such as those found in this book. The company's reaction to these requests will be telling.

Connect with Honorable People

Particularly early in your career, you are generally in an inferior power position relative to those with whom you work. As noted in the Standing Up to Power dilemma, this power imbalance can create ethical difficulties. One of the best ways of dealing with these dilemmas is through your social network.

Find mentors both within and without your organization who can provide wisdom, experience, and support. Ideally, they may have some authority to help you as well.

We give our students the assignment to identify, within their first six months of employment, a high-level mentor within the organization whom they would like to emulate. We encourage the students to find ways to connect with this individual without imposing unnecessarily on his or her time. Some students approach their would-be mentor by asking for advice on a real issue—keeping the ask brief and, afterward, expressing appreciation for the help. Other students find twenty seconds of courage, as portrayed in the movie *We Bought a Zoo*, and directly ask the individual to be their mentor.

Stay Out of Debt and Save

One of the most significant pressures on people to act unethically is financial dependence. The need to meet financial obligations, coupled with the desire to maintain a positive self-image, creates a powerful motivation for the mind to engage in crippling self-deception and rationalization. One of the best strategies for protecting yourself from the temptation to act unethically is becoming financially secure, or, in the words of the prominent philosopher Ed Freeman, "Make sure you have a 'go to hell' fund." Knowing you have enough in the bank to quit your job and still pay the bills for a few months shifts the balance of power in your favor—allowing you more freedom to act in ethical ways.

Develop a Reputation as an Honest and Ethical Person

In marketing, people often talk about "brand equity," or the value derived from the reputation of a product or service. Just as organizations have brands, so does each individual; and one important aspect of your brand is your ethical reputation.

Investing time and energy into developing your personal brand will yield significant benefits. For example, you may be able to avoid many ethical situations because your coworkers will know not to ask you to participate in anything questionable. You will also experience positive peer pressure: the expectation of others for you to do the right thing can help motivate you to act ethically. You will attract other ethical people to you and to your company. Coworkers experiencing an ethical dilemma will come to you for advice. This will enhance the positive impact you can have on the organization and its culture.

The following suggestions can help you establish your ethics brand.

Work Diligently at Your Job

The most fundamental duty of a worker is to work! Employees are expected to effectively perform the tasks they have been hired to do. Demonstrating your dedication to the organization through consistent hard work goes a long way in contributing to your reputation as an honorable person.

Act to Benefit Others

It is generally taken for granted that employees are self-interested: the employment relationship is premised on the idea that employees work to benefit themselves. However, research shows that many employees are also concerned with the welfare of the organization, its members, and its clients. In addition to caring about their own well-being, these employees are genuinely dedicated to serving others.

One's apparent self-interested or other-interested motivation becomes particularly important when dealing with ethical dilemmas. Employees with reputations for caring about others are likely to be given the benefit of the doubt when managing difficult ethical issues—including when others disagree with their choices or they make a mistake. In other words, consistent effort to benefit others can protect your ethical reputation.

Use Inspiring Stories

Organizational stories about how employees acted virtuously under difficult circumstances or proactively established a strong ethical culture can have tremendous power. Pay attention to others' positive actions and share your observations often—in meetings, trainings, publications and, especially, one-on-one. Help to socialize newcomers toward ethical behavior by retelling these stories often.

You can also use inspiring stories from other organizations or other parts of your own organization. For example, you might share the story of Merck and its decision in 1978 to invest in a cure for river blindness, a terrible disease afflicting millions of people in Africa and Central and South America even though their prospects for financial return were very low.[5] You could also mention Goldman Sachs's leadership in improving the work environment for employees: In October 2013 Goldman Sachs announced a new policy prohibiting junior bankers from working from 9:00 p.m. on Friday until 9:00 a.m. on Sunday.[6] Soon after Goldman's announcement, other banks such as JPMorganChase, Citigroup, Barclays, DeutscheBank, Bank of America, and Credit Suisse announced similar policies.

Avoid Judging Others

While being a voice for strong ethical principles is important, you should be careful to avoid seeming self-righteous. When others perceive you as being self-righteous, they are more likely to discount your ideas and scoff at your advice. You can avoid this by focusing on the accomplishments of others instead of your own. Share positive stories instead of negative ones, which could make you seem judgmental. Find ways to convey respect for others' values, even as you seek to live your own.

 ## Bill's Experiences

Your reputation as an honest and dependable person—someone who will look out for others and do what's right—will bring you new opportunities for ethical leadership. At Alcoa, it seemed I was always being handed new responsibilities where I would need to make hard choices and take a stand.

The Currency Hedge

One of these responsibilities was to direct our internal auditing. Whenever you run into auditing troubles, you know there will be uncomfortable choices to make.

I got a call from the auditor over our corporate treasury function. He told me he had uncovered what might be a significant deficiency. Earlier that year, to prepare for an international acquisition, the treasury had placed the biggest currency hedge in the history of our company (in the billions of dollars). Setting a currency hedge at Alcoa involves multiple parties: the controller's office determines the proper accounting; the treasury office selects the financial institution; and the back office handles all formal paperwork. Unfortunately, the auditor told me, our treasury function had handled the hedge alone.

I met with our treasurer, who was relatively new to the company. He said the CEO and CFO had told him to bypass the segregation of duties. So I met with the CEO and CFO. They said they had not asked him to go around proper procedure. They had simply asked him to try to keep the hedge secret. They didn't want word of the acquisition to leak prematurely. Evidently he misinterpreted their request.

We inspected the hedge more closely and found no issues arising from the breach in protocol. The treasury passed their corporate audit (just barely). Because they passed, I wasn't technically required to report the breach to the audit committee. This was before Sarbanes-Oxley, which now mandates reporting of all significant deficiencies.

On reflection, though, I felt the audit committee should know that the biggest currency hedge in the history of our company had been compromised by a failure to segregate duties. I left an email on Friday evening for the CEO and CFO, telling them I would report the deficiency to the audit committee at their meeting the following Tuesday. I did not say, "What do you think about this?" or "Let's discuss."

The CEO responded immediately. He told me to be in his office in New York City at 8 a.m. Monday. He was not pleased. But he knew better than to tell his auditor not to report something.

Our interview lasted exactly ten seconds. He said, "You've got to do what you've got to do. But if there's any discussion in the committee meeting, I'll handle it. Not you. Do you understand?"

The CEO attended the audit committee meeting and handled the discussion. He said the deficiency had been corrected and would not happen again. During a break, the committee chair asked our outside auditor how I was doing in my auditing job. The outside auditor said I was obviously doing well. After all, I'd just reported something that didn't reflect well on the CEO and CFO, a move that can put an internal auditor's career in jeopardy.

At the close of the meeting, the audit committee chairman told our CEO he should be proud. He had created an environment of openness, honesty, and trust—an environment "where Bill can feel free to tell us something he didn't have to tell us, but that we really should know." The chair was trying to cover for me, and I felt good about that.

But I did get sent to Russia a few months later.

Responsibility to Report

You'll encounter countless situations where saying nothing is the easiest answer. But, as you learned in the Intervention dilemma, even saying nothing is communicating.

When reporting is your job—maybe you're an auditor, a sheriff, or a teacher—speaking up honestly is your professional responsibility. Although it's difficult and should be approached with care, few actions build your reputation as an ethical person faster than being the one who is willing to report.

Create Habits of Ethical Reflection and Skill Building

Consistent effort is always a necessary ingredient of lasting change. Luckily, your habits of ethical reasoning and courage will reduce the effort needed to act ethically. In the words of Aristotle: "We are what we repeatedly do. Excellence, then, is not an act, but a habit."[7]

Charles Duhigg's *The Power of Habit* documents how successful agencies and individuals use routines that nearly automate their desired behaviors.[8] In order to become an ethical leader, your vision cannot be confined to merely making the right decision when a problem arises. Instead, you must cultivate a pattern of regular ethical reflection and skill building.

In fact, the act of ethical reflection, itself, may help you make better choices. Dan Ariely's research on honesty shows the value of keeping ethical considerations top of mind. His research demonstrates that most people cheat, but fortunately only by a little. However, when their values have been primed, people don't cheat. For example, test subjects cheated less when they had just been asked to list the ten commandments or to think about their university honor code—even when they couldn't name a single commandment, or their university didn't have an honor code![9]

Consider the following suggestions as you design your new habits.

Continue Learning

There are wonderful materials on the subject of ethics, including books, films, articles, TED talks, YouTube clips, and so on. Some specific examples include the books *Business with Integrity*,[10] *Giving Voice to Values*,[11] *Blind Spots*,[12] *The Road to Character*,[13] and the films *The Quiz Show*, *Codebreakers*, *Chariots of Fire*, *Amazing Grace*, and *Lincoln*. Visit ethics.byu.edu for more recommendations. Discuss with colleagues what you are learning and feeling.

Make Time to Think

You might set a calendar appointment a few times each year to re-read your company's value statements, policies, and code of ethics. During your review, think about your recent actions and the decisions that might come up in the future. Are there ways you can help your organization better live up to its values?

Spirituality is an important determinant in many people's ethical considerations. If spirituality is important to you, make time to participate in the practices that bring you strength or peace. For example, many business leaders find that prayer, meditation, or the study of sacred texts enhances their sense of connection to others and reinforces their commitment to integrity.

Develop Skills

Ethical decision making, courage, and leadership entail specific, learnable skills. For example, you must be able to communicate effectively in difficult conversations. We encourage our students to master the skills outlined in the book, *Crucial Conversations*.[14] In class we practice using the STATE model from that book: Share your facts, Tell your story, Ask for others' paths, Talk tentatively, and Encourage testing.

In addition to the skills you develop through your own experiences, you can practice ethical decision making and courage by thinking through others' situations. You might watch episodes from the TV show "What Would You Do?" and contemplate how you would handle the situations presented. Or you might ask colleagues or friends to share their ethical dilemmas with you.

Write It Out

Finally, maximize your learning by keeping a journal of your daily ethical challenges, your decisions and rationale, and the results. Document what went well and what you would do differently next time. Simply writing about current dilemmas can clarify your thoughts and feelings and help you arrive at a more ethical choice. As a bonus, your record could help when you're challenged on a decision or when you second-guess yourself.

Conclusion

Whether you're a seasoned executive or about to begin your first full-time job, opportunities for ethical decision making surround you. You can prevent or more easily handle the big dilemmas by doing some of the work right now. Start by identifying your values and committing to an ethical life. Make that commitment easier to keep by structuring your relationships and environment to support your goals, developing a reputation as an honest and ethical person, and engaging in regular habits of ethical reflection and skill building. Begin today.

CHAPTER 18

Leading in the Wilderness

We began this book by discussing how articulating and resolving value conflicts is a critical leadership skill. In the previous chapters, you learned a lot about how to develop this skill. This chapter gives insights from other research in ethical leadership. In particular, we will discuss the following topics: (1) ethical leadership, (2) ethical role modeling, (3) designing an ethical organizational culture, and (4) using an integrated ethical strategy model. The chapter concludes with a section particularly important for those in formal leadership positions. This section outlines important U.S. laws and regulations that encourage organizations maintain an ethical culture.

Ethical Leadership

In the early 2000s, Linda Treviño, Laura Hartman, and Michael Brown interviewed 20 senior executives and 20 corporate ethics officers to get a better understanding of ethical leadership.[1] They found two critical dimensions that determine whether people are perceived as *ethical* leaders. They described the dimensions as "moral person" and "moral manager."

Being a moral person refers to your own personal ethical behavior and is, of course, absolutely critical to developing a reputation as an ethical leader. However, contrary to what many executives thought, being a moral person is necessary but not sufficient for gaining a reputation as an ethical leader. The second dimension, being a moral manager, is also required. Leaders can become moral managers by doing things that make good ethics visible, things like (1) serving as a role model for ethical conduct in a way that is visible to employees; (2) communicating regularly with employees about ethical standards, principles, and values; and (3) using a consistent reward system to hold all employees accountable to ethical standards. Without this strong evidence of moral leadership, employees will more likely view you as morally neutral. So, to optimize the ethical behavior in your organization, make an effort to demonstrate your morality in public as well as personal ways.

Ethical Role Models

Another thing that Linda, Laura, and Michael found in their research on moral managers is that the leaders people considered ethical had their own ethical role models. Brad teamed up with Linda and another colleague, Gary Weaver, to investigate the characteristics of these ethical role models.[2] From interviews with dozens of executives, the research team identified four qualities of executives' role models.

Before providing more detail on these four qualities, we should note what these ethical role models were *not*. First, they were not perfect. Indeed, every interviewee could point to an imperfection in their ethical role model. Thus, one does not need to be or feel perfect in order to be an ethical role model for someone else. Second, they were not necessarily successful in their careers. In fact, in some cases interviewees pointed to times when their role model had made an ethical decision that harmed his or her career. Finally, these ethical role models were never distant figures, but were always people with whom the executives had had a close working relationship, at least for a short time. This seems to indicate that we predominantly rely on mentors with whom we have had direct experience, instead of trusting those we have only observed from afar. In selecting an ethical role model for yourself, or in striving to model ethical behavior for others, consider the following attributes.

1. **Interpersonal behaviors.** Role models were seen as individuals who were caring and showed concern and compassion for others. They were also hardworking and helpful, and they supported and took responsibility for others while valuing and maintaining relationships. Ethical role models tended to accentuate the positive. Finally, these ethical role models were also willing to accept others' failures. For the researchers, this was particularly interesting. While the role models didn't have unending tolerance for failure, they did recognize that all individuals make mistakes. By allowing people to be open about their failures, they were able to foster an honest and open environment.

2. **Ethical actions and self-expectations.** Role models were seen as having honesty, integrity, trustworthiness, and humility. They held themselves to a high ethical standard and were consistently ethical in both public and private life. Do not overlook the importance of this consistency; *no one* had an ethical role model who was outstanding in their public actions while failing morally in their private lives. Ethical role models also sacrificed for the benefit of others and, interestingly, accepted responsibility for and were open about their own ethical failings.

3. **Fairness toward others.** Role models distributed resources equitably. They respected people equally and were never condescending (even in disagreements). Further, role models were open to and solicitous of feedback, and they routinely offered explanations for their decisions.

4. **Articulating ethical standards.** Role models were non-compromising and consistent in their ethical values, and they communicated high ethical standards to others. They put

ethics above personal or company interests. In addition, they tended to have a long-term stakeholder orientation as opposed to a short-term shareholder-profit orientation. Finally, they held others ethically accountable. While, as noted above, they were understanding of people's mistakes, they had less tolerance than other leaders for deliberate violations of ethical standards.

Through their interpersonal behaviors, consistent ethical choices, fair treatment of others, and communication around ethical standards, these role models fostered an ethical culture within their organizations. In many cases, their influence as moral managers and role models continued long after their time in the organization came to an end.

Creating an Ethical Organizational Culture

Because research demonstrates that organizational culture has such a strong influence on the behavior of organizational members, it is critical that leaders create the kind of culture that facilitates and promotes ethical behavior.[3] Ed Shein "wrote the book" on organizational culture in 1980.[4] Among his insights is a list of the ways that leaders can and do embed their beliefs, values, and assumptions in their organizations. You can think of these embedding mechanisms as the levers by which one creates and changes organizational culture. Schein groups the levers into two categories: primary and secondary mechanisms. Let's apply these mechanisms to the task of developing an ethical organizational culture.

Primary Embedding Mechanisms

Primary embedding mechanisms involve specific leadership actions that signal the organization's priorities. These levers are critical to establishing and maintaining an ethical culture.

1. **What leaders pay attention to, measure, and control on a regular basis.** Your employees learn what's important to you by observing what you pay attention to. If ethical behavior is going to be an important element of your organizational cul-

ture, you must pay attention to it, measure it, and control it on a regular basis. There are many ways this can be done. Just as Paul O'Neill, the former CEO of Alcoa, made safety the first item on every company meeting agenda, you can emphasize ethics in many ways, both verbal and written. We suggest that managers regularly measure employees' perceptions about organizational ethics. By doing periodic surveys to assess the ethical culture of an organization, leaders both signal the importance of such a culture and gain valuable insights into the areas of strength and weakness in the current culture.

2. How leaders react to critical incidents and organizational crises. Your employees will learn a great deal about the values of your organization by observing how you respond to ethical challenges you face. Bill O'Rourke began this book by discussing his reaction to the trichloroethylene situation in Texas. During a critical incident, all eyes are (or will soon be) on you, making your response even more likely to influence your organization's culture.

3. How leaders allocate resources. How money and other resources are spent says much about the priorities of an organization. This is a primary reason that the budgeting process shapes organizational culture. If you allocate resources to ethics, it signals that this is important to you. Later in this chapter we discuss how to do that.

4. Deliberate role modeling, teaching, and coaching. In addition to the informal and non-deliberate ways culture is formed, some types of culture formation are very deliberate. For example, as a leader you should think about how your actions affect others around you. You should be thoughtful in mentoring employees and explicit about what is important to you and how you expect your subordinates to conduct themselves. Our earlier discussion of ethical role modeling should provide you with some help in selecting the model you want to present.

5. How leaders allocate rewards and status. The classic article "On the Folly of Rewarding 'A' while hoping for 'B'"[5] discusses the importance of aligning one's incentive system with one's desired outcomes. All too often organizations say they want one thing but then reward another. If you want ethical behavior in your organization, it must be rewarded. At the very least, unethical behavior must not be rewarded.

6. How leaders recruit, select, promote, and excommunicate. The beliefs, values and assumptions of those in your organization will have a profound effect on your ethical culture. Thus, choosing who to include in your organization, who will lead your organization, and who you will ask to leave your organization is critical. Organizations that are serious about creating ethical cultures recruit, promote, and fire based on ethical screens and criteria.

For example, to select those who would best fit your organization, use ethical dilemmas in your interviews. Choose only employees who impress you with their ethical reasoning, sensitivity, and ability to create solutions. Handle promotions strategically to ensure that only leaders who match the values of the company gain power in the company.

Many companies perform annual 360-degree evaluations of managers, which may include subordinates' evaluations of the manager's leadership and adherence to the values of the organization. Pay close attention to these evaluations: while leaders can sometimes fool their managers, it is very difficult to fool one's subordinates.

When organization members act unethically, it can be tempting to let the transgressions slide. Be aware that your response to this behavior shapes the expectations for other employees and speaks louder than any corporate values statement you could devise. If you need to let someone go, consider the rationale shared by Bill in the Intervention dilemma: "We're not firing him. He fired himself when he chose to cover up the safety issues." Beyond sending a clear message, dismissing employees who don't live the organization's values makes room for more ethically minded employees to take the lead.

Secondary Embedding Mechanisms

Secondary mechanisms involve structures, systems, and processes; the physical layout of the workplace; and organizational communication—both the informal sharing of stories and the formal publication of creeds or goals.

1. Organizational design and structure. Structural elements, like reporting channels and incentives, can heavily influence the culture of your organization. Research Brad did with his colleagues at the University of Washington[6] found that corporate crime increased when certain organizational design elements were present. For example, when a corporate reporting apparatus asked for very little information from its operating units, generally only financial information, corporate crime was more likely than when more information was requested from operating units. Likewise, when incentive systems were primarily tied to financial results, corporate crime increased.

2. Organizational systems and procedures. Organizations of any size need rules, systems, and procedures to operate. These systems signal important values about the organization. They also can facilitate or block ethical action in the organization. For example, highly rigid rules sometimes make it so difficult for organizational members to get important organizational work done that they are forced to resort to bending or circumventing the rules. The challenge is to set procedures and systems that encourage employees to make ethical decisions—not catalogues of rules that attempt to direct their every action.

3. Rites and rituals of the organization. Like many religious organizations, business organizations also have their rites and rituals. There are parties, celebrations, award ceremonies, trips, and so on. These occasions provide you with the opportunity to demonstrate what is really important in your organization. Consider ways you can weave ethics into your organization's rituals, or consider new rituals you might develop to reinforce ethical behavior.

4. Design of physical space, facades, and buildings. Beyond shaping employee interactions and sending messages about what your organization values, the physical layout of your workspace can encourage openness and transparency, or it can create barriers that allow unethical behavior to go unchecked. (See "Bill's Experiences" in this chapter for a fascinating example.)

Brad saw the power of physical spaces during his dissertation research, when he spent several days observing CEOs in action. He noted major differences among the leaders' office layouts. For example, at one major company, the CEO's office occupied a set of floors in a high-rise building exclusively for executives, with executive-only access. There were executive washrooms and an exclusive executive dining room. Brad had to go through multiple security screenings to get to the office suite. The chances of this company's leaders keeping a daily pulse on the ethical activities of their employees, or being accessed by an employee with ethically relevant information to share, were small.

Brad visited another high-powered CEO whose internal office looked exactly like every other office in the building. In fact, Brad struggled a bit to find it. This CEO took Brad to the employee cafeteria where he normally ate with the employees, most of whom called him by his first name. The CEO expressed to Brad a bit of embarrassment that while he could call many of his employees by their first names, the company had grown far too large for him to be able to call all of them by name. While each of these CEOs was very effective in terms of financial performance, the cultures felt very different.

5. Stories about important events and people. Over the years, in assessing organizational ethical cultures, we have found that stories are a powerful indicator of what matters to the company. Brad first became aware of the strong safety culture at Alcoa when he asked his executive MBA students at the University of Pittsburgh to share stories frequently told in their organizations. One student immediately regaled the class with the story of his CEO, Paul O'Neill, firing a top executive who put financial results above their safety culture—and then explaining the firing in an op-ed in the *Wall Street Journal*.

You may be familiar with the decades-old story of Nordstrom giving a refund for tires a customer said he purchased there. (No, Nordstrom has never sold tires—but the Fairbanks, Alaska, storefront where the return occurred had previously been occupied by a store that did.)[7] Nordstrom employees enjoy retelling the legend because it illustrates how important customer service is to the company. If you want a strong ethical culture, find stories that illustrate how your company has lived its values, particularly when doing so was challenging, and celebrate those stories. Further, inspire new stories with your own virtuous, ethical acts.

6. Formal statements of organizational philosophy, creeds, and charters. We often hear about setting the "tone from the top." That tone must be audible to be effective. Many executives tell us that the importance of ethics in their company "goes without saying." They are wrong. An organization is constantly sending messages about what is important. Organizational silence indicates that something is not important. Thus, if you want a strong ethical culture, your organizational values need to be articulated in your organization's documents and must be shared frequently by your organization's leaders.

 # Bill's Experiences

Throughout my career, I've been blessed by association with great leaders whose ethical actions I admire. The following experiences taught me about the many positive influences of an ethical leader.

On Ethical Culture through Office Layout

I learned about the influence of office layout when I was assigned to lead Alcoa Russia. My new office was on the top floor of our administration building. It was enormous! I had a main office, a private office, my own large conference room, and a luxurious lavatory—which only I could use. How could I possibly know what my employees were experiencing, when two very thick doors, a line of secretaries, and my own security guards protected my office from intrusion? This was not a good match for my leadership style.

I promptly converted a nearby auditorium into an office complex for me and my direct reports. I put all of us in cubicles. My workspace was in a central area through which employees had to travel during normal office movements. I learned this from Paul O'Neill, who took a thirty-one-story high rise corporate headquarters building in Pittsburgh, with 97% closed offices, gave it to the city, and built a five-story open office structure along the river. Paul's new building had 100% open offices—all the same size, all with the same type of furniture, and all within thirty feet of a window.

One day, a young clerk in the HR Department, who spoke some English, felt free enough to walk up to me in my cubicle. She told me that someone in her department was engaged in extortion (a story I tell in the Suspicions Without Enough Evidence dilemma). Had I stayed in my original fortress, I might never have learned of the situation.

On Ethical Role Models

My own ethical role models have influenced me in major ways. I don't just have a list of my role models' attributes. I have many of their pictures displayed in my den at home.

Some of these heroes are famous. I admire Thomas Jefferson's humility, Martin Luther King Jr.'s perseverance, Mother Teresa's compassion, and Ghandi's vision and sacrifice. Once I was speaking about the courage of astronauts at a dinner. I didn't know that someone at my table was good friends with Neil Armstrong. Three days later I received an envelope from Neil with two pictures he'd autographed and addressed to me. "If this is an imposition on your good nature, I apologize," he wrote in his cover letter. (An imposition!?)

The role models who influence me most, though, are leaders with whom I had close, personal interaction: Paul O'Neill, as I've mentioned, and my dad.

Let me be the first to admit that my role models aren't perfect, and all of their values don't perfectly align with mine. But their pictures remind me of the values I prize in each of them. There's great power in people who show you the way.

On Positive Ethical Leadership

I'm energized by the amount of good businesses can bring to the world when leaders are committed to do the right thing. This is especially true when companies determine to go beyond compliance to be good neighbors and to set industry standards for safety and sustainability. Here are a few choices leaders made at Alcoa that made me especially proud.

When our company built manufacturing facilities in Mexico, we needed to construct a wastewater treatment facility. At the time, the city had no wastewater treatment at all. Someone suggested that for about 20% more cost, we could increase the capacity of our treatment facility so we could treat the city's wastewater in addition to the wastewater from the plant. We did that. It's what a good neighbor in the community would do.

On another occasion, we built a factory in rural South Carolina, where less than 14% of the population had a high school education. Our new workforce would need substantial training to get up to speed. Rather than selecting our 400 prospective employees and educating only them, we opened these classes to everyone in the community. Again, we felt this was what a good neighbor does.

We also worked to reduce production risks within our industry. For instance, most governments allow certain levels of harmful components to be present in alloys. One of these components, beryllium, causes respiratory disease in workers who are exposed over time to fumes and dust. Our company set an objective to totally eliminate beryllium for our alloys. Finding substitutes required a considerable amount of research. (And research is expensive!) Eventu-

ally we identified and proved a suitable substitute. We then went to our customers and convinced them to switch to the beryllium-free alloy in the interest of our workers. Alcoa's proactive stance led to industry gains in health and safety.

Integrated Ethical Strategy Model

As you seek to become an ethical leader and role model, keep in mind that ethics is never found in a vacuum. Professor Ed Freeman at the University of Virginia argues that many executives erroneously adopt what he calls a "separation thesis"—the idea that business is over here and ethics is over there.[8] In reality, there is no separation. All business conduct has moral implications.

That's because the decisions you make as a business leader have real effects on your stakeholders; that is, on anyone with an interest in the management of your organization. For example, a decision to use one supplier over another might create harm for the supplier not chosen—and perhaps for the employees and families who rely on income from that supplier, and thus for the community where the supplier is based. Arguably, you also might create harm when you select one employee over another for a promotion, when you set policies that make work-life balance more difficult, or when you produce any item that will eventually make its way to a landfill. With so many stakeholders—and with their often competing needs—how will you decide which stakeholders your decisions should benefit, and which stakeholders it's okay to harm or ignore? That is a question with enormous ethical implications.

Fortunately, a rich literature on the "stakeholder theory of the firm," as popularized by Ed Freeman and others, offers some guidance.[9] Stakeholder experts insist that business leaders need to look beyond short-term return for investors to consider the needs of everyone impacted by firm actions. This is a daunting prospect. How can leaders prioritize stakeholders important for the organization's survival and success while also treating all stakeholders ethically? In the late 1990s, Ron Mitchell, Brad Agle, and Donna

Wood proposed an answer. They offered three attributes that deter-mine how essential a stakeholder is to the firm.[10]

1. Power. The first attribute refers to how much the stakeholder can influence the firm's success. Customers, employees, share-holders, major suppliers, and governments are a few stakehold-ers that often rank highly in terms of power. Ignoring entities whose cooperation the company needs to survive is not usually a good idea.

2. Legitimacy. The second attribute is legitimacy—how much the firm is morally obligated to meet the stakeholder's claim. Legitimacy is essentially the ethics piece of the model. Claims are considered legitimate when social norms, legal rights, or moral considerations substantiate the organization's duty to the stakeholder.

3. Urgency. The third attribute rates the time sensitivity of the stakeholders' claims, as well as the importance to the stake-holder of having these claims fulfilled. Claims that stakehold-ers believe need to be addressed right away, in order to achieve goals or to prevent substantial harm, often demand managers' urgent attention.

The Venn diagram in Figure 1 illustrates the way power, legitimacy, and urgency combine to signal how essential a stakeholder might be to the firm. When a stakeholder has all three attributes, man-agement should highly prioritize that stakeholder. When the stake-holder possesses two of those attributes, management should give lesser priority to that stakeholder. Finally, when the stakeholder only possesses one attribute, that stakeholder would have even lower priority.

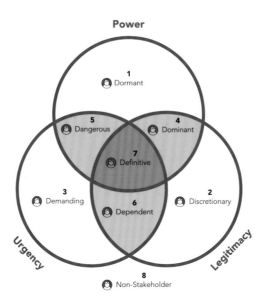

Stakeholder Types & Attributes

Power

1
Dormant

5
Dangerous

4
Dominant

7
Definitive

3
Demanding

6
Dependent

2
Discretionary

Urgency

Legitimacy

8
Non-Stakeholder

Figure 1. The Stakeholder Salience Model helps leaders to prioritize the competing demands of stakeholders by integrating ethical and strategic considerations.

The Stakeholder Salience Model is dynamic because stakeholders' attributes are always changing, relative to the power, urgency, and legitimacy of other stakeholders. Leaders can use the model regularly to ensure their actions toward stakeholders align with the company's ethical and strategic goals. Go to ethics.byu.edu to learn more about the stakeholder approach and to complete a guided stakeholder identification and prioritization exercise.

Laws and Regulations that Help Companies Be Ethical

Leaders need to be aware of the laws and regulations designed to encourage organizational ethics. Because a changing subset of organizations has a history of not meeting the standards of the general public, various entities have created laws, regulations, and best practices to help ensure against such expectations gaps. Companies have to meet various regulations about worker safety, product safety, pollution control, monopoly, and corruption, among others.

These laws were developed in the United States over the past two hundred years in response to public concern and various scandals. When great monopolies were being created in the late 1800s, the public pushed for (and got) anti-trust regulation. After the questionable actions that led to the stock market crash of 1929 and the Great Depression, the Securities Acts of 1933 and 1934 created the Securities and Exchange Commission.

Laws and Regulations on Ethical Issues

Some regulations and guidelines deal specifically with ethical issues. For example, after a number of U.S. companies were found to have bribed foreign officials, the U.S. passed the 1977 Foreign Corrupt Practices Act that made it illegal to pay bribes to foreign officials to gain business. Sarbanes-Oxley, passed in 2002 to protect investors from fraud, included several provisions dealing with ethical behavior in accounting. Likewise, the 2010 Dodd-Frank Act included provisions for ethics in financial transactions. The 2003 NYSE corporate governance guidelines call for a number of governance mechanisms, including an established code of ethics for listed companies.[11]

Guidelines for an Ethical Culture

Other regulations and guidelines deal specifically with creating ethical cultures in organizations. Specifically, the 1991 U.S. Sentencing Guidelines and the 2004 Amendments to those guidelines, while not regulatory, provide important guidance for organizations in creating an ethical culture. Commissions developed these guidelines after looking into the problems in organizations that engaged in improper acts. Chapter 8 of the 1991 guidelines included seven steps of due diligence that organizations are expected to follow to proactively develop an ethical culture. These seven steps follow.

1. Develop compliance standards and procedures. An organization needs to create a code of ethics that provides guidance for organizational members. It also needs to create procedures that enhance the probability that such guidance is heeded.

2. Give one executive overall responsibility. While organizations often say that everyone in the organization is responsible for ethics, like any other organizational function, if everyone is in charge, no one is charge. Thus, if an organization is to prioritize ethics, it needs to assign one person to be ultimately in charge.

3. Ensure executives are trustworthy. When individuals gain positions of power where they could do serious damage to the organization, it is important to do the best job possible of screening them for proclivity for engaging in unethical or illegal acts.

4. Communicate standards and procedures. While having an ethics code and procedures for implementing the code is important, if employees and stakeholders don't know about those standards and procedures, they will do very little good. Thus, communication and training are critical to developing a strong ethical culture. While on-line training is effective for certain types of compliance and ethics topics, in-person interaction is vital for transmitting values in areas where strong pressure exists to violate those values.

5. Create steps to ensure compliance. After communication and training have occurred, it is important to put in place other mechanisms to remind organizational members of their duties. It is also essential to create steps for reporting any ethical impediments. For example, all organizations should have a helpline that employees can call or email to get help with their ethical challenges.

6. Enforce standards consistently. Nothing undermines an ethics program quicker than treating individuals in the organization differently. Enforcing standards inconsistently creates a great deal of organizational cynicism.

7. Modify program appropriately. With an upfront design, no one can ever be sure how a code of ethics or program will function. Thus, it is critical to continually evaluate the effectiveness of the program and continue to modify as necessary.

After the major scandals of the early 2000s, the 1991 U.S. Sentencing Guidelines were reexamined for effectiveness. Amendments made in 2004 make them even more effective. Here's a recap of the enhanced guidelines.

1. Promote an organizational culture than supports ethical conduct. Organizations cannot be silent when it comes to ethics. They must be proactive in their commitment to complying with the law.

2. Assign boards and executives to oversee compliance and ethics programs. The top management of the organization cannot delegate ethics away. They are the most prominent organizational culture builders and must be active in ensuring that an organization develops an effective ethics program.

3. Define the content and operation of ethics programs. Once again, the leadership cannot fully delegate this responsibility. They must be involved in the details of the organization's program.

4. Identify ethics risks. Different organizations face different risks. For example, a manufacturing facility might have significant worker safety and environmental risks while a bank likely has significant currency risks. Each organization must determine the areas in which it needs to prioritize its efforts, with special attention to areas where criminal violations will occur.

5. Provide training at the top. Train high-level officials as well as employees in relevant legal standards and obligations. Like all members of an organization, leaders need training in their jobs. It is critical that they receive the information they need to perform their functions well. Many leaders first encounter duties involving legal standards and ethical obligations when they are promoted to executive or board levels. No one is born knowing about the U.S. Foreign Corrupt Practices Act, the NYSE corporate governance guidelines, or the U.S. Sentencing Guidelines. High-level officials need to be educated.

6. Empower ethics and compliance officers. In several high-profile cases of organizational misconduct, the organization had compliance and ethics officers in place. However, in many of these organizations, these officers had neither the authority nor resources to carry out their responsibilities effectively. Give compliance and ethics officers the authority and resources they need.

Conclusion

In this chapter, we've shared some research on how you can be an effective ethical leader. Ethical leaders understand the importance of being both a moral person and a moral manager. They understand that others watch them to discern the organization's true priorities. They also understand that all organizations have cultures, and they create, modify, and enhance their organization's culture to support ethical behavior. When choosing how to allocate resources, these leaders seek to be both strategic and ethical. Mapping stakeholders with a salience model helps them consider strategy and ethics together. Finally, they follow laws, regulations, and best-practice guidelines to create organizations that not only comply with the law but often go far beyond compliance.

In this book, you have practiced resolving the major ethical dilemmas of the business world. We hope you will continue to use this *Field Guide* as you become a leader for ethics in organizational life. When you're unsure how to act, refer to the ethics toolkit, the general questions to ask in any dilemma, and the specific questions and pitfalls for each dilemma type. Keep in mind the ethical dangers—especially the danger of rationalization—and work proactively to keep your decision making sharp. Review Bill's stories whenever you need a fresh perspective or boost of inspiration.

By strengthening your ethical leadership skills, you will bless those involved with your organization and will lift society as a whole.

We wish you well on your journey!

Appendix

The Business Ethics
FIELD GUIDE

The Big Question
By Brad Agle and Aaron Miller

Early each semester in our ethics courses, we find ourselves answering the Big Question people ask about ethics: "Why should I be ethical?" Of course, rarely do students put the question into those words, because stating it so directly would make the questioners feel conspicuously untrustworthy. Because of the reputational risk, students usually let the question simmer a few weeks before they're comfortable enough to ask it. We've found that it's best to discuss this question head-on. We feel it equally valuable to do the same here.

Before answering the Big Question, we should note that we've written this book based on the assumption that you want to be ethical. We are confident after years of teaching thousands of business students and executives that this is not an unreasonable assumption. In our experience, the vast majority of people want to do the right thing. They are not instinctively dishonest or manipulative. They consider themselves mostly moral and will generally try to match their behavior accordingly. As teachers of ethics, we have not had to convert very many people to the value of good ethics.

So the real question isn't, "Why should I *ever* be ethical?" Instead, it's, "Why should I *always* be ethical?" It's not that you want to act immorally, but that you will sometimes face pressure to do so. Not everyone is ethical all the time, and if we're on the other end of their bad behavior, we put ourselves at risk. For example, students constantly face the temptation to cheat, knowing that some of their classmates are cheating. But the dilemma doesn't end with school. Salespeople overpromise, applicants inflate their résumés, lawyers abuse the system, and people pay and take bribes. How do you compete in a world where someone is always getting a competitive edge unethically?

The reality is that there is no irrefutable, iron-clad argument proving that you should always be ethical. If there were such an argument, everyone would quickly discover it and everyone would make consistently right choices. But we do think there are very persuasive answers to the question, "Why should I always be ethical?" Here are the most important ones.

The Cost of Doing (Unethical) Business

The temptation to cheat, lie to, or take advantage of someone else always considers the short-term benefit of doing so. It is sadly often the case that an unethical choice will make you or your organization come out ahead. But that perspective ignores the costs that the unethical person bears because of their choices.

Unethical behavior hurts your reputation. The people you've mistreated are unlikely to do business with you again. They'll also tell others to avoid you. Because any career or company requires working with other people, the market of potential opportunities shrinks with each person that decides not to trust you. As a result, you have fewer opportunities to succeed.

Some ethical missteps are not merely expensive; they are catastrophic to your career. We regularly read in the news about incredibly talented people who destroy their legacies and future opportunities because of ethical failures. It's naïve to think that one indiscretion doesn't have the power to wreak havoc on your professional and personal life.

If people decide to work with you or your organization in spite of a bad reputation, they will require more assurances that you are worth the risk. You'll sign more complicated contracts, spend more money in showing good faith, face more scrutiny of your intentions, and wait through longer delays. In a very real and directly financial way, your cost of doing business goes up. Through the reputational cost of bad ethics, you basically invoke a tax on yourself, one that is likely to outweigh whatever gains you saw from your bad ethics. It's true that we hear stories of financially successful people who got there through dishonorable means, but there are also many competing stories of careers destroyed by bad ethical choices. On the other hand, when people can trust each other, doing business becomes much less expensive for everyone, because the costs of self-preservation go down. The fruits of cooperation, fundamental to any economic activity, grow more readily. You create value instead of merely extracting it.[1] You may not make a short-term killing, but you will build a career.

Personal Harmony

If you are like the vast majority of people, you *want* to be ethical. You see yourself as a fundamentally good person and prefer making choices that are in harmony with your self-image. Unethical choices conflict with how you see yourself. This is true even for small or rare missteps. Ethical failures invite regret.

It's unfortunately become cliché that immoral choices keep you up at night, but the long-term burden of doing the wrong thing is very real. Our research for this book bears that out. As we followed up with the professionals who shared their stories with us, we often heard them express sorrow and regret at the choices they made. In many cases, if they could do it over again, they would choose differently. The hard truth is that they can't.

Many, many people, on the other hand, told us about their coura-geous choices, some of which even led to switching companies or changing careers. In every case, they described their hard-but-ethical choices with confidence. They regularly told us that they were happy about the choice they made, even if it caused great personal uncertainty. They consistently referenced the personal peace they feel from having done the right thing.

It's hard to put a price on personal harmony, because it cannot be bought. Don't be naïve enough to think that losing your integrity won't matter to you. Instead, look forward to those hard choices as opportunities to build and show strong moral character.

Ethical Self-Defense

Too often we hear others discount ethical people as foolish rubes who get taken by savvier opponents. This version of good ethics is a strawman. Nothing in having good ethics requires you to be Pollyannaish or unwise. To the contrary, good ethics includes (and often requires) paying keen attention to the risk of being hurt by dishonest people. In fact, this book will help you be more sophisticated in dealing with others.

Your capacity for ethical self-defense should be part of every business calculation. How do you intend to succeed if you don't pay a bribe when a bribe is expected? How will you defend yourself if a partner turns into a false accuser? How can you help your bid win when you know that your competitors are cutting corners? There are good answers to all of these questions that lead to far greater long-run success.

Remember that being trustworthy doesn't always require you to be trusting. Exercise wisdom and caution. This will add to your reputation as an ethical person (or organization) and will bear fruit well into the future.

Sometimes You Lose (But So Does Everyone)

When we shared our book with a friend for feedback, he made the excellent point that there are times where ethical behavior does put you behind. Unless you're willing to lie, cheat, and steal like some competitors do, you may come up short while they walk away with the money. This can be especially true in markets or countries where unethical practices are the standard. If you're the nice guy or gal (or company), you might finish last *because* you are nice.

In these situations, you have to decide what you value. There will be times when your ethics and a moment of professional or organizational success will be at odds with each other. You'll have to decide if your ethical values are worth the setback. Just don't fall prey to the trap that unethical behavior is your *only* path to success. It might be the path in that moment or that market or that country, but with patience and integrity, you can find a career or build an organization where your ethics enable your success rather than obstruct it.

And finally, remember that we aren't making the case that being ethical is a guarantee for success. But neither is being unethical. An unethical player can get taken advantage of, too, and sometimes precisely because of his or her bad ethics. Your success involves a lot more than your ethical values alone. We just don't want you to leave them behind.

Conviction, not Conversion

As we noted above, our goal is not to convert you to the value of good ethics. Instead our goal is to help you better realize your good intentions. The skills we cover in this book will build your conviction to make the right choice because they will make you more capable in handling those tough moments. We want to help you be ethical *and* successful.

Acknowledgments
The Story of This Book, by Brad Agle

When values conflict and the course of action is not clear, what should you do?

This central, all-important question is one that we have been thinking about over the years as professors of business ethics. In that time, we have helped thousands of business students and managers to work through challenging ethical dilemmas.

As a field of inquiry, ethics has provided methodologies for thinking about these issues since the ancient Greeks. But the formal field of business-centered ethics is generally traced back about 50 years. Business ethics draws on classical ethical theories and philosophies to help guide the decisions of business people.

Like my professional colleagues, I have often utilized classical methodologies as an aid to think through business decisions. However, while that approach is helpful, I have found it to be woefully inadequate in providing the simple, practical advice that most students and business practitioners seek. For as long as I have been teaching business ethics, I have been on a quest to find a better way, or at least a helpful alternative to the classical approach.

Seven years ago I joined the Marriott School of Management at Brigham Young University, where I began working alongside Aaron Miller, a young JD who is an inspirational teacher of business ethics. One day I mentioned to Aaron that I thought that it might be possible to create a typology to classify all business ethics dilemmas. I had found that asking more targeted questions, based on the types of dilemmas in question, helped my students think them through and come to their own creative solutions. Aaron was intrigued by this idea, and a team was born.

With help from our research assistants, we began by examining hundreds of workplace ethical dilemmas I had collected from MBA and executive MBA students over the years. Ultimately we discovered thirteen dilemma types. For each type, we developed questions to help our students examine the ethical issues at play. In the classroom, we found this to be remarkably effective. When Aaron and I talked about different ways to disseminate our new approach to business ethics, a book seemed to be a natural option.

There was another person we wanted to add to our team. As a faculty member at the University of Pittsburgh, I had come to know and respect Bill O'Rourke, an executive at Alcoa. Over the past sixteen years he has been incredibly generous in speaking to each of my MBA business ethics classes at Pitt and BYU. Bill brings to class an ever-growing list of ethical dilemmas he has personally encountered, and he challenges the students to think about what they would do in those situations. Because of the various areas of business Bill has managed, the list covers a majority of the issues faced by business people. We hoped our readers could benefit from Bill's stories and his incredible wisdom, and we're grateful he agreed to join us in the effort.

A book like this one is a team effort. We are grateful for all those who have helped in this endeavor. We would like to begin our acknowledgements by expressing appreciation for the generous support of the Wheatley Institution at Brigham Young University.

The director, Richard Williams, and the assistant director, Emily Reynolds, are remarkable ethical leaders. They have been enthusiastic about this project from the beginning, and their support and encouragement greatly facilitated our completion of the book. We thank Jack Wheatley, the Wheatley Institution Board of Overseers, and all those who've donated to the Wheatley Institution. Your financial support for this project, and for other projects at the Wheatley Institution, makes an enormous difference.

Next, we express our profound thanks to two individuals without whose help this work could not have been completed. Camden Robinson, an incredibly bright and talented undergraduate student at BYU, worked closely with Brad in the writing of the book. Both the thinking and the prose in the book are greatly improved because of his involvement. Hilary Hendricks served as the editor of the book. We were incredibly fortunate to have her on our team, and it would be hard to overstate her contribution to this work. From her exemplary work ethic and dogged determination we learned the necessity of a good editor to the successful completion of a project such as this one. Her patience, writing instincts, encouragement, and editing talent were absolutely critical. Thank you, Hilary.

Dedicated administrators in the Marriott School of Management and the Romney Institute of Public Management have cheered on our efforts. Thank you to deans Ned Hill, Gary Cornia, and Lee Perry, and to directors David Hart and Jeff Thompson, each one an exemplary ethical leader.

We also express appreciation for those who have mentored us along our individual journeys. Brad thanks Charles Hill, Tom Jones, and Patricia Kelley, his wonderful PhD mentors; Jeff Sonnenfeld, who taught him to never forget those actually engaged in business while doing academic research; Donna Wood, Barry Mitnick and Jerry Zoffer, his mentors at Pitt; and Ron Mitchell, his primary academic collaborator. Aaron thanks those whose mentoring helped him find his way from the law into academia, including his world-class colleagues in the Romney Institute of Public Management, and in particular Gary Cornia, David Hart, and Jeff Thompson. He also thanks other key mentors, including Todd Manwaring, David Crandall, Stan Neeleman, Brett Scharffs, Doug Bush, Barbara Norman, Robert Orton, and not least, his coauthor and friend, Brad Agle. Bill has discussed his mentors in the text.

We thank our exceptional spouses, Kristi (Brad), Katie (Aaron), and Elena (Bill). They have each helped on the book in numerous ways, not the least of which is helping us stay motivated and feel appreciated in this work.

We also thank our research assistants through the years. Those who have helped on this project include Rachel Mahrt Degn, Michelle Allgood, Jared Miller, Matt Baker, Chase Bradshaw, and Sharla Kwarm.

We are incredibly appreciative of the time our friends in the business and academic communities spent reviewing this work. We sincerely thank the members of the Wheatley Ethics Advisory Council: Brian Agle, Amy Rees Anderson, Abdallah M. Assaf, Mindy Brown, Joe Cannon, Ray Carter, James Clarke, Stephen M.R. Covey, Robert Drewes, Dawn Eidelman, Bill Freedman, Charlie Freedman, Ron Gardner, George Harrington, Pat Hassey, Sharlene Wells Hawkes, Jeff Hill, Chris Hoke, Steve Larsen, Dan Nelson, Robert C. Oaks, Brad Oates, Greg Perry, Dale Prows, Craig Rasmussen, Greg Robinson, Jeff Rust, Kim Smith, Ruth Todd, Scott Wahlstrom and Art Wing. Others who reviewed the book include Jeff Agle, Sally Agle, Amy Benson, Bill Bridges, Kurt Brown, Tanner Clawson, Jan Dawson, Darin Gates, Steve Glover, Stacy Hall, Jim Harmon, Michael Hicks, Jim Hill, Michael Hsiung, Richard Hunter, Keith Lue, David Paradiso, Walt Parcell, Dan Peterson, Lindsay Agle Rasmussen, Leslie Snow, Emily Stallings, and Justin Swalberg. You made our work better.

Special appreciation goes to those who read our material and offered praise for the book. Their names are included in the front of the book along with their endorsements.

We also thank our colleagues in the Romney Institute who help us in all our work. Those not mentioned yet include Heather Chewning,

Rob Christensen, Catherine Cooper, Rex Facer, Tanya Harmon, Ray Nelson, Vicki Okerlund, Brad Owens, Chris Silvia, Kip Smith, Ty Turley, Lori Wadsworth, and Eva Witesman.

We are grateful for the passion of the business ethics community in its attempts at continually improving ethics pedagogy. In particular, we are grateful to the participants of the five Teaching Ethics in Universities Conferences hosted by the Wheatley Institution and sponsored by the Society for Business Ethics.

Finally, we express gratitude to the courageous individuals, across more than two decades, who have shared their experiences and insights with us. We are particularly grateful for those who gave us permission to share their stories in this volume. Working through your dilemmas has been a major source of guidance—for us as professors, for thousands of students, and, now, for countless readers as well. We owe this book, in large measure, to you.

Notes

Introduction

1. Leadership and management skills were first differentiated by Abraham Zaleznik and then later refined by John Kotter. See the following:

   Abraham Zaleznik, "Managers and Leaders," *Harvard Business Review*, 55 (1977): 67–78.

   Abraham Zaleznik, "The Leadership Gap," *The Executive*, 4.1 (1990): 7–22.

   John P. Kotter, *John P. Kotter on What Leaders Really Do* (Harvard Business Press, 1999).

   John P. Kotter, Force for Change: *How Leadership Differs from Management* (Simon and Schuster, 2008).

2. Confirming the idea that ethical leadership is more than good intentions, Linda Treviño and colleagues showed that being a moral person is not enough to be considered a moral manager. Their research showed that being a moral manager required more than just making good choices, but includes role modeling, use of a reward system, and communication about ethics. Note that these are all ethical skills, not just personal ethical intentions. See Linda Klebe Treviño, Laura Pincus Hartman, and Michael Brown, "Moral Person and Moral Manager: How Executives Develop a Reputation for Ethical Leadership,"

Harvard Business Review (July 1, 2000), https://hbr.org/product/moral-person-and-moral-manager-how-executives-deve/an/CMR183-PDF-ENG

3. A useful introduction to right-versus-right value conflicts is found in Joseph Badaracco Jr., *Defining Moments: When Managers Must Choose between Right and Right* (Harvard Business Press, 2013). Some people think of ethical dilemmas as right-versus-wrong issues, where one course of action is clearly confirmed by a moral obligation, while the other option contradicts that obligation. The ethical dilemmas in our book, on the other hand, are right-versus-right decisions in which two core moral values come into conflict. The justification for this distinction lies in the Greek roots of the word dilemma: An ethical dilemma is any situation that pits one deeply held lemma (fundamental proposition) against another (the prefix di- means "two"). While some use "dilemma" to describe a situation with two negative alternatives, the original meaning of the word carries no negative connotations. For more on this, see Rushworth M. Kidder, *How Good People Make Tough Choices* (Morrow, 1995).

4. During the past five years we have collected, compiled, and analyzed over five hundred ethical dilemmas faced by executive MBA and full-time MBA students. Using content analysis, we identified thirteen fundamental types of ethical dilemmas in business. For more on content analysis, see Hsiu-Fang Hsieh and Sarah E. Shannon, "Three Approaches to Qualitative Content Analysis," *Qualitative Health Research*, 15.9 (2005): 1277–1288; and Klaus Krippendorff, *Content Analysis: An Introduction to its Methodology* (Sage, 2012).

    We are not the first scholars to propose a typology for ethical issues. One of our colleagues at BYU, David Cherrington, along with his late brother and BYU colleague Owen Cherrington, examined the ethical issues in a week's worth of *Wall Street Journal* articles and published the resulting list of 12 ethical dilemmas in 1992. See J. Owen Cherrington and David J. Cherrington, "A Menu of Moral Issues: One Week in the Life of The Wall Street Journal," *Journal of Business Ethics*, 11.4 (1992): 255–265. The Cherrington list has significant overlap with our typology, but is more a list of unethical behaviors than a list of ethical dilemmas. Indeed, their 12th item is called "ethical dilemmas," situations in which it is not clear what to do. This last item is where most of our dilemmas reside.

    Later, Kidder suggested there are four fundamental ethical issues: 1) truth versus loyalty; 2) individual versus community, 3) justice versus mercy, and 4) short-term versus long-term. See Rushworth Kidder, *How Good People Make Tough Choices: Resolving the Dilemmas of Ethical Living* (Institute for Global Ethics, 2005). We have used this framework in the past and found it to be useful. However, it is sometimes too abstract to provide simple practical help. We hope this book will provide a practical approach to responding to the ethical dilemmas business people frequently face.

5. The idea of bringing your own experiences and identity to case work comes from Louise A. Mauffette-Leenders, James A. Erskine, and Michael R. Leenders, "Chapter 3: Individual Preparation," in *Learning with Cases*, 2nd ed., pp. 29–60 (Richard Ivey School of Business, 2001).

Chapter 1. Standing Up to Power

1. Potter Stewart (1915–1985), quoted at BrainyQuote.com (Xplore Inc, 2016), http://www.brainyquote.com/quotes/quotes/p/potterstew390058.html, accessed May 12, 2016.

2. The following resources describe social capital. James S. Coleman, "Social Capital in the Creation of Human Capital," *American Journal of Sociology*, 94 Supplement (1988): S95-S120; Alejandro Portes, "Social Capital: Its Origins and Applications in Modern Sociology," in Eric L. Lesser (Ed.), *Knowledge and Social Capital*, pp. 43–67 (Butterworth-Heinemann, 2000); Paul S. Adler and Seok-Woo Kwon, "Social Capital: Prospects for a New Concept," *Academy of Management Review*, 27.1 (2002): 17–40.

Chapter 2. Made a Promise (and the World Has Changed)

1. Richard J. Maynes, "The Eternal Importance of Honesty," *Ensign*, April 2010.

2. Amitai Etzioni, *The Moral Dimension: Toward a New Economics* (The Free Press, 1988).

3. Professor Adam Grant has done a great deal of research on prosocial behavior. See, for example, Adam M. Grant and Susan J. Ashford, "The Dynamics of Pro-activity at Work," *Research in Organizational Behavior*, 28 (2008): 3–34; Adam M. Grant and David M. Mayer, "Good Soldiers and Good Actors: Prosocial and Impression Management Motives as Interactive Predictors of Affiliative Citizenship Behaviors," *Journal of Applied Psychology*, 94.4 (2009): 900–912.

4. Patricia H. Werhane, *Moral Imagination* (John Wiley & Sons, 1999).

Chapter 4. Conflicts of Interest

1. The McCombs School of Business at the University of Texas at Austin has developed an engaging video series on business ethics. These videos can be found at http://ethicsunwrapped.utexas.edu/. One of these videos deals with the concept of moral imagination.

2. Daylian M. Cain, George Loewenstein, and Don A. Moore, "The Dirt on Coming Clean: Perverse Effects of Disclosing Conflicts of Interest," *The Journal of Legal Studies*, 34.1 (2005): 1–25; George Loewenstein, Sunita Sah, and Daylian M. Cain, "The Unintended Consequences of Conflict of Interest Disclosure," *Journal of the American Medical Association*, 307.7 (2012): 669–670.

Chapter 10. Sacrificing Personal Values

1. Associated Press, "Athlete's Fasting Puts a Spotlight on Islam," *Los Angeles Times* (February 17, 1996), http://articles.latimes.com/1996-02-17/local/me-37049_1_fasting-requirements

Chapter 12. Repair

1. This dilemma was based on Claire Lew, "What Kind of Company Are You?" Signal v. Noise (August 25, 2015), https://signalvnoise.com/posts/3920-what-kind-of-company-are-you

2. Rachel Zimmerman, "Doctors' New Tool to Fight Lawsuits: Saying 'I'm Sorry,'" *Wall Street Journal* (May 18, 2004), http://www.wsj.com/articles/SB108482777884713711

3. Lee Ross, "The Intuitive Psychologist and His Shortcomings: Distortions in the attribution process," *Advances in Experimental Social Psychology*, 10 (1977): 173–220.

4. Peter M. Madsen and Vinit Desai, "Failing to Learn?: The Effects of Failure and Success on Organizational Learning in the Global Orbital Launch Vehicle Industry," *Academy of Management Journal*, 53.3 (2010): 451–476; See also "Business-school Research: Failure to Launch," *The Economist Online* (April 13, 2010), http://www.economist.com/node/21009558

Chapter 15. Perils

1. Donald R. Cressey, "Why do Trusted Persons Commit Fraud? A Social-Psychological Study of Defalcators," *Journal of Accountancy*, 92.5 (1951): 576–581.

2. Steve W. Albrecht, "Iconic Fraud Triangle Endures," *Fraud Magazine*, August 2014: 1–7. Web.

3. The Arbinger Institute, *Leadership and Self-deception: Getting out of the Box* (Berrett-Koehler Publishers, 2010).

4. Denis Ribeaud and Manuel Eisner, "Are Moral Disengagement, Neutralization Techniques, and Self-Serving Cognitive Distortions the Same? Developing a Unified Scale of Moral Neutralization of Aggression," *International Journal of Conflict and Violence*, 4.2 (2010): 298–315.

5. Albert Bandura, "Moral Disengagement in the Perpetration of Inhumanities," *Personality and Social Psychology Review*, 3.3 (1999): 193–209.

6. Max H. Bazerman and Ann E. Tenbrunsel, *Blind Spots: Why We Fail to Do What's Right and What to Do about It* (Princeton University Press, 2011).

7. Gresham M. Sykes and David Matza, "Techniques of Neutralization: A Theory of Delinquency," *American Sociological Review*, 22.6 (1957): 664–670.

8. Dennis A. Gioia, "Pinto Fires and Personal Ethics: A Script Analysis of Missed Opportunities," *Journal of Business Ethics* 11.5–6 (1992): 379–389.

9. In these electric shock experiments, dozens of people administered what they thought were real electric shocks to an innocent person simply because a lab technically was instructing them to do so. See Stanley Milgram, *Obedience to Authority: An Experimental View* (Harper & Row, 1974).

10. The Stanford prison experiment was a study conducted by Philip Zimbardo in 1971. Zimbardo found that subjects acted on their behavioral expectations of their assigned roles, far beyond what the researchers had anticipated. For example, graduate students given the role of prison guards became abusive. For more information, see the film *The Stanford Prison Experiment* (2015) or read about it at www.prisonexp.org. See Philip G. Zimbardo, "Revisiting the Stanford Prison Experiment: A Lesson in the Power of Situation," *Chronicle of Higher Education*, 53.30 (2007).

11. While the original reporting of the case may have been partially inaccurate (i.e., there may have been fewer bystanders than originally reported; they may not have completely understood what was going on; and some bystanders did take some action), the Kitty Genovese story is still often used as a classic example of the bystander effect. See Kevin Cook, *Kitty Genovese: The Murder, the Bystanders, the Crime That Changed America* (W. W. Norton, 2014).

12. Jeffrey Sonnenfeld and Paul R. Lawrence, "Why Do Companies Succumb to Price Fixing?" *Harvard Business Review*, 56.4 (1978): 145–157.

Chapter 16. All-Purpose Tools

1. Thomas M. Jones, "Ethical Decision Making by Individuals in Organizations: An Issue-Contingent Model," *Academy of Management Review*, 16.2 (1991): 366–395.

2. Linda K. Treviño and Katherine A. Nelson, *Managing Business Ethics* (John Wiley & Sons, 2010).

3. The following are some foundational and some current academic sources for these various moral philosophies.

Deontology

Immanuel Kant, Allen W. Wood, and Jerome B. Schneewind, *Groundwork for the Metaphysics of Morals* (Yale University Press, 2002).

John Locke and Peter Laslett. Locke: *Two Treatises of Government, Student Edition* (Cambridge University Press, 1988).

John Rawls, *A Theory of Justice* (Harvard University Press, 2009).

Consequentialism

Jeremy Bentham, *The Collected Works of Jeremy Bentham: An Introduction to the Principles of Morals and Legislation* (Clarendon Press, 1996).

John Stuart Mill, *Utilitarianism* (Longmans, Green and Company, 1901).

Ayn Rand, *Atlas Shrugged* (1957; reprint, Penguin, 2005).

Henry Sidgwick, *The Methods of Ethics* (Hackett Publishing, 1907).

Peter Singer, *Practical Ethics* (Cambridge University Press, 2011).

Virtue Ethics

Alasdair MacIntyre, *After Virtue* (A&C Black, 2013).

Aristotle and Joe Sachs, *Nicomachean Ethics* (Focus Pub./R. Pullins, 2002)

Social Contracts

Thomas Donaldson and Thomas W. Dunfee, *Ties that Bind: A Social Contracts Approach to Business Ethics* (Harvard Business Press, 1999).

Thomas Hobbes, *Leviathan: Or the Matter, Forme and Power of a Commonwealth, Ecclesiasticall and Civil, Vol. 21* (Yale University Press, 1900).

Jean-Jacques Rousseau, *The Social Contract: & Discourses*, No. 660 (1762; reprint, JM Dent & Sons, 1920).

Ethics of Care

Carol Gilligan, *In a Different Voice: Psychological Theory and Women's Development* (Harvard University Press, 1982).

Virginia Held, *The Ethics of Care: Personal, Political, and Global.* (Oxford University Press, 2005).

4. John Rawls, *A Theory of Justice* (Harvard University Press, 2009).

Chapter 17. Being Ethically Proactive

1. Visit http://ethics.byu.edu/students/personal_mission.cfm for various values clarification exercises.

2. Clayton M. Christensen, James Allworth, and Karen Dillon. *How Will You Measure Your Life?* (Harper Business, 2012); Randy Pausch and Jeffrey Zaslow, *The Last Lecture* (Gale, 2008).

3. D. Todd Christofferson, "Moral Discipline," address from the General Conference of The Church of Jesus Christ of Latter-day Saints, Salt Lake City, UT, October 4, 2009 (available at lds.org).

4. David Brooks, *The Social Animal: The Hidden Sources of Love, Character, and Achievement* (Random House, 2012).

5. Denis G. Arnold, "Case 3: Merck and River Blindness," in Tom L. Beauchamp, Norman E. Bowie, and Denis Gordon Arnold (Eds.), *Ethical Theory and Business*, 8th ed., pp. 101–102 (Pearson/Prentice Hall, 2009), https://philosophia.uncg.edu/media/phi361-metivier/readings/Case-River%20Blindness.pdf. accessed July 2, 2016.

6. Lucy Tobin, "Never on a Saturday: Goldman Sachs...Tells Staff to Have a Weekend," *Independent* (November 7, 2013), http://www.independent.co.uk/

news/business/news/never-on-a-saturday-goldman-sachs-the-bank-famous-for-expecting-graduates-to-work-100-hour-weeks-8927870.html, accessed July 2, 2016.

7.   Terence Irwin (Trans.), *Aristotle: Nicomachean Ethics*, 2nd ed., (Hackett, 1999 [350 BC]).

8.   Charles Duhigg, *The Power of Habit: Why We Do What We Do in Life and Business* (Random House, 2012).

9.   Dan Ariely, "Our Buggy Moral Code," TED Talk, March 2009 (available at www.ted.com); Dan Ariely, *The (Honest) Truth about Dishonesty: How We Lie to Everyone, Especially Ourselves* (HarperCollins, 2012).

10.   Melody J. Murdock and Joseph D. Ogden, *Business with Integrity: Executives and Educators Share Experiences and Insights* (Brigham Young University Press, 2005).

11.   Mary C. Gentile, *Giving Voice to Values: How to Speak Your Mind When You Know What's Right* (Yale University Press, 2010).

12.   Max H. Bazerman and Ann E. Tenbrunsel, *Blind Spots: Why We Fail to Do What's Right and What to Do about It* (Princeton University Press, 2011).

13.   David Brooks, *The Road to Character* (Random House, 2015).

14.   Kerry Patterson, *Crucial Conversations: Tools for Talking When Stakes Are High* (McGraw-Hill, 2002).

Chapter 18. Leading in the Wilderness

1.   Linda K. Treviño, Laura P. Hartman, and Michael Brown, "Moral Person and Moral Manager: How Executives Develop a Reputation for Ethical Leadership," *California Management Review*, 42.4 (2000): 128–142. This article places the moral person and moral manager dimensions in a 2 x 2 matrix of different reputations an executive can develop, either as an ethical leader, an unethical leader, a hypocritical leader, or an ethically neutral leader. A strong moral manager and a strong moral person will, of course, be perceived as an ethical leader, while a weak moral manager and a weak moral person will be perceived as an unethical leader. A strong moral manager but a weak moral person will develop a reputation as a hypocritical leader. This is a leader who "talks the ethics talk" but does not "walk the ethics walk." And finally, a weak moral manager, even if she is a strong moral person, will be perceived as an ethically neutral leader, meaning that she is not perceived to be clearly unethical or clearly ethical. Such leaders are thought to focus on financial ends more than the means, with little concern about leaving the organization or the world a better place for the future.

2.   Gary R. Weaver, Linda K. Treviño, and Bradley R. Agle, " 'Somebody I Look Up To': Ethical Role Models in Organizations," *Organizational Dynamics*, 34.4 (2005): 313–330.

3. See for example the following: John Van Maanen and Edgar H. Schein, *Toward a Theory of Organizational Socialization* (Massachusetts Institute of Technology, 1977); Georgia T. Chao, Anne M. O'Leary-Kelly, Samantha Wolf, S., Howard J. Klein, and Philip D. Gardner (1994), "Organizational Socialization: Its content and consequences," *Journal of Applied Psychology*, 79.5 (1994): 730–743.

4. Edgar H. Schein, *Organizational Culture and Leadership*, Volume 2 (John Wiley & Sons, 2010).

5. Steven Kerr, "On the Folly of Rewarding A, while Hoping for B," *Academy of Management Journal*, 18.4 (1975): 769–783.

6. Charles W. Hill, Patricia C. Kelley, Bradley R. Agle, Michael A. Hitt, and Robert E. Hoskisson, "An Empirical Examination of the Causes of Corporate Wrongdoing in the United States," *Human Relations*, 45.10 (1992): 1055–1076.

7. Kristen Grind, "REI, Nordstrom and the Perils of No-Questions-Asked Returns," *Wall Street Journal* Moneybeat blog (September 18, 2013), http://blogs.wsj.com/moneybeat/2013/09/18/rei-nordstrom-and-the-perils-of-no-questions-asked-returns/

8. R. Edward Freeman, "The Politics of Stakeholder Theory: Some Future Directions," *Business Ethics Quarterly*, 4.4 (1994): 409–422.

9. R. Edward Freeman, *Strategic Management: A Stakeholder Approach* (Pitman, 1984); Robert A. Phillips and R. Edward Freeman (Eds.), Stakeholders (Edward Elgar, 2010).

10. Ronald K. Mitchell, Bradley R. Agle, and Donna J. Wood, "Toward a Theory of Stakeholder Identification and Salience: Defining the Principle of Who and What Really Counts," *Academy of Management Review*, 22.4 (1997): 853–886.

11. See sub-section "303A.10 Code of Business Conduct and Ethics" within "Section 3 - Corporate Responsibility" in the NYSE Listed Company Manual, http://nysemanual.nyse.com/LCM/Sections/

Appendix: The Big Question

1. For a full treatise on the benefits of honest dealings, we highly recommend Stephen M. R. Covey's excellent book, *The Speed of Trust* (Simon & Schuster, 2006). Covey describes in great detail the reasons that relationships of trust, built on ethical behavior, make everyone involved better off.

Story Index

Opening Dilemma	Bill's Experiences	Practice Dilemma	Other Examples
Preface: How to Use this Guidebook			
--	Trichloroethylene (TCE) in Texas drinking water, 1–4, 190 Returning golf club gift to sports store, 3 The "good name" plaque, 3	--	--
Introduction to the Challenges			
--	--	--	--

Opening Dilemma	Bill's Experiences	Practice Dilemma	Other Examples
Challenge 1: Standing Up to Power			
Frank wants Nathan to delete underpayment penalty from Mr. Bigglesworth's tax return, 15–16, 28–29	Clear assumptions in lifecycle analysis for metal vs. plastics and glass, 26 Severance policy appeal from recently laid-off employees, 26	Bicycle parts supplier in Brazil: Should Nisha disclose the upcoming liquidation? 29–30	Arthur Andersen accountants working for Enron, 20–21
Challenge 2: Made a Promise			
Susan could keep her promise to stay with nonprofit or accept a consultant's better offer, 31–33, 42–43	Involving customer when quality control equipment failed, 39–40 Bill attends wife's cancer treatments and coaches children's teams, 40 Chris honors commitment to work for medical center over Dick's Sporting Goods, 41–42	Natalia wants to hire Brian, but she promised the job to Rajeev, 43–45	Uncertainty in marriage promise, 33 Lawn mowing vs. hospital trip, 33–34 Scuba certification and swimming with dolphins, 34, 36 Richard Maynes airlifts bottling equipment to meet deadline, 35 Student backs out of job after wife's cancer diagnosis, 35, 37 Intern's reneging on job offer hurts university, 37
Challenge 3: Intervention			
Eric knows knee surgery will be needed, but physical therapist Jason won't tell Mr. Bell, 47–49, 59	Confederate flag in parking lot of North Carolina plant, 56–58	Andrea's boss has modified answers on their compliance questionnaire, 59–61	Uncle Ben to Peter Parker, 49

Opening Dilemma	Bill's Experiences	Practice Dilemma	Other Examples
Challenge 4: Conflicts of Interest			
Abed's double-sided notes (with StartNet info on one side) cause problems at his TerroTech exit interview, 63–65, 78–79	Avoiding nepotism in rubber procurement, 72–73 Medical director receives large wedding presents, 73–74 Bill's policies on trips, tickets, negotiation gifts, and meals, 74–75 Refusing to pay company bribes in Russia and Middle East, 75–76 Third party verifies Alcoa's gift to school, 76	Baby gift from flatware supplier worries Clyde, 79–81	Bad examples: Andy Fastow (Enron); Darleen Druyun (Air Force) and Michael Sears (Boeing); Hillary Clinton and Donald Trump (presidential candidates), 66–67 Brad refuses orchestra fundraising offer, 67–68 Policies on "nominal" gifts and time use, 68–69, 74–75 Selecting Olympic judges for synchronized swimming, 77–78
Challenge 5: Suspicions Without Enough Evidence			
Marco wonders if Cindy has bribed Chinese export officials so his crafting product will arrive in time, 83–84, 96–97	Australian plant manager "fired himself" by hiding safety incidents, 90–92 HR director in Russia demands kickbacks for severance pay, 92–93 Benedictine nun claims Alcoa hurting employees in Mexico, 93 General manager accused of buying office art from son, 94–95	Ashley and two friends want to be transferred out of Mr. Francis's math class: Should Craig investigate their harassment complaints?, 97–98	--

Opening Dilemma	Bill's Experiences	Practice Dilemma	Other Examples
Challenge 6: Playing Dirty			
David's summer sales team could trick the CEO into paying what the company owes them, 99–101, 107	Patent for heat treating plastic offered at higher royalties, 105 Electrical connector for ship sold at premium after contract obligations met, 105–106	Ethan could switch suppliers—leaving Westbrook, who violated the brokerage agreement, with surplus custom corkboard, 108–109	Abraham Lincoln pays bribes to help abolish slavery, 103
Challenge 7: Skirting the Rules			
If Nick reports Mr. Sandoval's invalid Social Security number, the consequences could be drastic for his company and his customer, 111–113, 124	Telling the truth about employee's tourist visa, 121 Reporting U.S. investment income to Russian tax authorities, 121–122 Reducing factory emissions legitimately, 122	Kim could get office air conditioning fixed for tenants today, or wait to follow expenditure rules, 124–125	Civil disobedience by Mahatma Ghandi and Martin Luther King, Jr., 114–115
Challenge 8: Dissemblance			
HR director asks Shelley to keep GMAT waiver secret, but VP wants to know her test score, 127–128, 139–140	Bill tells plant workers his salary, 136 Bill testifies in court about master cutoff switch, 136–137 Bill communicates directly in budgeting conversations, 137-138 Law partner offers to spin patent infringement opinion, 138	In a negotiation, the Carterville School District rep asks Jeff if his fleet maintenance company is facing bankruptcy, 140	--

	Opening Dilemma	Bill's Experiences	Practice Dilemma	Other Examples
Challenge 9: Loyalty				
	Ellie is being forced to quit—and a lawsuit to obtain severance might hurt Ellie's former boss, Paul, 141–143, 151–152	Vice president dismissed for viewing pornography at work, 149 Secretary dismissed while on maternity leave, 150	Dr. Costa wants Keyshawn to sign a letter in support of Dr. Pennington, 152–154	--
Challenge 10: Sacrificing Personal Values				
	Arthur does not want to do business with a pornography company, and this offends their benefits consultant, Joe, 155–157, 166–167	Bill refuses paying bribes to traffic police and airport officials, 162–163 Alcoa's safety dress code, 163–164 Asking suppliers to donate to a charity that was honoring the CEO, 164 Declining award from environmental charity that expects large contributions, 164–165	Selma will be fired if she refuses to work the call center on Sundays, 167–168	Alcohol norms in Russia vs. Sudan, 157 Tagg Romney reassigned to avoid state lottery client, 158 Hakeem Olajuwon observes Ramadan while playing in the NBA, 160
Challenge 11: Unfair Advantage				
	Liza quietly included a fee in the contract with Peter, and Stephen must decide whether to make Peter's company pay, 169–170, 179	Bill introduces himself to negotiators he overhears in the airport, 176–177 When payment cycle moves from 30 to 60 days, Bill softens the blow to suppliers, 178	Information from Phil's sales pitch to HealthTe ch will benefit Derrick—but Derrick has no intention of buying Phil's product, 180–181	--

	Opening Dilemma	Bill's Experiences	Practice Dilemma	Other Examples
Challenge 12: Repair				
	A software glitch exposed clients' information to new hires, and Claire must decide what to do, 183–184, 193–194	Broken Christmas lights on the newspaper route, 190–191 Sharing Pepsi at a football game solves boys' quarrel, 191	The supplier is fixing the problem for free, but Annie's company is probably at fault, 194–195	Expectations of safety while skydiving, 187
Challenge 13: Showing Mercy				
	Alan's many mistakes are beginning to effect Julie's law practice, 197–199, 207–208	Flex time for employee, Mike, 204 Second chance for business unit president who make mistakes with antitrust compliance, 204–205 Dealing with employees' substance abuse, 205–206	Omar is frustrated with Bridget's frequent errors in the general ledger, 208–209	--
Chapter 14: Becoming an Ethical Guide				
	--	--	--	Driving hospital tractor for Boy Scout fundraising task, 212 Hospital jobs for the boss's sons, 212 Brad learns from accidental overtime payment at IBM, 212–213 Bank makes false recruiting promises, 213 Hospital parking remains free to community, 214 Patt Hassey given union shirts, 214

Opening Dilemma	Bill's Experiences	Practice Dilemma	Other Examples
			Aaron sees unethical behavior as an attorney, 215
			Aaron tries to sell Fiat Spider to man who sabotaged fuel line and runs into him years later as a car salesman, 216
Chapter 15: Perils			
--	--	--	Denny Gioia overlooks defect in Ford Pinto, 225–226
			Milgram shock trials expose risks of obedience, 226
			Role taking in the Stanford prison experiments, 227
			Bystanders ignore Kitty Genovese, 227
			Norms for drug use by baseball players and cyclists, 228

Opening Dilemma	Bill's Experiences	Practice Dilemma	Other Examples
Chapter 16: All-Purpose Tools			
--	--	--	Moral intensity of choosing office paint color vs. other decisions, 231
			Lying to Nazi soldiers, 236
			Voting as demonstration of fairness, 238
			Utilitarianism in attorney-client privilege, 240
Chapter 17: Being Ethically Proactive			
--	Reporting to board an improper procedure on currency hedge, 253–254	--	Brad congratulates CEO on ethical culture, 250
			Merck combats river blindness, 253
			Goldman Sachs announces no-work Saturdays, 253
			Individuals cheat less when primed to think about ethics, 256

Opening Dilemma	Bill's Experiences	Practice Dilemma	Other Examples
Chapter 18: Leading in the Wilderness			
--	Bill's changes to office layout enables HR clerk to report extortion, 267–268 Bill displays photos of ethical role models, 268–269 Constructing extra wastewater treatment facility for city near Mexico plant, 269 Creating training classes for community when opening South Carolina factory, 269 Eliminating a harmful substance from alloys, 269–270	--	Paul O'Neill puts safety first on every agenda, 263 Brad notes differences in office layouts and visits employee cafeteria with CEO, 266 Nordstrom gives refund on tires, 267 History of U.S. laws and regulations on ethics, 272–276
Appendix: The Big Question			
--	--	--	Students ask "Why be ethical?", 281–282 Reports from students who shared dilemmas for this book, 283–284
Appendix: Acknowledgements			
--	--	--	Brad and Aaron categorize dilemmas for classroom discussion and invite Bill to share experiences, 288–290

Index

The research and writing of this book received generous support from The Wheatley Institution at Brigham Young University.

—— T H E ——
WHEATLEY INSTITUTION

LIFTING SOCIETY BY PRESERVING
AND STRENGTHENING ITS CORE INSTITUTIONS

wheatley.byu.edu

The Wheatley Institution
Brigham Young University
392 Hinckley Center
Provo, UT 84602

Main: (801) 422-5883

Email: wheatley_institution@byu.edu

Donor Liaison: Doug Perry
Email: doug_perry@byu.edu

About The Wheatley Institution

The mission of The Wheatley Institution is to enhance the academic climate and scholarly reputation of BYU, and to enrich faculty and student experiences, by contributing recognized scholarship that lifts society by preserving and strengthening its core institutions.

Named for Jack and Mary Lois Wheatley, the Wheatley Institution at Brigham Young University produces consequential scholarship on key topics consistent with its core mission, including work on faith and intellect, family, education, ethics, and civic virtue. The Institution convenes leading scholars from BYU and from beyond campus to research and publish collaboratively, as well as individually, enriching the academic environment for BYU students and faculty and expanding the influence of BYU and its faculty within the scholarly disciplines and in the broader culture. The emphasis is on application of sound scholarly work to important real-world problems. The Institution also seeks to expand its contribution and influence through conferences and seminars, as well as through the dissemination of scholarly products.

Put The Business Ethics Field Guide to work in your organization

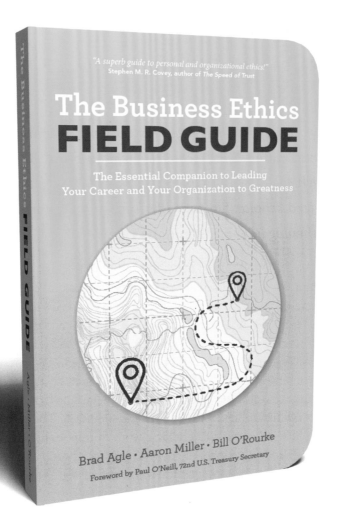

"A superb guide to personal and organizational ethics!"
Stephen M. R. Covey, author of The Speed of Trust

The Business Ethics
FIELD GUIDE

The Essential Companion to Leading
Your Career and Your Organization to Greatness

Brad Agle · Aaron Miller · Bill O'Rourke

Foreword by Paul O'Neill, 72nd U.S. Treasury Secretary

Protect your organization and make sure everyone on your team is equipped to handle the ethical challenges they face everyday.

Whether you want simple, self-paced online training for your employees, more advanced leadership courses, keynote speakers, or even an organizational Ethics Audit™, we can help you put the principles and ideas of the leading book on business ethics to work.

- Keynotes
- Employee training
- Leadership training
- Organizational Ethics Audit™
- Consulting
- Volume discount book pricing

The authors of the book and our expert training and consulting staff will help protect your company from ethical missteps that can damage your reputation. Equip your employees with the tools they need to make the best decisions.

www.EthicsFieldGuide.com
(888) 717-1226

MERIT
LEADERSHIP

Left to right: Aaron Miller, Brad Agle, Bill O'Rourke

About the Authors

With decades of combined experience as educators and experts in business ethics, Brad Agle, Aaron Miller and Bill O'Rourke offer distilled, practical advice.

Brad Agle

(PhD, University of Washington) is the George W. Romney Endowed Professor, and Professor of Ethics and Leadership in the Marriott School of Management at Brigham Young University. He is also a Fellow in the Wheatley Institution at BYU, where he chairs the ethics initiative, including the biannual Teaching Ethics at Universities Conference. He currently serves on the advisory board of RLG Capital, the ethics committee of USA Synchro, the editorial board of *Business Ethics Quarterly*, and as President-Elect of the International Association for Business and Society. Previously, he spent seventeen years as a professor in the Katz Graduate School of Business at the University of Pittsburgh, where he also served for eight years as the inaugural director of the Berg Center for Ethics and Leadership.

Brad is an active researcher concentrating on business ethics, stakeholder management, CEO leadership and religious influences on business. His writings appear in journals such as the *Academy of Management Review*, *Academy of Management Journal*, *Business Ethics Quarterly*, *Journal of*